THE SUNDAY SERVICE OF THE METHODISTS; WITH OTHER OCCASIONAL SERVICES

Published @ 2017 Trieste Publishing Pty Ltd

ISBN 9780649716173

The Sunday Service of the Methodists; With Other Occasional Services by John Wesley

Edited by Trieste Publishing Pty Ltd.
Cover @ 2017

www.triestepublishing.com

JOHN WESLEY

THE SUNDAY SERVICE OF THE METHODISTS; WITH OTHER OCCASIONAL SERVICES

Trieste

THE

SUNDAY SERVICE

OF THE

METHODISTS;

WITH

OTHER OCCASIONAL SERVICES.

LONDON:

PUBLISHED BY JOHN MASON,

AT THE WESLEYAN CONFERENCE OFFICE, 14, CITY-ROAD;

AND SOLD AT 66, PATERNOSTER-ROW

1846.

ROCHE, PRINTER, 25, HOXTON-SQUARE, LONDON.

I BELIEVE there is no LITURGY in the world, either in ancient or modern language, which breathes more of a solid, scriptural, rational piety, than the COMMON PRAYER of the CHURCH of ENGLAND: and though the main of it was compiled considerably more than two hundred years ago, yet is the language of it not only pure, but strong and elegant in the highest degree.

Little alteration is made in the following edition of it, except in the following instances :—

1. Most of the holy-days (so called) are omitted, as at present answering no valuable end.

2. The Service of the LORD's DAY, the length of which has been often complained of, is considerably shortened.

3. Some sentences in the offices of Baptism, and for the Burial of the Dead, are omitted ; and,

4. Many Psalms left out, and many parts of the others, as being highly improper for the mouths of a Christian congregation.

JOHN WESLEY.

Bristol, Sept. 9, 1784.

PROPER LESSONS

TO BE READ AT

MORNING AND EVENING PRAYER,

ON THE SUNDAYS THROUGHOUT THE YEAR.

Sundays in Advent.	*Morning.*		*Evening.*	
The first.	Isaiah	1	Isaiah	2
2 ———	———	5	———	24
3 ———	———	25	———	26
4 ———	———	30	———	32
Sundays aft. Christ.				
The first.	———	37	———	38
2 ———	———	41	———	43
3 ———	———	44	———	46
4 ———	———	51	———	53
5 ———	———	55	———	56
6 ———	———	57	———	58
7 ———	———	59	———	64
8 ———	———	65	———	66
9 ———	Genesis	1	G nesis	2
10 ———	———	3	———	6
11 ———	———	7	———	18
12 ———	19 to ver.	30	———	22
13 ———	———	24	———	37
14 ———	———	39	———	42
15 ———	———	43	— 44 and 45	
Sunday bef. Easter.				
1 Lesson.	Exodus	9	Exodus	10
2 Lesson.	Matthew	26	Heb. 5 to v. 11	

PROPER LESSONS FOR SUNDAYS.

	Morning.	Evening.
Easter-Day.		
1 Lesson.	Exodus 12	Exodus 14
2 Lesson.	Romans 6	Acts 2 v. 22
Sundays aft. Easter.		
The first.	Numbers 16	Numbers 22
2 ———	— 23 and 24	——— 25
3 ———	Deuter. 4	Deuter. 5
4 ———	——— 6	——— 7
5 ———	——— 8	——— 9
Sunday after Ascension-Day.	Deuter. 12	Deuter. 13
Whitsunday.		
1 Lesson.	16 to ver. 18	Isaiah 11
2 Lesson.	Acts 10 ver. 34	Acts 19 to v. 21
Trinity Sunday.		
1 Lesson.	Genesis 1	Genesis 18
2 Lesson.	Matthew 3	1 John 5
Sundays after Trinity Sunday.		
The first.	Joshua 10	Joshua 23
2 ———	Judges 4	Judges 5
3 ———	1 Samuel 2	1 Samuel 3
4 ———	——— 12	——— 13
5 ———	——— 15	——— 17
6 ———	2 Samuel 12	2 Samuel 19
7 ———	——— 21	——— 24
8 ———	1 Kings 13	1 Kings 17
9 ———	——— 18	——— 19
10 ———	——— 21	——— 22
11 ———	2 Kings 5	2 Kings 9
12 ———	——— 10	——— 18
13 ———	——— 19	——— 23
14 ———	Jeremiah 5	Jeremiah 22
15 ———	——— 35	——— 36

PROPER LESSONS FOR SUNDAYS.

Sundays after Trinity Sunday.	Morning.		Evening.	
16 ———	Ezekiel	2	Ezekiel	13
17 ———	———	14	———	18
18 ———	———	20	———	24
19 ———	Daniel	3	Daniel	6
20 ———	Joel	2	Micah	6
21 ———	Habakkuk	2	Proverbs	1
22 ———	Proverbs	2	———	3
23 ———	———	11	———	12
24 ———	———	13	———	14
25 ———	———	15	———	16
26 ———	———	17	———	19

N.B. Let the Second Lesson in the Morning be a Chapter out of the Four Gospels, or the Acts of the Apostles, and the Second Lesson in the Evening be a Chapter out of the Epistles, in regular rotation; excepting where it is otherwise provided.

PROPER LESSONS FOR PARTICULAR DAYS.

Nativity of Christ.	Morning.	Evening.
1 Lesson.	Isaiah 9 to ver. 8	Isaiah 7, ver. 10 [to 17
2 Lesson.	Luke 2 to v. 15	Tit. 3, v. 4 to 9
Good-Friday.		
1 Lesson.	Gen. 22 to v. 20	Isaiah 53
2 Lesson.	John 18	1 Peter 2
Ascension-Day.		
1 Lesson.	Deuter. 10	2 Kings 2
2 Lesson.	Luke 24, v. 44	Eph. 4 to v. 17

PROPER PSALMS ON CERTAIN DAYS.

	Morning.	Evening.
Christmas-Day.	Psalm 19	Psalm 89
	———— 45	————
	———— 85	————
Good-Friday.	Psalm 22	Psalm 69
	———— 40	————
Easter-Day.	Psalm 2	Psalm 113
	———— 57	———— 114
	———— 111	———— 118
Ascension-Day.	Psalm 8	Psalm 24
	———— 15	———— 47
Whitsunday.	Psalm 48	Psalm 104
	———— 68	———— 145

DAYS OF FASTING OR ABSTINENCE.

All the Fridays in the Year, except *Christmas-Day.*

A TABLE

OF

MOVEABLE SABBATH-DAYS.

Year.	Easter Sunday.		Whitsunday.		Adv. Sunday.	
1825	April	3	May	22	Nov.	27
1826	March	26	————	14	Dec.	3
1827	April	15	June	3	————	2
1828	————	6	May	25	Nov.	30
1829	————	19	June	7	————	29
1830	————	11	May	30	————	28
1831	————	3	————	22	————	27
1832	————	22	June	10	Dec.	2
1833	————	7	May	26	————	1
1834	March	30	————	18	Nov.	30
1835	April	19	June	7	————	29
1836	————	3	May	22	————	27
1837	March	26	————	14	Dec.	3
1838	April	15	June	3	————	2
1839	March	31	May	19	————	1
1840	April	19	June	7	Nov.	29
1841	————	11	May	30	————	28
1842	March	27	————	15	————	27
1843	April	16	June	4	Dec.	3
1844	————	7	May	26	————	1
1845	March	23	————	11	Nov.	30
1846	April	12	————	31	————	29
1847	————	4	————	23	————	28
1848	————	23	June	11	Dec.	3
1849	————	8	May	27	————	2
1850	March	31	————	19	————	1
1851	April	20	June	8	Nov.	30
1852	————	11	May	30	————	28
1853	March	27	————	15	————	27
1854	April	16	June	4	Dec.	3

A TABLE OF MOVEABLE SABBATH-DAYS.

Year.	Easter Sunday.		Whitsunday.		Adv. Sunday.	
1855	April	8	May	27	Dec.	2
1856	March	23	————	11	Nov.	30
1857	April	12	————	31	————	29
1858	————	4	————	23	————	28
1859	————	24	June	12	————	27
1860	————	8	May	27	Dec.	2
1861	March	31	————	19	————	1
1862	April	20	June	8	Nov.	30
1863	————	5	May	24	————	29
1864	March	27	————	15	————	27
1865	April	16	June	4	Dec.	3
1866	————	1	May	20	————	2
1867	————	21	June	9	————	1
1868	————	12	May	31	Nov.	29
1869	March	28	————	16	————	28
1870	April	17	June	5	————	27
1871	————	9	May	28	Dec.	3
1872	March	31	————	19	————	1
1873	April	13	June	1	Nov.	30
1874	————	5	May	24	————	29
1875	March	28	————	16	————	28
1876	April	16	June	4	Dec.	3
1877	————	1	May	20	————	2
1878	————	21	June	9	————	1
1879	————	13	————	1	Nov.	30
1880	March	28	May	16	————	28
1881	April	17	June	5	————	27
1882	————	9	May	28	Dec.	3
1883	March	25	————	13	————	2
1884	April	18	June	1	Nov.	30
1885	————	5	May	24	————	29
1886	————	25	June	13	————	28
1887	————	10	May	29	————	27
1888	————	1	————	20	Dec.	2

THE ORDER FOR

MORNING PRAYER,

EVERY LORD'S DAY.

At the beginning of Morning Prayer, the Minister shall read with a loud voice some one or more of these Sentences of the Scriptures that follow: And then he shall say that which is written after the said Sentences.

WHEN the wicked man turneth away from his wickedness that he hath committed, and doeth that which is lawful and right, he shall save his soul alive.   Ezek. xviii. 27.

The sacrifices of God are a broken spirit: a broken and a contrite heart, O God, thou wilt not despise. Psalm li. 17.

To the Lord our God belong mercies and forgivenesses, though we have rebelled against him: neither have we obeyed the voice of the Lord our God, to walk in his laws which he set before us.   Dan. ix. 9, 10.

I will arise, and go to my father, and will say unto him, Father, I have sinned against Heaven and before thee, and am no more worthy to be called thy son. Luke xv. 18, 19.

Enter not into judgment with thy servant, O Lord; for in thy sight shall no man living be justified. Psal. cxliii. 2.

DEARLY beloved brethren, the Scripture moveth us, in sundry places, to acknowledge and confess our manifold sins and wickedness, and that we should not dissemble nor cloak them before the face of Almighty God our heavenly Father; but confess them with an humble, lowly, penitent, and obedient heart; to the end that we may obtain forgiveness of the same, by his infinite goodness and mercy. Wherefore, I pray and beseech you, as many as are here present, to accompany me with a pure heart and humble voice, unto the throne of the heavenly grace, saying after me:

A general Confession, to be said by the whole Congregation, after the Minister, all kneeling.

ALMIGHTY and most merciful Father, We have erred, and strayed from thy ways like lost sheep. We have followed too much the devices and desires of our own hearts. We have offended against thy holy laws. We have left undone those things which we ought to have done; and we have done those things which we ought not to have done; And there is no health in us. But thou, O Lord, have mercy upon us, miserable offenders. Spare thou them, O God, who confess their faults. Restore thou them that are penitent; According to thy promises declared unto mankind in Christ Jesus our Lord. And grant, O most merciful Father, for his sake, That we may hereafter live a godly, righteous, and sober life; to the glory of thy holy Name. *Amen.*

Then the Minister shall say,

O LORD, we beseech thee, absolve thy people from their offences; that through thy bountiful goodness we may be delivered from the bands of those sins, which by our frailty we have committed. Grant this,

O heavenly Father, for Jesus Christ's sake, our blessed Lord and Saviour.

The People shall answer here, and at the end of all other Prayers, Amen.

Then the Minister shall say the Lord's Prayer; the People also repeating it with him, both here and wheresoever else it is used in Divine Service.

OUR Father, who art in heaven, Hallowed be thy Name. Thy kingdom come. Thy will be done on earth, As it is in heaven. Give us this day our daily bread. And forgive us our trespasses, As we forgive them that trespass against us. And lead us not into temptation; But deliver us from evil: For thine is the kingdom, and the power, and the glory, For ever and ever. *Amen.*

Then likewise he shall say,

O Lord, open thou our lips;
Answ. *And our mouth shall show forth thy praise.*
Minist. O God, make speed to save us;
Answ. *O Lord, make haste to help us.*

Here, all standing up, the Minister shall say,

Glory be to the Father, and to the Son, and to the Holy Ghost.
Answ. *As it was in the beginning, is now, and ever shall be, world without end.* Amen.
Minist. Praise ye the Lord.
Answ. *The Lord's name be praised.*

Then shall follow the Psalms, in order as they are appointed; and at the end of every Psalm shall be repeated,

Glory be to the Father, and to the Son, and to the Holy Ghost;
As it was in the beginning, is now, and ever shall be, world without end. Amen.

Then shall be read distinctly the First Lesson, taken out of the
Old Testament, as it is appointed in the Table of proper Lessons:
He that readeth, so standing, and turning himself, as he may
best be heard of all.   And after that shall be said the following
Hymn :

WE praise thee, O God ; we acknowledge thee to
be the Lord.
All the earth doth worship thee, the Father everlasting.
To thee all angels cry aloud : the Heavens, and all
the Powers therein.
To thee Cherubim and Seraphim continually do cry,
Holy, holy, holy, Lord God of Sabaoth ;
Heaven and earth are full of the Majesty of thy glory.
The glorious company of the Apostles praise thee.
The goodly fellowship of the Prophets praise thee.
The noble army of Martyrs praise thee.
*The Holy Church throughout all the world doth ac-
knowledge thee ;*
The Father of an infinite Majesty ;
Thine honourable, true, and only Son.
Also the Holy Ghost, the Comforter.
Thou art the King of Glory, O Christ ;
Thou art the everlasting Son of the Father.
*When thou tookest upon thee to deliver man, thou didst
not abhor the Virgin's womb.*
When thou hadst overcome the sharpness of death,
thou didst open the kingdom of Heaven to all believers.
*Thou sittest at the right hand of God, in the glory of
the Father.*
We believe that thou shalt come to be our Judge.
*We therefore pray thee, help thy servants, whom thou
hast redeemed with thy precious blood.*
Make them to be numbered with thy saints in glory
everlasting.
O Lord, save thy people, and bless thine heritage.
Govern them, and lift them up for ever.
Day by day we magnify thee.

And we worship thy name ever, world without end.

Vouchsafe, O Lord, to keep us this day without sin.

O Lord, have mercy upon us : have mercy upon us.

O Lord, let thy mercy lighten upon us, as our trust is in thee.

O Lord, in thee have I trusted : let me never be confounded.

Then shall be read in like manner the Second Lesson, taken out of the New Testament; and, after that, the following Psalm :

O BE joyful in the Lord, all ye lands ; serve the Lord with gladness, and come before his presence with a song.

Be ye sure that the Lord he is God : it is he that hath made us, and not we ourselves : we are his people, and the sheep of his pasture.

O go your way into his gates with thanksgiving, and into his courts with praise ; be thankful unto him, and speak good of his name.

For the Lord is gracious, his mercy is everlasting ; and his truth endureth from generation to generation.

Glory be to the Father, and to the Son, and to the Holy Ghost;

As it was in the beginning, is now, and ever shall be, world without end. Amen.

Then shall be said the Apostles' Creed, by the Minister and the People, standing.

I BELIEVE in God, the Father Almighty, Maker of heaven and earth :

And in Jesus Christ, his only Son our Lord; Who was conceived by the Holy Ghost ; Born of the Virgin Mary ; Suffered under Pontius Pilate ; Was crucified, dead, and buried : He descended into hell ; The third day he rose again from the dead; He ascended into heaven, And sitteth on the right hand of God the Father Almighty; From thence he shall come to judge the quick and the dead.

I believe in the Holy Ghost; The Holy Catholic Church; The Communion of Saints; The Forgiveness of Sins; The Resurrection of the Body; And the Life everlasting. *Amen.*

And, after that, the Minister shall pronounce with a loud Voice,

The Lord be with you;
Answ. *And with thy spirit.*

Minister. Let us pray.

Lord, have mercy upon us.
Answ. *Christ, have mercy upon us.*
Minist. Lord, have mercy upon us.

Then shall follow three Collects; the first of the Day, which shall be the same that is appointed at the Communion; the second for Peace; the third for Grace to live well: all devoutly kneeling.

The second Collect for Peace.

O GOD, who art the author of peace, and lover of concord, in knowledge of whom standeth our eternal life, whose service is perfect freedom; Defend us, thy humble servants, in all assaults of our enemies; that we, surely trusting in thy defence, may not fear the power of any adversaries, through the might of Jesus Christ our Lord. *Amen.*

O LORD, our heavenly Father, Almighty and ever-lasting God, who hast safely brought us to the beginning of this day; Defend us in the same with thy mighty power; and grant that this day we fall into no sin, neither run into any kind of danger; but that all our doings may be ordered by thy governance, to do always that is righteous in thy sight; through Jesus Christ our Lord. *Amen.*

O LORD, our heavenly Father, high and mighty, King of kings, Lord of lords, who dost from thy throne behold all the dwellers upon earth; Most heartily we beseech thee with thy favour to behold our gracious Sovereign, Queen VICTORIA; and so replenish her with the grace of thy Holy Spirit, that she may alway incline to thy will, and walk in thy way: Endue her plenteously with heavenly gifts; grant her in health and wealth long to live; strengthen her that she may vanquish and overcome all her enemies; and finally, after this life, she may attain everlasting joy and felicity; through Jesus Christ our Lord. *Amen.*

ALMIGHTY God, the fountain of all goodness, we humbly beseech thee to bless ADELAIDE the Queen Dowager, the Prince ALBERT, ALBERT Prince of WALES, and all the Royal Family: Endue them with thy Holy Spirit; enrich them with thy heavenly grace; prosper them with all happiness; and bring them to thine everlasting kingdom; through Jesus Christ our Lord. *Amen.*

ALMIGHTY and everlasting God, who alone workest great marvels; Send down upon all the Ministers of thy Gospel the healthful Spirit of thy grace; and that they may truly please thee, pour upon them the continual dew of thy blessing. Grant this, O Lord, for the honour of our Advocate and Mediator, Jesus Christ. *Amen.*

A Prayer for all Conditions of Men.

O GOD, the Creator and Preserver of all mankind, we humbly beseech thee for all sorts and conditions of men, that thou wouldest be pleased to make thy ways known unto them, thy saving health unto all nations. More especially we pray for the good estate of the Catholic Church; that it may be so guided and governed by thy good Spirit, that all who profess and call themselves Christians may be led into the way of truth, and hold the faith in unity of spirit, in the bond of peace, and in righteousness of life. Finally, we commend to thy fatherly goodness all those who are any ways afflicted or distressed in mind, body, or estate; [*especially those for whom our prayers are desired;] that it may please thee to comfort and relieve them according to their several necessities; giving them patience under their sufferings, and a happy issue out of all their afflictions: And this we beg for Jesus Christ's sake. Amen.

* This is to be said when any desire the prayers of the congregation.

A General Thanksgiving.

A LMIGHTY God, Father of all mercies, we thine unworthy servants do give thee most humble and hearty thanks for all thy goodness and loving-kindness to us and to all men; [*particularly to those who desire now to offer up their praises and thanksgivings for thy late mercies vouchsafed unto them.] We bless thee for our creation, preservation, and all the blessings of this life; but above all, for thine inestimable love in the redemption of the world by our Lord Jesus Christ; for the means of grace, and for the hope of glory. And, we beseech thee, give us that due sense of all thy mer-

* This is to be said when any desire to return thanks.

cies, that our hearts may be unfeignedly thankful, and that we may show forth thy praise, not only with our lips, but in our lives; by giving up ourselves to thy service, and by walking before thee in holiness and righteousness all our days; through Jesus Christ our Lord, to whom with thee and the Holy Ghost be all honour and glory, world without end. *Amen.*

ALMIGHTY God, who hast given us grace at this time with one accord to make our common supplications unto thee, and dost promise that when two or three are gathered together in thy name, thou wilt grant their requests; Fulfil now, O Lord, the desires and petitions of thy servants as may be most expedient for them; granting us in this world knowledge of thy truth, and in the world to come life everlasting. *Amen.*

2 *Cor.* xiii. 14.

THE grace of our Lord Jesus Christ, and the love of God, and the fellowship of the Holy Ghost, be with you all evermore. *Amen.*

EVENING PRAYER,

EVERY LORD'S DAY.

At the beginning of Evening Prayer, the Minister shall read with a loud Voice some one or more of these Sentences of the Scriptures that follow: And then he shall say that which is written after the said Sentences.

WHEN the wicked man turneth away from his wickedness that he hath committed, and doeth that which is lawful and right, he shall save his soul alive. Ezek. xviii. 27.

The sacrifices of God are a broken spirit: a broken and a contrite heart, O God, thou wilt not despise. Psalm li. 17.

To the Lord our God belong mercies and forgivenesses, though we have rebelled against him; neither have we obeyed the voice of the Lord our God, to walk in his laws which he set before us. Dan. ix. 9, 10.

I will arise, and go to my father, and will say unto him, Father, I have sinned against Heaven and before thee, and am no more worthy to be called thy son. Luke xv. 18, 19.

Enter not into judgment with thy servant, O Lord; for in thy sight shall no flesh living be justified. Psalm cxliii. 2.

DEARLY beloved brethren, the Scripture moveth us, in sundry places, to acknowledge and confess our manifold sins and wickedness, and that we should not dissemble nor cloak them before the face of Almighty God, our heavenly Father; but confess them with an humble, lowly, penitent, and obedient heart; to the end that we may obtain forgiveness of the same, by his infinite goodness and mercy. Wherefore I pray and beseech you, as many as are here present, to accompany me with a pure heart and humble voice, unto the throne of the heavenly grace, saying after me:

A general Confession, to be said by the whole Congregation, after the Minister, all kneeling.

ALMIGHTY and most merciful Father, we have erred and strayed from thy ways like lost sheep. We have followed too much the devices and desires of our own hearts. We have offended against thy holy laws. We have left undone those things which we ought to have done; And we have done those things which we ought not to have done; And there is no health in us. But thou, O Lord, have mercy upon us, miserable offenders. Spare thou them, O God, who confess their faults. Restore thou them that are penitent; According to thy promises declared unto mankind in Christ Jesus our Lord. And grant, O most merciful Father, for his sake, That we may hereafter live a godly, righteous, and sober life, To the glory of thy holy name. *Amen.*

Then the Minister shall say,

O LORD, we beseech thee, absolve thy people from their offences; that through thy bountiful goodness, we may be delivered from the bands of those sins,

which by our frailty we have committed. Grant this,
O heavenly Father, for Jesus Christ's sake, our blessed
Lord and Saviour. *Amen.*

Then the Minister shall say the Lord's Prayer; the People also
repeating it with him.

OUR Father, who art in heaven, Hallowed be thy
Name. Thy kingdom come. Thy will be done on
earth, As it is in heaven. Give us this day our daily
bread. And forgive us our trespasses, As we forgive
them that trespass against us. And lead us not into
temptation ; But deliver us from evil ; For thine is the
kingdom, and the power, and the glory, For ever and
ever. *Amen.*

Then likewise he shall say,

O Lord, open thou our lips,
Answ. *And our mouth shall show forth thy praise.*
Minist. O God, make speed to save us.
Answ. *O Lord, make haste to help us.*

Here all standing up, the Minister shall say,

Glory be to the Father, and to the Son, and to the
Holy Ghost ;
Answ. *As it was in the beginning, is now, and ever
shall be, world without end.*   Amen.
Minist. Praise ye the Lord.
Answ. *The Lord's name be praised.*

Then shall be said the Psalms in order as they are appointed.
Then a Lesson out of the Old Testament, as is appointed : and
after that the following Psalm :

O SING unto the Lord a new song ; for he hath
done marvellous things.

With his own right hand, and with his holy arm, hath he gotten himself the victory.

The Lord declareth his salvation; his righteousness hath he openly showed in the sight of the heathen.

He hath remembered his mercy and truth towards the house of Israel; and all the ends of the world have seen the salvation of our God.

Show yourselves joyful unto the Lord, all ye lands; sing, rejoice, and give thanks.

Let the sea make a noise, and all that therein is; the round world, and they that dwell therein.

Let the floods clap their hands, and let the hills be joyful together before the Lord: for he cometh to judge the earth.

With righteousness shall he judge the world; and the people with equity.

Glory be to the Father, &c.

As it was in the beginning, &c.

Then a Lesson out of the New Testament, as it is appointed: And after that the following Psalm:

G OD be merciful unto us, and bless us; and show us the light of his countenance, and be merciful unto us.

That thy way may be known upon earth; thy saving health among all nations.

Let the people praise thee, O God; yea, let all the people praise thee.

O let the nations rejoice and be glad; for thou shalt judge the people righteously, and govern the nations upon the earth.

Let the people praise thee, O God; yea, let all the people praise thee.

Then shall the earth bring forth her increase: and God, even our own God, shall give us his blessing.

God shall bless us; and all the ends of the world shall fear him.

Glory be to the Father, &c.

As it was in the beginning, &c.

Then shall be said the Apostles' Creed, by the Minister and the People, standing.

I BELIEVE in God, the Father Almighty, Maker of heaven and earth:

And in Jesus Christ, his only Son our Lord: Who was conceived by the Holy Ghost; Born of the Virgin Mary; suffered under Pontius Pilate; Was crucified, dead, and buried: He descended into hell; The third day he rose again from the dead: He ascended into heaven, And sitteth on the right hand of God the Father Almighty; From thence he shall come to judge the quick and the dead.

I believe in the Holy Ghost; The Holy Catholic Church; The Communion of Saints; The Forgiveness of Sins; The Resurrection of the Body; And the Life everlasting. *Amen.*

Then shall the Minister pronounce with a loud voice,

The Lord be with you,

Answ. *And with thy spirit.*

Minist. Let us pray.

Lord, have mercy upon us.

Answ. *Christ, have mercy upon us.*

Minist. Lord, have mercy upon us.

Then shall follow three Collects; the first of the Day; the second for Peace; the third for Aid against all Perils.

The second Collect at Evening Prayer.

O GOD, from whom all holy desires, all good counsels, and all just works do proceed; Give unto thy servants that peace which the world cannot give; that both our hearts may be set to obey thy commandments, and also that by thee we being defended from the fear of our enemies, may pass our time in rest and quietness; through the merits of Jesus Christ our Saviour. *Amen.*

The third Collect, for Aid against all Perils.

LIGHTEN our darkness, we beseech thee, O Lord; and by thy great mercy defend us from all perils and dangers of this night, for the love of thy only Son our Saviour Jesus Christ. *Amen.*

A Prayer for the Queen.

O LORD, our heavenly Father, high and mighty, King of kings, Lord of lords, who dost from thy throne behold all the dwellers upon earth; Most heartily we beseech thee with thy favour to behold our gracious Sovereign, Queen VICTORIA; and so replenish her with the grace of thy Holy Spirit, that she may alway incline to thy will, and walk in thy way: Endue her plenteously with heavenly gifts; grant her in health and wealth long to live; strengthen her that she may vanquish and overcome all her enemies; and finally, after this life, she may attain everlasting joy and felicity; through Jesus Christ our Lord. *Amen.*

A Prayer for the Royal Family.

ALMIGHTY God, the fountain of all goodness, we humbly beseech thee to bless ADELAIDE the Queen Dowager, the Prince ALBERT, ALBERT Prince of WALES, and all the Royal Family: Endue them with thy Holy Spirit; enrich them with thy heavenly grace; prosper them with all happiness; and bring them to thine everlasting kingdom; through Jesus Christ our Lord. *Amen.*

B

A Prayer for the Ministers of the Gospel.

ALMIGHTY and everlasting God, who alone workest great marvels; Send down upon all the Ministers of thy Gospel the healthful Spirit of thy grace; and that they may truly please thee, pour upon them the continual dew of thy blessing. Grant this, O Lord, for the honour of our Advocate and Mediator Jesus Christ. *Amen.*

A Prayer for all Conditions of Men.

O GOD, the Creator and Preserver of all mankind, we humbly beseech thee for all sorts and conditions of men, that thou wouldest be pleased to make thy ways known unto them, thy saving health unto all nations. More especially we pray for the good estate of the Catholic Church; that it may be so guided and governed by thy good Spirit, that all who profess and call themselves Christians may be led into the way of truth, and hold the faith in unity of spirit, in the bond of peace, and in righteousness of life. Finally, we commend to thy fatherly goodness all those who are any ways afflicted or distressed, in mind, body, or estate; [* *especially those for whom our prayers are desired ;*] that it may please thee to comfort and relieve them according to their several necessities; giving them patience under their sufferings, and a * This is to be said when any desire the prayers of the congregation. happy issue out of all their afflictions: And this we beg for Jesus Christ's sake. *Amen.*

A General Thanksgiving.

ALMIGHTY God, Father of all mercies, we thine unworthy servants do give thee most humble and hearty thanks for all thy goodness and loving-kindness to us and to all men; [*particularly to those who desire now to offer up their praises and thanksgivings for thy late mercies vouchsafed unto them.] We bless

* This is to be said when any desire to return thanks.

thee for our creation, preservation, and all the blessings of this life; but above all, for thine inestimable love in the redemption of the world by our Lord Jesus Christ; for the means of grace, and for the hope of glory. And, we beseech thee, give us that due sense of all thy mercies, that our hearts may be unfeignedly thankful, and that we may show forth thy praise, not only with our lips, but in our lives; by giving up ourselves to thy service, and by walking before thee in holiness and righteousness all our days; through Jesus Christ our Lord, to whom with thee and the Holy Ghost, be all honour and glory, world without end. *Amen.*

ALMIGHTY God, who hast given us grace at this time, with one accord, to make our common supplications unto thee; and dost promise, that when two or three are gathered together in thy Name, thou wilt grant their requests; Fulfil now, O Lord, the desires and petitions of thy servants, as may be most expedient for them; granting us in this world knowledge of thy truth, and in the world to come life everlasting. *Amen.*

2 *Cor.* xiii. 14.

THE grace of our Lord Jesus Christ, and the love of God, and the fellowship of the Holy Ghost, be with you all evermore. *Amen.*

THE LITANY

OR

GENERAL SUPPLICATION,

TO BE SAID UPON WEDNESDAYS AND FRIDAYS.

O GOD the Father, of heaven, have mercy upon us miserable sinners.

O God the Father, of heaven, have mercy upon us miserable sinners.

O God the Son, Redeemer of the world, have mercy upon us miserable sinners.

O God the Son, Redeemer of the world, have mercy upon us miserable sinners.

O God the Holy Ghost, proceeding from the Father and the Son, have mercy upon us miserable sinners.

O God the Holy Ghost, proceeding from the Father and the Son, have mercy upon us miserable sinners.

O holy, blessed, and glorious Trinity, three persons and one God, have mercy upon us miserable sinners.

O holy, blessed, and glorious Trinity, three persons and one God, have mercy upon us miserable sinners.

Remember not, Lord, our offences, nor the offences of our forefathers; neither take thou vengeance of our sins; spare us, good Lord, spare thy people, whom thou hast redeemed with thy most precious blood, and be not angry with us for ever.

Spare us, good Lord.

From all evil and mischief; from sin, from the crafts and assaults of the devil: from thy wrath, and from everlasting damnation,

Good Lord, deliver us.

From all blindness of heart; from pride, vain-glory, and hypocrisy; from envy, hatred, and malice, and all uncharitableness,

Good Lord, deliver us.

From fornication, and all other deadly sin ; and from all the deceits of the world, the flesh, and the devil,

Good Lord, deliver us.

From lightning and tempest; from plague, pestilence, and famine ; from battle, and murder, and from sudden death,

Good Lord, deliver us.

From all sedition, privy conspiracy, and rebellion; from all false doctrine, heresy, and schism; from hardness of heart, and contempt of thy word and commandment,

Good Lord, deliver us.

By the mystery of thy holy incarnation; by thy holy Nativity and Circumcision ; by thy Baptism, Fasting, and Temptation,

Good Lord, deliver us.

By thine Agony and bloody Sweat; by thy Cross and Passion; by thy precious Death and Burial; by thy glorious Resurrection and Ascension ; and by the coming of the Holy Ghost,

Good Lord, deliver us.

In all time of our tribulation ; in all time of our wealth ; in the hour of death, and in the day of judgment,

Good Lord, deliver us.

We sinners do beseech thee to hear us, O Lord God ; and that it may please thee to rule and govern thy holy Church universal in the right way ;

We beseech thee to hear us, good Lord.

That it may please thee to keep and strengthen in the true worshipping of thee, in righteousness and holiness of life, thy servant VICTORIA, our most gracious Queen and Governor;

We beseech thee to hear us, good Lord.

That it may please thee to rule her heart in thy faith, fear, and love, that she may evermore have affiance in thee, and ever seek thy honour and glory;

We beseech thee to hear us, good Lord.

That it may please thee to be her Defender and Keeper, giving her the victory over all her enemies;

We beseech thee to hear us, good Lord.

That it may please thee to bless and preserve ADE-LAIDE the Queen Dowager, the Prince ALBERT, ALBERT Prince of WALES, and all the Royal Family;

We beseech thee to hear us, good Lord.

That it may please thee to illuminate all the Ministers of thy Gospel with true knowledge and understanding of thy Word; that both by their preaching and living they may set it forth, and show it accordingly;

We beseech thee to hear us, good Lord.

That it may please thee to bless and keep the Magistrates, giving them grace to execute justice, and to maintain truth;

We beseech thee to hear us, good Lord.

That it may please thee to bless and keep all thy people;

We beseech thee to hear us, good Lord.

That it may please thee to give to all nations unity, peace, and concord;

We beseech thee to hear us, good Lord.

That it may please thee to give us an heart to love and dread thee, and diligently to live after thy commandments;

We beseech thee to hear us, good Lord.

That it may please thee to give to all thy people increase of grace, to hear meekly thy word, and to receive it with pure affection, and to bring forth the fruits of the Spirit.

We beseech thee to hear us, good Lord.

That it may please thee to bring into the way of truth all such as have erred, and are deceived;

We beseech thee to hear us, good Lord.

That it may please thee to strengthen such as do stand, and to comfort and help the weak-hearted, and to raise up them that fall, and finally to beat down Satan under our feet;

We beseech thee to hear us, good Lord.

That it may please thee to succour, help, and comfort all that are in danger, necessity, and tribulation;

We beseech thee to hear us, good Lord.

That it may please thee to preserve all that travel by land or by water, all women labouring with child, all sick persons and young children; and to show thy pity upon all prisoners and captives;

We beseech thee to hear us, good Lord.

That it may please thee to defend, and provide for, the fatherless children, and widows, and all that are desolate and oppressed;

We beseech thee to hear us, good Lord.

That it may please thee to have mercy upon all men;

We beseech thee to hear us, good Lord.

That it may please thee to forgive our enemies, persecutors, and slanderers, and to turn their hearts;

We beseech thee to hear us, good Lord.

That it may please thee to give and preserve to our use the kindly fruits of the earth, so as in due time we may enjoy them;

We beseech thee to hear us, good Lord.

That it may please thee to give us true repentance; to forgive us all our sins, negligences, and ignorances; and to endue us with the grace of thy Holy Spirit, to amend our lives according to thy holy Word;

We beseech thee to hear us, good Lord.

Son of God, we beseech thee to hear us.

Son of God, we beseech thee to hear us.

O Lamb of God, that takest away the sins of the world ;

Grant us thy peace.

O Lamb of God, that takest away the sins of the world ;

Have mercy upon us.

O Christ, hear us.

O Christ, hear us.

Lord, have mercy upon us.

Lord, have mercy upon us.

Christ, have mercy upon us.

Christ, have mercy upon us.

Lord, have mercy upon us.

Lord, have mercy upon us.

Then shall the Minister, and the People with him, say the
Lord's Prayer.

OUR Father, who art in heaven, Hallowed be thy Name. Thy kingdom come. Thy will be done on earth, As it is in heaven. Give us this day our daily bread. And forgive us our trespasses, As we forgive them that trespass against us. And lead us not into temptation ; But deliver us from evil. *Amen.*

Minist. O Lord, deal not with us after our sins.

Answ. Neither reward us after our iniquities.

Let us pray.

O GOD, merciful Father, that despisest not the sighing of a contrite heart, nor the desire of such as be sorrowful ; Mercifully assist our prayers that we make before thee, in all our troubles and adversities, whensoever they oppress us ; and graciously hear us, that those evils, which the craft and subtilty of the devil or man worketh against us, be brought to nought, and by the providence of thy goodness be dispersed; that we thy servants, being hurt by no persecutions, may evermore give thanks unto thee in thy holy Church, through Jesus Christ our Lord.

O Lord, arise, help us, and deliver us, for thy Name's sake.

O GOD, we have heard with our ears, and our fathers have declared unto us, the noble works that thou didst in their days, and in the old time before them.

O Lord, arise, help us, and deliver us, for thine honour.

Glory be to the Father, and to the Son, and to the Holy Ghost;

As it was in the beginning, is now, and ever shall be, world without end. Amen.

From our enemies defend us, O Christ.
Graciously look upon our afflictions.
Pitifully behold the sorrows of our hearts.
Mercifully forgive the sins of thy people.
Favourably with mercy hear our prayers.
O Son of David, have mercy upon us.
Both now and ever, vouchsafe to hear us, O Christ.
Graciously hear us, O Christ; graciously hear us, O Lord Christ.
O Lord, let thy mercy be showed upon us;
As we do put our trust in thee.

Let us pray.

WE humbly beseech thee, O Father, mercifully to look upon our infirmities; and for the glory of thy Name turn from us all those evils that we most righteously have deserved; and grant that in all our troubles we may put our whole trust and confidence in thy mercy, and evermore serve thee in holiness and pureness of living, to thy honour and glory; through our only Mediator and Advocate, Jesus Christ our Lord. *Amen.*

ALMIGHTY God, who hast given us grace at this time, with one accord, to make our common supplications unto thee, and dost promise that when two or three are gathered together in thy name, thou wilt grant their requests; Fulfil now, O Lord, the desires and petitions of thy servants, as may be most expedient for them; granting us in this world knowledge of thy truth, and in the world to come life everlasting. *Amen.*

2 *Cor.* xiii. 14.

THE grace of our Lord Jesus Christ, and the love of God, and the fellowship of the Holy Ghost, be with you all evermore. *Amen.*

COLLECTS, EPISTLES, AND GOSPELS,

TO BE USED THROUGHOUT THE YEAR.

THE FIRST SUNDAY IN ADVENT.

The Collect.

ALMIGHTY God, give us grace that we may cast away the works of darkness, and put upon us the armour of light, now in the time of this mortal life, in which thy Son Jesus Christ came to visit us in great humility; that in the last day, when he shall come again in his glorious Majesty, to judge both the quick and dead, we may rise to the life immortal through him who liveth and reigneth with thee and the Holy Ghost, now and ever. *Amen.*

The Epistle. Rom. xiii. 8.

OWE no man any thing, but to love one another: for he that loveth another hath fulfilled the law. For this, Thou shalt not commit adultery, Thou shalt not kill, Thou shalt not steal, Thou shalt not bear false witness, Thou shalt not covet; and if there be any other commandment, it is briefly comprehended in this saying, namely, Thou shalt love thy neighbour as thy-self. Love worketh no ill to his neighbour : therefore love is the fulfilling of the law. And that knowing the time, that now it is high time to awake out of sleep : for now is our salvation nearer than when we believed. The night is far spent, the day is at hand : let us therefore cast off the works of darkness, and let us put on the armour of light. Let us walk honestly, as in the day ; not in rioting and drunkenness, not in chambering and wantonness, not in strife and envying. But put ye on the Lord Jesus Christ, and make not provision for the flesh, to fulfil the lusts thereof.

The Gospel. Matt. xxi. 1.

WHEN they drew nigh unto Jerusalem, and were come to Bethphage, unto the Mount of Olives, then sent Jesus two disciples, saying unto them, Go into the village over against you, and straightway ye shall find an ass tied, and a colt with her : loose them, and bring them unto me. And if any man say aught unto you, ye shall say, The Lord hath need of them ; and straightway he will send them. All this was done, that it might be fulfilled which was spoken by the pro-phet, saying, Tell ye the daughter of Sion, Behold, thy King cometh unto thee, meek, and sitting upon an ass, and a colt the foal of an ass. And the disciples went, and did as Jesus commanded them ; and brought the ass, and the colt, and put on them their clothes, and they set him thereon. And a very great multitude spread their garments in the way ; others cut down branches from the trees, and strawed them in the way. And the multitudes that went before, and that followed, cried, saying, Hosanna to the Son of David : Blessed is he that cometh in the name of the Lord ; Hosanna in the highest. And when he was come into Jerusalem, all the city was moved, saying, Who is this ? And the multitude said, This is Jesus the Prophet of Nazareth of Galilee. And Jesus went into the temple of God, and cast out all them that sold and bought in the temple; and overthrew the tables of the money-changers, and the seats of them that sold doves ; and said unto them, It is written, My house shall be called the house of prayer ; but ye have made it a den of thieves.

THE SECOND SUNDAY IN ADVENT.

The Collect.

BLESSED Lord, who hast caused all holy Scriptures to be written for our learning ; Grant that we may in such wise hear them, read, mark, learn, and inwardly digest them, that by patience and comfort of thy holy Word, we may embrace and ever hold fast the blessed hope of everlasting life, which thou hast given us in our Saviour Jesus Christ. *Amen.*

The Epistle.   Rom. xv. 4.

WHATSOEVER things were written aforetime were written for our learning ; that we through patience and comfort of the Scriptures might have hope. Now the God of patience and consolation grant you to be like-minded one toward another, according to Christ Jesus ; that ye may with one mind and one mouth glorify God, even the Father of our Lord Jesus Christ. Wherefore receive ye one another, as Christ also received us to the glory of God. Now I say, that Jesus Christ was a minister of the circumcision for the truth of God, to confirm the promises made unto the fathers : and that the Gentiles might glorify God for his mercy ; as it is written, For this cause I will confess to thee among the Gentiles, and sing unto thy name.

And again he saith, Rejoice, ye Gentiles, with his people. And again, Praise the Lord, all ye Gentiles; and laud him, all ye people. And again, Esaias saith, There shall be a root of Jesse, and he that shall rise to reign over the Gentiles; in him shall the Gentiles trust. Now the God of hope fill you with all joy and peace in believing, that ye may abound in hope, through the power of the Holy Ghost.

The Gospel. Luke xxi. 25.

AND there shall be signs in the sun, and in the moon, and in the stars; and upon the earth distress of nations with perplexity; the sea and the waves roaring; men's hearts failing them for fear, and for looking after those things which are coming on the earth: for the powers of heaven shall be shaken. And then shall they see the Son of Man coming in a cloud with power and great glory. And when these things begin to come to pass, then look up, and lift up your heads; for your redemption draweth nigh. And he spake to them a parable; Behold the fig-tree, and all the trees; when they now shoot forth, ye see and know of your own selves that summer is now nigh at hand. So likewise ye, when ye see these things come to pass, know ye that the kingdom of God is nigh at hand. Verily I say unto you, This generation shall not pass away, till all be fulfilled. Heaven and earth shall pass away: but my words shall not pass away.

THE THIRD SUNDAY IN ADVENT.

The Collect.

O LORD Jesus Christ, who at thy first coming didst send thy messenger to prepare thy way before thee; Grant that the ministers and stewards

of thy mysteries may likewise so prepare and make
ready thy way, by turning the hearts of the disobedient
to the wisdom of the just, that at thy second coming
to judge the world we may be found an acceptable
people in thy sight, who livest and reignest with the
Father and the Holy Spirit, ever one God, world
without end. *Amen.*

The Epistle. 1 Cor. iv. 1.

LET a man so account of us, as of the ministers
of Christ, and stewards of the mysteries of God.
Moreover it is required in stewards, that a man be
found faithful. But with me it is a very small thing
that I should be judged of you, or of man's judgment:
yea, I judge not mine own self. For I know nothing
by myself; yet am I not hereby justified: but he that
judgeth me is the Lord. Therefore judge nothing
before the time, until the Lord come, who both will
bring to light the hidden things of darkness, and will
make manifest the counsels of the hearts: and then
shall every man have praise of God.

The Gospel. Matt. xi. 2.

NOW when John had heard in the prison the works
of Christ, he sent two of his disciples, and said
unto him, Art thou he that should come, or do we look
for another? Jesus answered and said unto them, Go
and show John again those things which ye do hear and
see: The blind receive their sight, and the lame walk,
the lepers are cleansed, and the deaf hear, the dead are
raised, and the poor have the Gospel preached unto
them. And blessed is he, whosoever shall not be offended in me. And as they departed, Jesus began to
say unto the multitude concerning John, What went ye
out into the wilderness to see? A reed shaken with the

wind ? But what went ye out for to see ? A man clothed
in soft raiment ? Behold, they that wear soft clothing
are in kings' houses. But what went ye out for to see ?
A prophet ? yea, I say unto you, and more than a prophet. For this is he of whom it is written, Behold, I
send my messenger before thy face, which shall prepare
thy way before thee.

THE FOURTH SUNDAY IN ADVENT.

The Collect.

O LORD, raise up, we pray thee, thy power, and
come among us, and with great might succour us;
that whereas, through our sins and wickedness, we are
sore let and hindered in running the race that is set
before us, thy bountiful grace and mercy may speedily
help and deliver us; through the satisfaction of thy
Son our Lord; to whom with thee and the Holy Ghost
be honour and glory, world without end. *Amen.*

The Epistle. Phil. iv. 4.

REJOICE in the Lord alway: and again I say,
Rejoice. Let your moderation be known unto all
men. The Lord is at hand. Be careful for nothing;
but in every thing by prayer and supplication, with
thanksgiving, let your requests be made known unto
God. And the peace of God, which passeth all understanding, shall keep your hearts and minds through
Christ Jesus.

The Gospel. John i. 19.

THIS is the record of John, when the Jews sent
Priests and Levites from Jerusalem to ask him,
Who art thou ? And he confessed, and denied not ;

but confessed, I am not the Christ. And they asked him, What then ? Art thou Elias ? And he saith, I am not. Art thou that Prophet ? And he answered, No. Then said they unto him, Who art thou, that we may give an answer to them that sent us ? What sayest thou of thyself ? He said, I am the voice of one crying in the wilderness, Make straight the way of the Lord, as said the prophet Esaias. And they which were sent were of the Pharisees. And they asked him, and said unto him, Why baptizest thou then, if thou be not that Christ, nor Elias, neither that Prophet ? John answered them, saying, I baptize with water : but there standeth one among you whom ye know not ; he it is, who coming after me is preferred before me, whose shoe's latchet I am not worthy to unloose. These things were done in Bethabara, beyond Jordan, where John was baptizing.

The Nativity of our Lord, or the Birth-day of CHRIST, commonly called

CHRISTMAS-DAY.

The Collect.

ALMIGHTY God, who hast given us thy only be-gotten Son to take our nature upon him, and as at this time to be born of a pure Virgin ; Grant that we being regenerate, and made thy children by adoption and grace, may daily be renewed by thy Holy Spirit ; through the same our Lord Jesus Christ, who liveth and reigneth with thee and the same Spirit, ever one God, world without end. *Amen.*

The Epistle. Heb. i. 1.

GOD, who at sundry times, and in divers manners, spake in time past unto the fathers by the pro-phets, hath in these last days spoken unto us by his

Son, whom he hath appointed heir of all things, by
whom also he made the worlds; who being the brightness of his glory, and the express image of his person,
and upholding all things by the word of his power,
when he had by himself purged our sins, sat down on
the right hand of the Majesty on high; being made so
much better than the angels, as he hath by inheritance
obtained a more excellent name than they. For unto
which of the angels said he at any time, Thou art my
Son, this day have I begotten thee? And again, I will
be to him a Father, and he shall be to me a Son? And
again, when he bringeth in the first-begotten into the
world, he saith, And let all the angels of God worship
him. And of the angels he saith, Who maketh his
angels spirits, and his ministers a flame of fire. But
unto the Son he saith, Thy throne, O God, is for ever
and ever: a sceptre of righteousness is the sceptre of
thy kingdom. Thou hast loved righteousness, and
hated iniquity; therefore God, even thy God, hath
anointed thee with the oil of gladness above thy fellows.
And, Thou, Lord, in the beginning hast laid the foundation of the earth; and the heavens are the works of
thine hands: they shall perish, but thou remainest;
and they all shall wax old as doth a garment; and as
a vesture shalt thou fold them up, and they shall be
changed: but thou art the same, and thy years shall
not fail.

The Gospel. John i. 1.

IN the beginning was the Word, and the Word was
with God, and the Word was God. The same was
in the beginning with God. All things were made by
him; and without him was not any thing made that
was made. In him was life; and the life was the light
of men. And the light shineth in darkness, and the
darkness comprehended it not. There was a man sent
from God, whose name was John. The same came for

a witness, to bear witness of the Light, that all men through him might believe. He was not that Light, but was sent to bear witness of that Light. That was the true Light, which lighteth every man that cometh into the world. He was in the world, and the world was made by him, and the world knew him not. He came unto his own, and his own received him not. But as many as received him, to them gave he power to become the sons of God, even to them that believe on his name: which were born, not of blood, nor of the will of the flesh, nor of the will of man, but of God. And the Word was made flesh, and dwelt among us, (and we beheld his glory, the glory as of the only begotten of the Father,) full of grace and truth.

THE FIRST SUNDAY AFTER CHRISTMAS.

The Collect.

ALMIGHTY God, who hast given us thy only begotten Son to take our nature upon him, and as at this time to be born of a pure Virgin; Grant that we being regenerate, and made thy children by adoption and grace, may daily be renewed by thy Holy Spirit; through the same our Lord Jesus Christ, who liveth and reigneth with thee and the same Spirit, ever one God, world without end. *Amen.*

The Epistle. Gal. iv. 1.

NOW I say, That the heir, as long as he is a child, differeth nothing from a servant, though he be lord of all; but is under tutors and governors until the time appointed of the father. Even so we, when we were children, were in bondage under the elements of the world: but when the fulness of the time was come, God sent forth his Son, made of a woman, made under the law, to redeem them that were under the law, that we might receive the adoption of sons. And because ye are sons, God hath sent forth the Spirit of his Son into your hearts, crying, Abba, Father. Wherefore thou art no more a servant, but a son; and if a son, then an heir of God through Christ.

The Gospel. Matt. i. 18.

THE birth of Jesus Christ was on this wise : When as his mother Mary was espoused to Joseph, before they came together, she was found with child of the Holy Ghost. Then Joseph her husband, being a just man, and not willing to make her a public example, was minded to put her away privily. But while he thought on these things, behold, the angel of the Lord appeared unto him in a dream, saying, Joseph, thou son of David, fear not to take unto thee Mary thy wife ; for that which is conceived in her is of the Holy Ghost. And she shall bring forth a Son, and thou shalt call his name Jesus : for he shall save his people from their sins. Now all this was done, that it might be fulfilled which was spoken of the Lord by the prophet, saying, Behold, a virgin shall be with child, and shall bring forth a Son, and they shall call his name Emmanuel, which, being interpreted, is, God with us. Then Joseph being raised from sleep did as the angel of the Lord had bidden him, and took unto him his wife ; and knew her not till she had brought forth her first-born Son : and he called his name JESUS.

THE SECOND SUNDAY AFTER CHRISTMAS.

The Collect.

O LORD, we beseech thee mercifully to receive the prayers of thy people which call upon thee ; and grant that they may both perceive and know what things they ought to do, and also may have grace and power faithfully to fulfil the same; through Jesus Christ our Lord. *Amen.*

The Epistle. Rom. xii. 1.

I BESEECH you, therefore, brethren, by the mercies of God, that ye present your bodies a living sacrifice, holy, acceptable unto God, which is your reasonable service. And be not conformed to this world; but be ye transformed by the renewing of your mind, that ye may prove what is that good, and acceptable, and perfect will of God. For I say, through the grace given unto me, to every man that is among you, not to think of himself more highly than he ought to think; but to think soberly, according as God hath dealt to every man the measure of faith. For as we have many members in one body, and all members have not the same office; so we, being many, are one body in Christ, and every one members one of another.

The Gospel. Luke ii. 41.

NOW his parents went to Jerusalem every year at the feast of the passover. And when he was twelve years old, they went up to Jerusalem after the custom of the feast. And when they had fulfilled the days, as they returned, the child Jesus tarried behind in Jerusalem; and Joseph and his mother knew not of it. But they, supposing him to have been in the company, went a day's journey; and they sought him among their kinsfolk and acquaintance. And when they found him not, they turned back again to Jerusalem, seeking him. And it came to pass, that after three days they found him in the temple, sitting in the midst of the doctors, both hearing them, and asking them questions. And all that heard him were astonished at his understanding and answers. And when they saw him, they were amazed: and his mother said unto him, Son, why hast thou thus dealt with us? behold, thy father and I have sought thee sorrowing. And he said unto them, How is it that ye sought me? knew ye not that I must be about my Father's business? And they understood not the saying which he spake unto them. And he went down with them, and came to Nazareth, and was subject unto them: but his mother kept all these sayings in her heart. And Jesus increased in wisdom and stature, and in favour with God and man.

THE THIRD SUNDAY AFTER CHRISTMAS.

The Collect.

A LMIGHTY and everlasting God, who dost govern all things in heaven and earth; Mercifully hear the supplications of thy people, and grant us thy peace all the days of our life; through Jesus Christ our Lord. *Amen.*

The Epistle. Rom. xii. 6.

H AVING then gifts differing according to the grace that is given to us, whether prophecy, let us prophesy according to the proportion of faith; or ministry, let us wait on our ministering; or he that teacheth, on teaching; or he that exhorteth, on exhortation: he that giveth, let him do it with simplicity; he that ruleth, with diligence; he that showeth mercy, with cheerfulness. Let love be without dissimulation. Abhor that which is evil; cleave to that which is good. Be kindly affectioned one to another with brotherly love; in honour preferring one another: not slothful in business; fervent in spirit; serving the Lord; rejoicing in hope;

patient in tribulation; continuing instant in prayer; distributing to the necessity of saints; given to hospitality. Bless them which persecute you: bless, and curse not. Rejoice with them that do rejoice, and weep with them that weep. Be of the same mind one toward another. Mind not high things, but condescend to men of low estate.

The Gospel. John ii. 1.

AND the third day there was a marriage in Cana of Galilee: and the mother of Jesus was there: and both Jesus was called, and his disciples, to the marriage. And when they wanted wine, the mother of Jesus saith unto him, They have no wine. Jesus saith unto her, Woman, what have I to do with thee? Mine hour is not yet come. His mother saith unto the servants, Whatsoever he saith unto you, do it. And there were set there six water-pots of stone, after the manner of the purifying of the Jews, containing two or three firkins apiece. Jesus saith unto them, Fill the water-pots with water. And they filled them up to the brim. And he saith unto them, Draw out now, and bear unto the governor of the feast. And they bare it. When the ruler of the feast had tasted the water that was made wine, and knew not whence it was; (but the servants who drew the water knew;) the governor of the feast called the bridegroom, and saith unto him, Every man at the beginning doth set forth good wine; and when men have well drunk, then that which is worse: but thou hast kept the good wine until now. This beginning of miracles did Jesus in Cana of Galilee, and manifested forth his glory; and his disciples believed on him.

THE FOURTH SUNDAY AFTER CHRISTMAS

The Collect.

A LMIGHTY and everlasting God, mercifully look upon our infirmities, and in all our dangers and necessities stretch forth thy right hand to help and defend us ; through Jesus Christ our Lord. *Amen.*

The Epistle. Rom. xii. 16.

B E not wise in your own conceits. Recompense to no man evil for evil. Provide things honest in the sight of all men. If it be possible, as much as lieth in you, live peaceably with all men. Dearly beloved, avenge not yourselves, but rather give place unto wrath : for it is written, Vengeance is mine ; I will repay, saith the Lord. Therefore if thine enemy hunger, feed him ; if he thirst, give him drink : for in so doing thou shalt heap coals of fire on his head. Be not overcome of evil, but overcome evil with good.

The Gospel. Matt. viii. 1.

W HEN he was come down from the mountain, great multitudes followed him. And, behold, there came a leper, and worshipped him, saying, Lord, if thou wilt, thou canst make me clean. And Jesus put forth his hand, and touched him, saying, I will ; be thou clean. And immediately his leprosy was cleansed. And Jesus saith unto him, See thou tell no man ; but go thy way, show thyself to the priest, and offer the gift that Moses commanded for a testimony unto them. And when Jesus was entered into Capernaum, there came unto him a centurion, beseeching him, and saying, Lord, my servant lieth at home sick of the palsy, grievously tormented. And Jesus saith unto him, I will come and heal him. The centurion answered and said, Lord, I am not worthy that thou shouldest come under my roof; but speak the word only, and my servant shall be healed. For I am a man under authority, having soldiers under me: and I say unto this man, Go, and he goeth; and to another, Come, and he cometh; and to my servant, Do this, and he doeth it. When Jesus heard it, he marvelled, and said to them that followed, Verily I say unto you, I have not found so great faith, no, not in Israel. And I say unto you, that many shall come from the east and west, and shall sit down with Abraham, and Isaac, and Jacob, in the kingdom of heaven. But the children of the kingdom shall be cast out into outer darkness: there shall be weeping and gnashing of teeth. And Jesus said unto the centurion, Go thy way; and as thou hast believed, so be it done unto thee. And his servant was healed in the selfsame hour.

THE FIFTH SUNDAY AFTER CHRISTMAS.

The Collect.

O GOD, who knowest us to be set in the midst of so many and great dangers, that by reason of the frailty of our nature we cannot always stand upright; Grant to us such strength and protection as may support us in all dangers, and carry us through all temptations; through Jesus Christ our Lord. *Amen.*

The Epistle. Rom. xiii. 1.

LET every soul be subject unto the higher powers. For there is no power but of God: the powers that be are ordained of God. Whosoever, therefore, resisteth the power, resisteth the ordinance of God: and they that resist, shall receive to themselves damna-

tion. For rulers are not a terror to good works, but to
the evil. Wilt thou then not be afraid of the power?
do that which is good, and thou shalt have praise of the
same: for he is the minister of God to thee for good.
But if thou do that which is evil, be afraid; for he
beareth not the sword in vain: for he is the minister of
God, a revenger to execute wrath upon him that doeth
evil. Wherefore ye must needs be subject, not only
for wrath, but also for conscience' sake. For for this
cause pay ye tribute also: for they are God's ministers,
attending continually upon this very thing. Render,
therefore, to all their dues: tribute to whom tribute is
due; custom to whom custom; fear to whom fear:
honour to whom honour.

The Gospel. Matt. viii. 23.

A ND when he was entered into a ship, his disciples
followed him. And, behold, there arose a great
tempest in the sea, insomuch that the ship was covered
with the waves: but he was asleep. And his disciples
came to him, and awoke him, saying, Lord, save us:
we perish. And he saith unto them, Why are ye fearful, O ye of little faith? Then he arose, and rebuked
the winds and the sea; and there was a great calm.
But the men marvelled, saying, What manner of man is
this, that even the winds and the sea obey him! And
when he was come to the other side into the country
of the Gergesenes, there met him two possessed with
devils, coming out of the tombs, exceeding fierce, so
that no man might pass by that way. And, behold, they
cried out, saying, What have we to do with thee, Jesus,
thou Son of God? art thou come hither to torment us
before the time? And there was a good way off from
them an herd of many swine feeding. So the devils
besought him, saying, If thou cast us out, suffer us to
go away into the herd of swine. And he said unto

them, Go. And when they were come out, they went into the herd of swine : and, behold, the whole herd of swine ran violently down a steep place into the sea, and perished in the waters. And they that kept them fled, and went their ways into the city, and told every thing, and what was befallen to the possessed of the devils. And, behold, the whole city came out to meet Jesus : and when they saw him, they besought him that he would depart out of their coasts.

THE SIXTH SUNDAY AFTER CHRISTMAS.

The Collect.

O LORD, we beseech thee to keep thy church and household continually in thy true religion ; that they who do lean only upon the hope of thy heavenly grace may evermore be defended by thy mighty power ; through Jesus Christ our Lord. *Amen.*

The Epistle. Col. iii. 12.

PUT on therefore, as the elect of God, holy and beloved, bowels of mercies, kindness, humbleness of mind, meekness, long-suffering ; forbearing one an- other, and forgiving one another, if any man have a quarrel against any : even as Christ forgave you, so also do ye. And above all these things put on love, which is the bond of perfectness. And let the peace of God rule in your hearts, to which also ye are called in one body ; and be ye thankful. Let the word of Christ dwell in you richly in all wisdom ; teaching and admonishing one another in psalms and hymns and spiritual songs, singing with grace in your hearts to the Lord. And whatsoever ye do in word or deed, do all in the Name of the Lord Jesus, giving thanks to God and the Father by him.

c 2

The Gospel. Matt. xiii. 24.

THE kingdom of heaven is likened unto a man who sowed good seed in his field : but while men slept, his enemy came and sowed tares among the wheat, and went his way. But when the blade was sprung up, and brought forth fruit, then appeared the tares also. So the servants of the householder came, and said unto him, Sir, didst not thou sow good seed in thy field? from whence then hath it tares? He said unto them, An enemy hath done this. The servants said unto him, Wilt thou then that we go and gather them up? But he said, Nay; lest while ye gather up the tares, ye root up also the wheat with them. Let both grow together until the harvest : and in the time of harvest, I will say to the reapers, Gather ye together first the tares, and bind them in bundles to burn them : but gather the wheat into my barn.

THE SEVENTH SUNDAY AFTER CHRISTMAS.

The Collect.

O GOD, whose blessed Son was manifested that he might destroy the works of the devil, and make us the sons of God, and heirs of eternal life ; Grant us, we beseech thee, that, having this hope, we may purify ourselves even as he is pure ; that when he shall appear again, with power and great glory, we may be made like unto him in his eternal and glorious kingdom ; where with thee, O Father, and thee, O Holy Ghost, he liveth and reigneth, ever one God, world without end. *Amen.*

The Epistle. 1 John iii. 1.

BEHOLD, what manner of love the Father hath bestowed upon us, that we should be called the

sons of God : therefore the world knoweth us not, because it knew him not.   Beloved, now are we the sons
of God, and it doth not yet appear what we shall be ;
but we know that, when he shall appear, we shall be
like him, for we shall see him as he is.   And every man
that hath this hope in him purifieth himself, even as he
is pure.   Whosoever committeth sin transgresseth also
the law ; for sin is the transgression of the law.   And
ye know that he was manifested to take away our sins ;
and in him is no sin.   Whosoever abideth in him, sinneth not : whosoever sinneth hath not seen him, neither
known him.   Little children, let no man deceive you :
he that doeth righteousness is righteous, even as he is
righteous.   He that committeth sin is of the devil ; for
the devil sinneth from the beginning.   For this purpose
the Son of God was manifested, that he might destroy
the works of the devil.

The Gospel.   Matt. xxiv. 23.

THEN if any man shall say unto you, Lo, here is
Christ, or there, believe it not.   For there shall
arise false Christs, and false prophets, and shall show
great signs and wonders ; insomuch that, if it were
possible, they shall deceive the very elect.   Behold, I
have told you before.   Wherefore, if they shall say unto
you, Behold, he is in the desert ; go not forth : Behold,
he is in the secret chambers ; believe it not.   For as the
lightning cometh out of the east, and shineth even unto
the west, so shall also the coming of the Son of man be.
For wheresoever the carcase is, there will the eagles be
gathered together.   Immediately after the tribulation of
those days shall the sun be darkened, and the moon
shall not give her light, and the stars shall fall from
heaven, and the powers of the heavens shall be shaken.
And then shall appear the sign of the Son of man in
heaven : and then shall all the tribes of the earth

mourn, and they shall see the Son of man coming in the clouds of heaven with power and great glory. And he shall send his angels with a great sound of a trumpet, and they shall gather together his elect from the four winds, from one end of heaven to the other.

THE EIGHTH SUNDAY AFTER CHRISTMAS.

The Collect.

O LORD, we beseech thee favourably to hear the prayers of thy people; that we who are justly punished for our offences, may be mercifully delivered by thy goodness, for the glory of thy name, through Jesus Christ our Saviour, who liveth and reigneth with thee and the Holy Ghost, ever one God, world without end. *Amen.*

The Epistle. 1 Cor. ix. 24.

KNOW ye not that they which run in a race run all, but one receiveth the prize? So run, that ye may obtain. And every man that striveth for the mastery is temperate in all things. Now they do it to obtain a corruptible crown; but we an incorruptible. I therefore so run, not as uncertainly; so fight I, not as one that beateth the air; but I keep under my body, and bring it into subjection, lest that by any means, when I have preached to others, I myself should be a castaway.

The Gospel. Matt. xx. 1.

THE kingdom of heaven is like unto a man that is an householder, which went out early in the morning to hire labourers into his vineyard. And when he had agreed with the labourers for a penny a day, he sent them into his vineyard. And he went out about the third hour, and saw others standing idle in the market-place, and said unto them, Go ye also into the vineyard, and whatsoever is right I will give you. And they went their way. Again he went out about the sixth and ninth hour, and did likewise. And about the eleventh hour he went out, and found others standing idle, and saith unto them, Why stand ye here all the day idle? They say unto him, Because no man hath hired us. He saith unto them, Go ye also into the vineyard; and whatsoever is right, that shall ye receive. So when even was come, the Lord of the vineyard saith unto his steward, Call the labourers, and give them their hire, beginning from the last unto the first. And when they came that were hired about the eleventh hour, they received every man a penny. But when the first came, they supposed that they should have received more; and they likewise received every man a penny. And when they had received it, they murmured against the good man of the house, saying, These last have wrought but one hour, and thou hast made them equal unto us, who have borne the burden and heat of the day. But he answered one of them, and said, Friend, I do thee no wrong. Didst thou not agree with me for a penny? Take that thine is, and go thy way: I will give unto this last even as unto thee. Is it not lawful for me to do what I will with mine own? Is thine eye evil because I am good? So the last shall be first, and the first last; for many are called, but few chosen.

THE NINTH SUNDAY AFTER CHRISTMAS.

The Collect.

O LORD God, who seest that we put not our trust in any thing that we do; Mercifully grant that by thy power we may be defended against all adversity; through Jesus Christ our Lord. *Amen.*

The Epistle. 2 Cor. xi. 19.

YE suffer fools gladly, seeing ye yourselves are wise. For ye suffer if a man bring you into bondage, if a man devour you, if a man take of you, if a man exalt himself, if a man smite you on the face. I speak as concerning reproach, as though we had been weak. Howbeit, whereinsoever any is bold, (I speak foolishly,) I am bold also. Are they Hebrews? so am I. Are they Israelites? so am I. Are they the seed of Abraham? so am I. Are they ministers of Christ? (I speak as a fool,) I am more: in labours more abundant, in stripes above measure, in prisons more frequent, in deaths oft. Of the Jews five times received I forty stripes save one. Thrice was I beaten with rods, once was I stoned, thrice I suffered shipwreck, a night and a day have I been in the deep; in journeyings often, in perils of waters, in perils of robbers, in perils by mine own countrymen, in perils by the heathen, in perils in the city, in perils in the wilderness, in perils in the sea, in perils among false brethren; in weariness and painfulness, in watchings often, in hunger and thirst, in fastings often, in cold and nakedness. Beside those things that are without, that which cometh upon me daily, the care of all the churches. Who is weak, and I am not weak? Who is offended, and I burn not? If I must needs glory, I will glory of the things which concern mine infirmities. The God and Father of our Lord Jesus Christ, who is blessed for evermore, knoweth that I lie not.

The Gospel. Luke viii. 4.

WHEN much people were gathered together, and were come to him out of every city, he spake by a parable. A sower went out to sow his seed: and as he sowed, some fell by the way-side; and it was trodden down, and the fowls of the air devoured it. And some fell upon a rock; and as soon as it was sprung up, it withered away, because it lacked moisture. And some fell among thorns; and the thorns sprang up with it, and choked it. And other fell on good ground, and sprang up, and bare fruit an hundred-fold. And when he had said these things, he cried, He that hath ears to hear, let him hear. And his disciples asked him, saying, What might this parable be? And he said, Unto you it is given to know the mysteries of the kingdom of God; but to others in parables; that seeing they might not see, and hearing they might not understand. Now the parable is this: The seed is the word of God. Those by the way-side are they that hear. Then cometh the devil, and taketh away the word out of their hearts, lest they should believe and be saved. They on the rock are they who, when they hear, receive the word with joy; and these have no root, who for a while believe, and in time of temptation fall away. And that which fell among thorns are they who, when they have heard, go forth, and are choked with cares and riches and pleasures of this life, and bring no fruit to perfection. But that on the good ground are they who, in an honest and good heart, having heard the word, keep it, and bring forth fruit with patience.

THE TENTH SUNDAY AFTER CHRISTMAS.

The Collect.

O LORD, who hast taught us that all our doings without love are nothing worth; Send thy Holy Spirit, and pour into our hearts that most excellent gift of love, the very bond of peace, and of all virtues, without which whosoever liveth is counted dead before thee: Grant this for thine only Son Jesus Christ's sake. *Amen.*

The Epistle. 1 Cor. xiii. 1.

THOUGH I speak with the tongues of men and of angels, and have not love, I am become as sounding brass, or a tinkling cymbal. And though I have the gift of prophecy and understand all mysteries, and all knowledge; and though I have all faith, so that I could remove mountains, and have not love, I am nothing. And though I bestow all my goods to feed the poor, and though I give my body to be burned, and have not love, it profiteth me nothing. Love suffereth long, and is kind; love envieth not; love vaunteth not itself, is not puffed up, doth not behave itself unseemly, seeketh not her own, is not provoked, thinketh no evil; rejoiceth not in iniquity, but rejoiceth in the truth; covereth all things, believeth all things, hopeth all things, endureth all things. Love never faileth: but whether there be prophecies, they shall fail; whether there be tongues, they shall cease; whether there be knowledge, it shall vanish away. For we know in part, and we prophesy in part. But when that which is perfect is come, then that which is in part shall be done away. When I was a child, I spake as a child, I understood as a child, I thought as a child; but when I became a man, I put away childish things. For now we see through a glass darkly; but then face to face: now I know in part; but then shall I know even as also I am known. And now abide faith, hope, love, these three; but the greatest of these is love.

The Gospel. Luke xviii. 31.

THEN Jesus took unto him the twelve, and said unto them, Behold, we go up to Jerusalem, and all things that are written by the prophets concerning the Son of man shall be accomplished. For he shall be delivered unto the Gentiles, and shall be mocked, and spitefully entreated, and spitted on: and they shall scourge him, and put him to death: and the third day he shall rise again. And they understood none of these things: and this saying was hid from them, neither knew they the things which were spoken. And it came to pass, that as he was come nigh unto Jericho, a certain blind man sat by the way-side begging: and hearing the multitude pass by, he asked what it meant. And they told him that Jesus of Nazareth passed by. And he cried, saying, Jesus, thou Son of David, have mercy on me. And they who went before rebuked him, that he should hold his peace: but he cried so much the more, Thou Son of David, have mercy on me. And Jesus stood, and commanded him to be brought unto him: and when he was come near, he asked him, saying, What wilt thou that I should do unto thee? And he said, Lord, that I may receive my sight. And Jesus said unto him, Receive thy sight: thy faith hath saved thee. And immediately he received his sight, and followed him, glorifying God: and all the people, when they saw it, gave praise to God.

THE ELEVENTH SUNDAY AFTER CHRISTMAS.

The Collect.

O LORD, who for our sake didst fast forty days and forty nights; Give us grace to use such abstinence, that our flesh being subdued to the Spirit, we may ever obey thy godly motions in righteousness, and true holiness, to thy honour and glory, who livest and reignest with the Father and the Holy Ghost, one God, world without end. *Amen.*

The Epistle. 2 Cor. vi. 1.

WE then, as workers together with him, beseech you also that ye receive not the grace of God in

vain. (For he saith, I have heard thee in a time accepted, and in the day of salvation have I succoured
thee: behold, now is the accepted time; behold, now
is the day of salvation.) Giving no offence in any thing,
that the ministry be not blamed: but in all things
approving ourselves as the ministers of God, in much
patience, in afflictions, in necessities, in distresses, in
stripes, in imprisonments, in tumults, in labours, in
watchings, in fastings; by pureness, by knowledge, by
long-suffering, by kindness, by the Holy Ghost, by love
unfeigned, by the word of truth, by the power of God,
by the armour of righteousness on the right hand and
on the left, by honour and dishonour, by evil report
and good report; as deceivers, and yet true; as un-
known, and yet well known; as dying, and, behold, we
live; as chastened, and not killed; as sorrowful, yet
alway rejoicing; as poor, yet making many rich; as
having nothing, and yet possessing all things.

The Gospel. Matt. iv. 1.

THEN was Jesus led up of the Spirit into the wilderness, to be tempted of the devil. And when he
had fasted forty days and forty nights, he was afterwards an hungred. And when the tempter came to
him, he said, If thou be the Son of God, command that
these stones be made bread. But he answered and
said, It is written, Man shall not live by bread alone,
but by every word that proceedeth out of the mouth of
God. Then the devil taketh him up into the holy city,
and setteth him on a pinnacle of the temple, and saith
unto him, If thou be the Son of God, cast thyself
down: for it is written, He shall give his angels charge
concerning thee, and in their hands shall they bear thee
up, lest at any time thou dash thy foot against a stone.
Jesus said unto him, It is written again, Thou shalt not

tempt the Lord thy God. Again, the devil taketh him
up into an exceeding high mountain, and showeth him
all the kingdoms of the world, and the glory of them;
and saith unto him, All these things will I give thee, if
thou wilt fall down and worship me. Then saith Jesus
unto him, Get thee hence, Satan: for it is written,
Thou shalt worship the Lord thy God, and him only
shalt thou serve. Then the devil leaveth him, and,
behold, angels came and ministered unto him.

THE TWELFTH SUNDAY AFTER CHRISTMAS.

The Collect.

ALMIGHTY God, who seest that we have no
power of ourselves to help ourselves; Keep us
both outwardly in our bodies, and inwardly in our
souls; that we may be defended from all adversities
which may happen to the body, and from all evil
thoughts which may assault and hurt the soul; through
Jesus Christ our Lord. *Amen.*

The Epistle. 1 Thess. iv. 1.

WE beseech you, brethren, and exhort you by the
Lord Jesus, that as ye have received of us how
ye ought to walk, and to please God, so ye would
abound more and more. For ye know what commandments we gave you by the Lord Jesus. For this is the
will of God, even your sanctification, that ye should
abstain from fornication: that every one of you should
know how to possess his vessel in sanctification and
honour; not in the lust of concupiscence, even as the
Gentiles who know not God: that no man go beyond
and defraud his brother in any matter: because that the

Lord is the avenger of all such, as we also have fore-warned you and testified. For God hath not called us to uncleanness, but unto holiness. He therefore tha despiseth, despiseth not man, but God, who hath also given unto us his Holy Spirit.

The Gospel. Matt. xv. 21.

JESUS went thence, and departed into the coasts of Tyre and Sidon. And behold, a woman of Canaan came out of the same coasts, and cried unto him, say-ing, Have mercy on me, O Lord, thou Son of David· my daughter is grievously vexed with a devil. But he answered her not a word. And his disciples came and besought him, saying, Send her away; for she crieth after us. But he answered and said, I am not sent but unto the lost sheep of the house of Israel. Then came she and worshipped him, saying, Lord, help me. But he answered and said, It is not meet to take the child-ren's bread, and to cast it to dogs. And she said, Truth, Lord: yet the dogs eat of the crumbs which fall from their masters' table. Then Jesus answered and said unto her, O woman, great is thy faith: be it unto thee even as thou wilt. And her daughter was made whole from that very hour.

THE THIRTEENTH SUNDAY AFTER CHRISTMAS.

The Collect.

WE beseech thee, Almighty God, look upon the hearty desires of thy humble servants, and stretch forth the right hand of thy Majesty, to be our defence against all our enemies; through Jesus Christ our Lord. Amen.

The Epistle.   Ephes. v. 1.

BE ye therefore followers of God, as dear children ; and walk in love, as Christ also hath loved us, and hath given himself for us, an offering and a sacrifice to God for a sweet-smelling savour.   But fornication, and all uncleanness, or covetousness, let it not be once named amongst you, as becometh saints ; neither fil-thiness, nor foolish talking, nor jesting, which are not convenient : but rather giving of thanks.   For this ye know, that no whoremonger, or unclean person, or covetous man, who is an idolater, hath any inheritance in the kingdom of Christ and of God.   Let no man deceive you with vain words : for because of these things cometh the wrath of God upon the children of disobedience.   Be not ye therefore partakers with them. For ye were sometimes darkness, but now are ye light in the Lord : walk as children of light ; (for the fruit of the Spirit is in all goodness, and righteousness, and truth ;) proving what is acceptable unto the Lord.   And have no fellowship with the unfruitful works of darkness, but rather reprove them.   For it is a shame even to speak of those things which are done of them in secret. But all things that are reproved are made manifest by the light : for whatsoever doth make manifest is light. Wherefore he saith, Awake thou that sleepest, and arise from the dead, and Christ shall give thee light.

The Gospel.   Luke xi. 14.

JESUS was casting out a devil, and it was dumb. And it came to pass, when the devil was gone out, the dumb spake ; and the people wondered.   But some of them said, He casteth out devils through Beelzebub the chief of the devils.   And others, tempting him, sought of him a sign from heaven.   But he, knowing their thoughts, said unto them, Every kingdom divided against itself is brought to desolation ; and a house divided against a house falleth. If Satan also be divided against himself, how shall his kingdom stand? because ye say that I cast out devils through Beelzebub. And if I by Beelzebub cast out devils, by whom do your sons cast them out? therefore shall they be your judges. But if I with the finger of God cast out devils, no doubt the kingdom of God is come upon you. When a strong man armed keepeth his palace, his goods are in peace: but when a stronger than he shall come upon him and overcome him, he taketh from him all his armour wherein he trusted, and divideth his spoils. He that is not with me is against me: and he that gathereth not with me scattereth. When the unclean spirit is gone out of a man, he walketh through dry places, seeking rest; and finding none, he saith, I will return unto my house whence I came out. And when he cometh, he findeth it swept and garnished. Then goeth he, and taketh to him seven other spirits more wicked than himself; and they enter in and dwell there: and the last state of that man is worse than the first. And it came to pass, as he spake these things, a certain woman of the company lifted up her voice, and said unto him, Blessed is the womb that bare thee, and the paps which thou hast sucked. But he said, Yea rather, blessed are they that hear the word of God, and keep it.

THE FOURTEENTH SUNDAY AFTER CHRISTMAS.

The Collect.

G RANT, we beseech thee, Almighty God, that we, who for our evil deeds do worthily deserve to be punished, by the comfort of thy grace may mercifully be relieved; through our Lord and Saviour Jesus Christ. *Amen.*

The Epistle. **Gal. iv. 21.**

TELL me, ye that desire to be under the law, do ye not hear the law? For it is written, that Abraham had two sons, the one by a bond-maid, the other by a free-woman. But he who was of the bond-woman was born after the flesh; but he of the free-woman was by promise. Which things are an allegory: for these are the two covenants; the one from the mount Sinai which gendereth to bondage, which is Agar. For this Agar is mount Sinai in Arabia, and answereth to Jerusalem which now is, and is in bondage with her children. But Jerusalem which is above is free, which is the mother of us all. For it is written, Rejoice, thou barren that bearest not; break forth and cry, thou that travailest not: for the desolate hath many more children than she who hath an husband. Now we, brethren, as Isaac was, are the children of promise. But as then he that was born after the flesh persecuted him that was born after the Spirit, even so it is now. Nevertheless what saith the Scripture? Cast out the bond-woman and her son: for the son of the bond-woman shall not be heir with the son of the free-woman. So then, brethren, we are not children of the bond-woman, but of the free.

The Gospel. **John vi. 1.**

JESUS went over the sea of Galilee, which is the sea of Tiberias. And a great multitude followed him, because they saw his miracles which he did on them that were diseased. And Jesus went up into a mountain, and there he sat with his disciples. And the passover, a feast of the Jews, was nigh. When Jesus then lifted up his eyes, and saw a great company come unto him, he saith unto Philip, Whence shall we buy bread, that these may eat? And this he said to prove him: for he himself knew what he would do. Philip answered him, Two hundred pennyworth of bread is not sufficient for them, that every one of them may take a little. One of his disciples, Andrew, Simon Peter's brother, saith unto him, There is a lad here, who hath five barley loaves, and two small fishes: but what are they among so many? And Jesus said, Make the men sit down. Now there was much grass in the place So the men sat down, in number about five thousand And Jesus took the loaves ; and when he had given thanks, he distributed to the disciples, and the disciples to them that were sat down ; and likewise of the fishes as much as they would. When they were filled, he said unto his disciples, Gather up the fragments that remain, that nothing be lost. Therefore they gathered them together, and filled twelve baskets with the fragments of the five barley loaves, which remained over and above unto them that had eaten. Then those men, when they had seen the miracle that Jesus did, said, This is of a truth that Prophet that should come into the world.

THE FIFTEENTH SUNDAY AFTER CHRISTMAS.

The Collect.

WE beseech thee, Almighty God, mercifully to look upon thy people ; that by thy great goodness they may be governed and preserved evermore, both in body and soul; through Jesus Christ our Lord. *Amen.*

The Epistle. Heb. ix. 11.

CHRIST being come an High Priest of good things to come, by a greater and more perfect tabernacle, not made with hands, that is to say, not of this building; neither by the blood of goats and calves, but by his own blood, he entered in once into the holy place, having obtained eternal redemption for us. For if the blood of bulls and of goats, and the ashes of an heifer sprinkling the unclean, sanctifieth to the purifying of the flesh; how much more shall the blood of Christ, who through the eternal Spirit offered himself without spot to God, purge your conscience from dead works to serve the living God? And for this cause he is the Mediator of the New Testament, that by means of death, for the redemption of the transgressions that were under the first testament, they who are called might receive the promise of eternal inheritance.

The Gospel.   John viii. 46.

JESUS said, Which of you convinceth me of sin? And if I say the truth, why do ye not believe me? He that is of God heareth God's words: ye therefore hear them not, because ye are not of God. Then answered the Jews, and said unto him, Say we not well, that thou art a Samaritan, and hast a devil? Jesus answered, I have not a devil; but I honour my Father, and ye do dishonour me. And I seek not mine own glory: there is one that seeketh and judgeth. Verily, verily, I say unto you, If a man keep my saying, he shall never see death. Then said the Jews unto him, Now we know that thou hast a devil. Abraham is dead, and the prophets; and thou sayest, If a man keep my saying, he shall never taste of death. Art thou greater than our father Abraham, who is dead? and the prophets are dead: whom makest thou thyself? Jesus said, If I honour myself, my honour is nothing: it is my Father that honoureth me; of whom ye say, that he is your God: yet ye have not known him; but I know him: and if I should say, I know him not, I should be a liar like unto you: but I know him, and keep his saying. Your father Abraham rejoiced to see my day: and he saw it, and was glad. Then said the Jews unto him, Thou art not yet fifty years old, and hast thou seen Abraham? Jesus said unto them, Verily, verily, I say unto you, Before Abraham was, I am. Then took they up stones to cast at him; but Jesus hid himself, and went out of the temple.

THE SUNDAY NEXT BEFORE EASTER.

The Collect.

ALMIGHTY and everlasting God, who, of thy tender love towards mankind, hast sent thy Son, our Saviour Jesus Christ, to take upon him our flesh, and to suffer death upon the cross, that all mankind should follow the example of his great humility; Mercifully grant, that we may both follow the example of his patience, and also be made partakers of his resurrection; through the same Jesus Christ our Lord. *Amen.*

The Epistle. Phil. ii. 5.

LET this mind be in you, which was also in Christ Jesus: who, being in the form of God, thought it not robbery to be equal with God; but made himself of no reputation, and took upon him the form of a servant, and was made in the likeness of men: and being found in fashion as a man, he humbled himself, and became obedient unto death, even the death of the cross. Wherefore God also hath highly exalted him, and given him a name which is above every name; that at the name of Jesus every knee should bow, of things in heaven, and things in earth, and things under the earth; and that every tongue should confess that Jesus Christ is Lord, to the glory of God the Father.

The Gospel. Matt. xxvii. 1.

WHEN the morning was come, all the chief priests and elders of the people took counsel against

Jesus, to put him to death. And when they had bound him, they led him away, and delivered him to Pontius Pilate the governor. Then Judas, who had betrayed him, when he saw that he was condemned, repented himself, and brought again the thirty pieces of silver to the chief priests and elders, saying, I have sinned, in that I have betrayed the innocent blood. And they said, What is that to us? see thou to that. And he cast down the pieces of silver in the temple, and departed, and went and hanged himself. And the chief priests took the silver pieces, and said, It is not lawful to put them into the treasury, because it is the price of blood. And they took counsel, and bought with them the potter's field, to bury strangers in. Wherefore that field was called, The field of blood, unto this day. Then was fulfilled that which was spoken by Jeremy the prophet, saying, And they took the thirty pieces of silver, the price of him that was valued, whom they of the children of Israel did value; and gave them for the potter's field, as the Lord appointed me. And Jesus stood before the governor: and the governor asked him, saying, Art thou the King of the Jews? And Jesus said unto him, Thou sayest. And when he was accused of the chief priests and elders, he answered nothing. Then said Pilate unto him, Hearest thou not how many things they witness against thee? And he answered him to never a word; insomuch that the governor marvelled greatly. Now at that feast the governor was wont to release unto the people a prisoner, whom they would. And they had then a notable prisoner, called Barabbas. Therefore when they were gathered together, Pilate said unto them, Whom will ye that I release unto you? Barabbas, or Jesus who is called Christ? For he knew that for envy they had delivered him. When he was set down on the judgment-seat, his wife sent unto him, saying, Have thou nothing to do with that just man : for I have suffered many things this day in a dream, because of him. But the chief priests and elders persuaded the multitude that they should ask Barabbas, and destroy Jesus. The governor answered and said unto them, Whether of the twain will ye that I release unto you? They said, Barabbas. Pilate saith unto them, What shall I do then with Jesus who is called Christ? They all say unto him, Let him be crucified. And the governor said, Why, what evil hath he done? But they cried out the more, saying, Let him be crucified. When Pilate saw that he could prevail nothing, but that rather a tumult was made, he took water, and washed his hands before the multitude, saying, I am innocent of the blood of this just person : see ye to it. Then answered all the people, and said, His blood be on us, and on our children. Then released he Barabbas unto them : and when he had scourged Jesus, he delivered him to be crucified. Then the soldiers of the governor took Jesus into the common hall, and gathered unto him the whole band of soldiers. And they stripped him, and put on him a scarlet robe. And when they had platted a crown of thorns, they put it upon his head, and a reed in his right hand : and they bowed the knee before him, and mocked him, saying, Hail, King of the Jews! And they spit upon him, and took the reed, and smote him on the head. And after that they had mocked him, they took the robe off from him, and put his own raiment on him, and led him away to crucify him. And as they came out, they found a man of Cyrene, Simon by name : him they compelled to bear the cross. And when they were come into a place called Golgotha, that is to say, A place of a skull, they gave him vinegar to drink. And they crucified him, and parted his garments, casting lots : that it might be fulfilled which was spoken by the prophet, They parted my garments among them, and upon my vesture did they cast lots. And sitting down, they watched him there ; and set up over his head his

accusation written, THIS IS JESUS THE KING OF
THE JEWS. Then were there two thieves crucified
with him, one on the right hand, and another on the
left. And they that passed by reviled him, wagging
their heads, and saying, Thou that destroyest the
temple, and buildest it in three days, save thyself. If
thou be the Son of God, come down from the cross.
Likewise also the chief priests mocking him, with the
scribes and elders, said, He saved others; himself he
cannot save. If he be the King of Israel, let him now
come down from the cross, and we will believe him.
He trusted in God ; let him deliver him now, if he will
have him : for he said, _ _ n the Son of God. The
thieves also, who were crucified with him, cast the
same in his teeth. Now from the sixth hour there
was darkness over all the land until the ninth hour.
And about the ninth hour Jesus cried with a loud
voice, saying, *Eli, Eli, lama sabacthani?* that is to say,
My God, my God, why hast thou forsaken me? Some
of them that stood there, when they heard that, said,
This man calleth for Elias. And straightway one of
them ran, and took a sponge, and filled it with vinegar,
and put it on a reed, and gave him to drink. The rest
said, Let be, let us see whether Elias will come to save
him. Jesus, when he had cried again with a loud voice,
yielded up the ghost. And behold, the veil of the
temple was rent in twain from the top to the bottom;
and the earth did quake, and the rocks rent; and the
graves were opened ; and many bodies of the saints
which slept arose, and came out of the graves after his
resurrection, and went into the holy city and appeared
unto many. Now when the centurion and they that
were with him, watching Jesus, saw the earthquake,
and those things that were done, they feared greatly,
saying, Truly this was the Son of God.

GOOD FRIDAY.

The Collects.

ALMIGHTY God, we beseech thee graciously to behold this thy family, for which our Lord Jesus Christ was contented to be betrayed, and given up into the hands of wicked men, and to suffer death upon the cross, who now liveth and reigneth with thee and the Holy Ghost, ever one God, world without end. *Amen.*

ALMIGHTY and everlasting God, by whose Spirit the whole body of the church is governed and sanctified; Receive our supplications and prayers which we offer before thee for all estates of men in thy holy church, that every member of the same, in his vocation and ministry, may truly and godly serve thee; through our Lord and Saviour Jesus Christ. *Amen.*

O MERCIFUL God, who hast made all men, and hatest nothing thou hast made, nor wouldest the death of a sinner, but rather that he should be converted and live; Have mercy upon all Jews, Turks, Infidels, and Heretics, and take from them all ignorance, hardness of heart, and contempt of thy word; and so fetch them home, blessed Lord, to thy flock, that they may be saved among the remnant of the true Israelites, and be made one fold under one Shepherd, Jesus Christ our Lord, who liveth and reigneth with thee and the Holy Spirit, one God, world without end. *Amen.*

The Epistle. Heb. x. 1.

THE law naving a shadow of good things to come, and not the very image of the things, can never with those sacrifices which they offered year by year continually, make the comers thereunto perfect. For then would they not have ceased to be offered? because that the worshippers once purged, should have had no more conscience of sins. But in those sacrifices there is a remembrance again made of sins every year. For it is not possible that the blood of bulls and of goats should take away sins. Wherefore when he cometh into the world, he saith, Sacrifice and offering thou wouldest not, but a body hast thou prepared me: in burnt offerings and sacrifices for sin thou hast had no pleasure. Then said I, Lo, I come (in the volume of the book it is written of me) to do thy will, O God. Above, when he said, Sacrifice and offering, and burnt offerings, and offering for sin, thou wouldest not, neither hadst pleasure therein; which are offered by the law: then said he, Lo, I come to do thy will, O God. He taketh away the first, that he may establish the second. By which will we are sanctified through the offering of the body of Jesus Christ once for all. And every priest standeth daily ministering and offering oftentimes the same sacrifices, which can never take away sins; but this man, after he had offered one sacrifice for sins, for ever sat down on the right hand of God: from henceforth expecting till his enemies be made his footstool. For by one offering he hath perfected for ever them that are sanctified. Whereof the Holy Ghost also is a witness to us: for that after he had said before, This is the covenant that I will make with them after those days, saith the Lord, I will put my laws into their hearts, and in their minds will I write them; and their sins and iniquities will I remember no more. Now where remission of these is, there is no more offering for sin. Having therefore, brethren, boldness to enter into the holiest by the blood of Jesus, by a new and living way, which he hath consecrated for us, through the veil, that is to say, his flesh; and having an High Priest over the house of God; let us draw near with a true heart, in full assurance of faith, having our hearts sprinkled from an evil conscience, and our bodies washed

D

with pure water. Let us hold fast the profession of our faith without wavering; (for he is faithful that promised;) and let us consider one another to provoke unto love and to good works : not forsaking the assembling of ourselves together, as the manner of some is ; but exhorting one another: and so much the more, as ye see the day approaching.

The Gospel. John xix. 1.

PILATE therefore took Jesus, and scourged him. And the soldiers platted a crown of thorns, and put it on his head, and they put on him a purple robe, and said, Hail, King of the Jews! and they smote him with their hands. Pilate therefore went forth again, and saith unto them, Behold, I bring him forth to you, that ye may know that I find no fault in him. Then came Jesus forth, wearing the crown of thorns, and the purple robe. And Pilate saith unto them, Behold the man! When the chief priests therefore and officers saw him, they cried out, Crucify him, crucify him. Pilate saith unto them, Take ye him, and crucify him : for I find no fault in him. The Jews answered him, We have a law, and by our law he ought to die, because he made himself the Son of God. When Pilate therefore heard that saying, he was the more afraid; and went again into the judgment-hall, and saith unto Jesus, Whence art thou? But Jesus gave him no answer. Then saith Pilate unto him, Speakest thou not unto me? Knowest thou not that I have power to crucify thee, and have power to release thee? Jesus answered, Thou couldest have no power at all against me, except it were given thee from above: therefore he that delivered me unto thee hath the greater sin. And from thenceforth Pilate sought to release him : but the Jews cried out, saying, If thou let this man go, thou art not Cæsar's friend. Whosoever maketh himself a king speaketh against Cæsar. When Pilate therefore heard that saying, he brought Jesus forth, and sat down in the judgment-seat in a place which is called the Pavement, but in the Hebrew, Gabbatha. And it was the preparation of the Passover, and about the sixth hour: and he saith unto the Jews, Behold your King! But they cried out, Away with him, away with him, crucify him! Pilate saith unto them, Shall I crucify your King? The chief priests answered, We have no King but Cæsar. Then delivered he him therefore unto them to be crucified. And they took Jesus, and led him away. And he, bearing his cross, went forth into a place called the place of a skull, which is called in the Hebrew, Golgotha, where they crucified him, and two other with him, on either side one, and Jesus in the midst. And Pilate wrote a title, and put it on the cross. And the writing was, JESUS OF NAZARETH THE KING OF THE JEWS. This title then read many of the Jews; for the place where Jesus was crucified was nigh to the city: and it was written in Hebrew, and Greek, and Latin. Then said the chief priests of the Jews to Pilate, Write not, The King of the Jews; but that he said, I am the King of the Jews. Pilate answered, What I have written I have written. Then the soldiers, when they had crucified Jesus, took his garments, and made four parts, to every soldier a part; and also his coat. Now the coat was without seam, woven from the top throughout. They said therefore among themselves, Let us not rend it, but cast lots for it, whose it shall be: that the Scripture might be fulfilled, which saith, They parted my raiment among them, and for my vesture they did cast lots. These things therefore the soldiers did. Now there stood by the cross of Jesus his mother, and his mother's sister, Mary the wife of Cleophas, and Mary Magdalene. When Jesus therefore saw his mother, and the disciple standing by whom he loved, he saith unto his mother, Woman, behold thy son! Then saith he to

the disciple, Behold thy mother! And from that hour
that disciple took her unto his own home. After this,
Jesus knowing that all things were now accomplished,
that the Scripture might be fulfilled, saith, I thirst.
Now there was set a vessel full of vinegar; and they
filled a sponge with vinegar, and put it upon hyssop,
and put it to his mouth. When Jesus therefore had
received the vinegar, he said, It is finished: and he
bowed his head, and gave up the ghost. The Jews
therefore, because it was the preparation, that the bodies
should not remain upon the cross on the sabbath-day,
(for that sabbath-day was an high day,) besought Pilate
that their legs might be broken, and that they might be
taken away. Then came the soldiers, and brake the legs
of the first, and of the other, who was crucified with
him. But when they came to Jesus, and saw that he
was dead already, they brake not his legs; but one of
the soldiers with a spear pierced his side, and forthwith
came thereout blood and water. And he that saw it
bare record, and his record is true: and he knoweth
that he saith true, that ye might believe. For these
things were done, that the Scripture should be fulfilled,
A bone of him shall not be broken. And again, another
Scripture saith, They shall look on him whom they
pierced.

EASTER-DAY.

At Morning Prayer, before the Psalms, these sentences shall be
said.

CHRIST our passover is sacrificed for us: therefore
let us keep the feast;
Not with the old leaven, neither with the leaven of
malice and wickedness; but with the unleavened bread
of sincerity and truth. 1 *Cor.* v. 7, 8.

CHRIST being raised from the dead dieth no more; death hath no more dominion over him.

For in that he died, he died unto sin once : but in that he liveth, he liveth unto God.

Likewise reckon ye also yourselves to be dead indeed unto sin, but alive unto God through Jesus Christ our Lord. *Rom.* vi. 9—11.

CHRIST is risen from the dead, and become the first-fruits of them that slept.

For since by man came death, by man came also the resurrection of the dead.

For as in Adam all die, even so in Christ shall all be made alive. 1 *Cor.* xv. 20—22.

Glory be to the Father, and to the Son, and to the Holy Ghost;

Answ. *As it was in the beginning, is now, and ever shall be, world without end.* Amen.

The Collect.

ALMIGHTY God, who through thine only begotten Son Jesus Christ hast overcome death, and opened unto us the gate of everlasting life; We humbly beseech thee, that as by thy special grace preventing us, thou dost put into our minds good desires; so by thy continual help we may bring the same to good effect; through Jesus Christ our Lord, who liveth and reigneth with thee and the Holy Ghost, ever one God, world without end. *Amen.*

The Epistle. Col. iii. 1.

IF ye then be risen with Christ, seek those things which are above, where Christ sitteth on the right hand of God. Set your affection on things above, not on things on the earth. For ye are dead, and your life is hid with Christ in God. When Christ, who is our life, shall appear, then shall ye also appear with him in glory. Mortify therefore your members which are upon the earth; fornication, uncleanness, inordinate affection, evil concupiscence, and covetousness, which is idolatry: for which things' sake the wrath of God cometh on the children of disobedience: in the which ye also walked some time, when ye lived in them.

The Gospel. John xx. 1.

THE first day of the week cometh Mary Magdalene early, when it was yet dark, unto the sepulchre, and seeth the stone taken away from the sepulchre. Then she runneth, and cometh to Simon Peter, and to the other disciple whom Jesus loved, and saith unto them, They have taken the Lord out of the sepulchre, and we know not where they have laid him. Peter therefore went forth, and that other disciple, and came to the sepulchre. So they ran both together; and the other disciple did outrun Peter, and came first to the sepulchre. And he stooping down, and looking in, saw the linen clothes lying; yet went he not in. Then cometh Simon Peter following him, and went into the sepulchre, and seeth the linen clothes lie, and the napkin, that was about his head, not lying with the linen clothes, but wrapped together in a place by itself. Then went in also that other disciple who came first to the sepulchre, and he saw, and believed. For as yet they knew not the Scripture, that he must rise again from the dead. Then the disciples went away again unto their own home.

THE FIRST SUNDAY AFTER EASTER.

The Collect.

ALMIGHTY Father, who hast given thine only Son to die for our sins, and to rise again for our justification; Grant us so to put away the leaven of malice and wickedness, that we may alway serve thee in pureness of living and truth; through the merits of the same thy Son Jesus Christ our Lord. *Amen.*

The Epistle. 1 John v. 4.

WHATSOEVER is born of God overcometh the world; and this is the victory that overcometh the world, even our faith. Who is he that overcometh the world, but he that believeth that Jesus is the Son of God? This is he that came by water and blood, even Jesus Christ; not by water only, but by water and blood: and it is the Spirit that beareth witness, because the Spirit is truth. For there are three that bear record in heaven, the Father, the Word, and the Holy Ghost: and these three are one. And there are three that bear witness in earth, the Spirit, and the water, and the blood: and these three agree in one. If we receive the witness of men, the witness of God is greater: for this is the witness of God, which he hath testified of his Son. He that believeth on the Son of God hath the witness in himself: he that believeth not God, hath made him a liar, because he believeth not the record that God gave of his Son. And this is the record, that God hath given to us eternal life; and this life is in his Son. He that hath the Son hath life, and he that hath not the Son hath not life.

The Gospel. John xx. 19.

THE same day at evening, being the first day of the week, when the doors were shut where the disciples were assembled for fear of the Jews, came Jesus, and stood in the midst, and saith unto them, Peace be unto you. And when he had so said, he showed unto them his hands and his side. Then were the disciples glad when they saw the Lord. Then said Jesus to them again, Peace be unto you: as my Father hath sent me, even so send I you. And when he had said this, he breathed on them, and saith unto them, Receive ye the Holy Ghost. Whose soever sins ye remit, they are remitted unto them; and whose soever sins ye retain, they are retained.

THE SECOND SUNDAY AFTER EASTER.

The Collect.

ALMIGHTY God, who hast given thine only Son to be made unto us both a sacrifice for sin, and also an ensample of godly life; Give us grace, that we may always most thankfully receive that his inestimable benefit, and also daily endeavour ourselves to follow the blessed steps of his most holy life; through the same Jesus Christ our Lord. *Amen.*

The Epistle. 1 Pet. ii. 19.

THIS is thankworthy, if a man for conscience toward God endure grief, suffering wrongfully. For what glory is it, if when ye be buffeted for your faults, ye shall take it patiently? But if when ye do well, and suffer for it, ye take it patiently, this is acceptable with God. For even hereunto were ye called: because Christ also suffered for us, leaving us an example, that ye should follow his steps : who did no sin, neither was guile found in his mouth : who, when he was reviled, reviled not again; when he suffered, he threatened not; but committed himself to him that judgeth righteously : who his own self bare our sins in his own body on the tree, that we, being dead to sins, should live unto righteousness : by whose stripes ye were healed. For ye were as sheep going astray ; but are now returned unto the Shepherd and Bishop of your souls.

The Gospel. John x. 11.

JESUS said, I am the good shepherd : the good shepherd giveth his life for the sheep. But he that is an hireling, and not the shepherd, whose own the sheep are not, seeth the wolf coming, and leaveth the sheep, and fleeth ; and the wolf catcheth them, and scattereth the sheep. The hireling fleeth because he is an hireling, and careth not for the sheep. I am the good shepherd, and know my sheep, and am known of mine. As the Father knoweth me, even so know I the Father : and I lay down my life for the sheep. And other sheep I have, which are not of this fold : them also I must bring, and they shall hear my voice ; and there shall be one fold, and one shepherd.

THE THIRD SUNDAY AFTER EASTER.

The Collect.

ALMIGHTY God, who showest to them that are in error the light of thy truth, to the intent that they may return into the way of righteousness; Grant unto all them that are admitted into the fellowship of Christ's religion, that they may eschew those things that are contrary to their profession, and follow all such things as are agreeable to the same ; through our Lord Jesus Christ. *Amen.*

D 5

The Epistle.   1 Peter ii. 11.

DEARLY beloved, I beseech you as strangers and pilgrims, abstain from fleshly lusts, which war against the soul; having your conversation honest among the Gentiles : that whereas they speak against you as evil-doers, they may, by your good works which they shall behold, glorify God in the day of visitation. Submit yourselves to every ordinance of man for the Lord's sake ; whether it be to the King, as supreme ; or unto governors, as unto them that are sent by him for the punishment of evil-doers, and for the praise of them that do well. For so is the will of God, that with well-doing ye may put to silence the ignorance of foolish men : as free, and not using your liberty for a cloak of maliciousness ; but as the servants of God. Honour all men. Love the brotherhood. Fear God. Honour the King.

The Gospel.   John xvi. 16.

JESUS said to his disciples, A little while and ye shall not see me ; and again, a little while, and ye shall see me ; because I go to the Father. Then said some of his disciples among themselves, What is this that he saith unto us: A little while, and ye shall not see me ; and again, a little while and ye shall see me ; and, Because I go to the Father? They said therefore, What is this that he saith, A little while? we cannot tell what he saith. Now Jesus knew that they were desirous to ask him, and said unto them, Do ye inquire among yourselves of that I said, A little while, and ye shall not see me ; and again, a little while, and ye shall see me? Verily, verily, I say unto you, That ye shall weep and lament, but the world shall rejoice : and ye shall be sorrowful, but your sorrow shall be turned into joy. A woman, when she is in travail, hath sorrow, because her hour is come : but as soon as she is delivered of the child, she remembereth no more the anguish, for joy that a man is born into the world. And ye now therefore have sorrow : but I will see you again, and your heart shall rejoice, and your joy no man taketh from you.

THE FOURTH SUNDAY AFTER EASTER.

The Collect.

O ALMIGHTY God, who alone canst order the unruly wills and affections of sinful men ; Grant unto thy people, that they may love the thing which thou commandest, and desire that which thou dost promise ; that so, among the sundry and manifold changes of the world, our hearts may surely there be fixed, where true joys are to be found ; through Jesus Christ our Lord. *Amen.*

The Epistle. James i. 17.

EVERY good gift, and every perfect gift, is from above, and cometh down from the Father of lights, with whom is no variableness, neither shadow of turning. Of his own will begat he us with the word of truth, that we should be a kind of first-fruits of his creatures. Wherefore, my beloved brethren, let every man be swift to hear, slow to speak, slow to wrath ; for the wrath of man worketh not the righteousness of God. Wherefore lay apart all filthiness and superfluity of naughtiness, and receive with meekness the engrafted word, which is able to save your souls.

The Gospel. John xvi. 5.

JESUS said unto his disciples, Now I go my way to him that sent me, and none of you asketh me, Whither goest thou ? But, because I have said these things unto you, sorrow hath filled your heart. Nevertheless, I tell you the truth ; It is expedient for you that I go away : for if I go not away, the Comforter will not come unto you ; but if I depart, I will send him unto you. And when he is come, he will convince the world of sin, and of righteousness, and of judgment : of sin, because they believe not on me ; of righteousness, because I go to my Father, and ye see me no more ; of judgment, because the prince of this world is judged. I have yet many things to say unto you, but ye cannot bear them now. Howbeit, when he, the Spirit of truth, is come, he will guide you into all truth : for he shall not speak of himself ; but whatsoever he shall hear, that shall he speak : and he will show you things to come. He shall glorify me : for he shall receive of mine, and shall show it unto you. All things that the Father hath are mine : therefore said I, that he shall take of mine, and shall show it unto you.

THE FIFTH SUNDAY AFTER EASTER.

The Collect.

O LORD, from whom all good things do come ; Grant to us thy humble servants, that by thy holy inspiration we may think those things that are good, and by thy merciful guiding may perform the same ; through our Lord Jesus Christ. *Amen.*

The Epistle. James i. 22.

BE ye doers of the word, and not hearers only, deceiving your ownselves. For if any be a hearer of the word, and not a doer, he is like unto a man beholding his natural face in a glass. For he beholdeth himself, and goeth his way, and straightway forgetteth what manner of man he was. But whoso looketh into the perfect law of liberty, and continueth therein, he being not a forgetful hearer, but a doer of the work, this man shall be blessed in his deed. If any man among you seem to be religious, and bridleth not his tongue, but deceiveth his own heart, this man's religion is vain. Pure religion and undefiled before God and the Father is this, To visit the fatherless and widows in their affliction, and to keep himself unspotted from the world.

The Gospel. John xvi. 23.

VERILY, verily, I say unto you, Whatsoever ye shall ask the Father in my name, he will give it you. Hitherto have ye asked nothing in my name : Ask, and ye shall receive, that your joy may be full. These things have I spoken unto you in proverbs : but the time cometh when I shall speak no more unto you in proverbs, but I shall show you plainly of the Father. At that day ye shall ask in my name : and I say not unto you, that I will pray the Father for you; for the Father himself loveth you, because ye have loved me, and have believed that I came out from God. I came forth from the Father, and am come into the world : again, I leave the world, and go to the Father. His disciples said unto him, Lo, now speakest thou plainly, and speakest no proverb. Now are we sure that thou knowest all things, and needest not that any man should ask thee. By this we believe that thou camest forth from God. Jesus answered them, Do ye now believe ? Behold, the hour cometh, yea, is now come, that ye shall be scattered every man to his own, and shall leave me alone; and yet I am not alone, because the Father is with me. These things I have spoken unto you, that in me ye might have peace. In the world ye shall have tribulation : but be of good cheer ; I have overcome the world.

THE ASCENSION-DAY.

The Collect.

G RANT, we beseech thee, Almighty God, that like as we do believe thy only begotten Son our Lord Jesus Christ to have ascended into the heavens; so we may also in heart and mind thither ascend, and with him continually dwell, who liveth and reigneth with thee and the Holy Ghost, one God, world without end. *Amen.*

The Epistle. Acts i. 1.

T HE former treatise have I made, O Theophilus, of all that Jesus began both to do and teach, until the day in which he was taken up, after that he through the Holy Ghost had given commandments unto the apostles whom he had chosen: to whom also he showed himself alive after his passion, by many infallible proofs; being seen of them forty days, and speaking of the things pertaining to the kingdom of God: and being assembled together with them, commanded them that they should not depart from Jerusalem, but wait for the promise of the Father, which, saith he, ye have heard of me. For John truly baptized with water, but ye shall be baptized with the Holy Ghost not many days hence. When they therefore were come together, they asked of him, saying, Lord, wilt thou at this time restore again the kingdom to Israel? And he said unto them, It is not for you to know the times or the seasons, which the Father hath put in his own power. But ye shall receive power after that the Holy Ghost is come upon you; and ye shall be witnesses unto me, both in Jerusalem, and in all Judea, and in Samaria, and unto the uttermost part of the earth. And when he had spoken these things, while they beheld, he was taken

up, and a cloud received him out of their sight. And
while they looked steadfastly toward heaven, as he went
up, behold, two men stood by them in white apparel,
who also said, Ye men of Galilee, why stand ye gazing
up into heaven? This same Jesus, who is taken up
from you into heaven, shall so come in like manner as
ye have seen him go into heaven.

The Gospel. Mark xvi. 14.

JESUS appeared unto the eleven as they sat at meat,
and upbraided them with their unbelief and hardness
of heart, because they believed not them who had seen
him after he was risen. And he said unto them, Go
ye into all the world, and preach the Gospel to every
creature. He that believeth and is baptized shall be
saved; but he that believeth not shall be damned. And
these signs shall follow them that believe: In my name
shall they cast out devils; they shall speak with new
tongues; they shall take up serpents; and if they drink
any deadly thing, it shall not hurt them; they shall lay
hands on the sick, and they shall recover. So then
after the Lord had spoken unto them, he was received
into heaven, and sat on the right hand of God. And
they went forth and preached every where, the Lord
working with them, and confirming the word with signs
following.

THE SUNDAY AFTER ASCENSION-DAY.

The Collect.

O GOD the King of glory, who hast exalted thine
only Son Jesus Christ with great triumph unto
thy kingdom in heaven; We beseech thee leave us not
comfortless; but send to us thine Holy Ghost to comfort
us, and exalt us unto the same place whither our Saviour

Christ is gone before, who liveth and reigneth with thee and the Holy Ghost, one God, world without end. *Amen.*

The Epistle. 1 Pet. iv. 7.

THE end of all things is at hand; be ye therefore sober, and watch unto prayer. And above all things have fervent love among yourselves: for love shall cover a multitude of sins. Use hospitality one to another, without grudging. As every man hath received the gift, even so minister the same one to another, as good stewards of the manifold grace of God. If any man speak, let him speak as the oracles of God: if any man minister, let him do it as of the ability which God giveth; that God in all things may be glorified through Jesus Christ; to whom be praise and dominion for ever and ever. *Amen.*

The Gospel. John xv. 26, *and part of the* xvith *Chapter.*

WHEN the Comforter is come, whom I will send unto you from the Father, even the Spirit of truth, who proceedeth from the Father, he shall testify of me. And ye also shall bear witness, because ye have been with me from the beginning. These things have I spoken unto you, that you should not be offended. They shall put you out of the synagogues: yea, the time cometh, that whosoever killeth you will think that he doeth God service. And these things will they do unto you, because they have not known the Father nor me. But these things have I told you, that, when the time shall come, ye may remember that I told you of them.

WHIT-SUNDAY.

The Collect.

O GOD, who as at this time didst teach the hearts of thy faithful people, by the sending to them the light of thy Holy Spirit; Grant us, by the same Spirit, to have a right judgment in all things, and evermore to rejoice in his holy comfort; through the merits of Christ Jesus our Saviour, who liveth and reigneth with thee, in the unity of the same Spirit, one God, world without end. *Amen.*

For the Epistle. Acts ii. 1.

WHEN the day of Pentecost was fully come, they were all with one accord in one place. And suddenly there came a sound from heaven, as of a rushing mighty wind, and it filled all the house where they were sitting. And there appeared unto them cloven tongues, like as of fire, and it sat upon each of them : and they were all filled with the Holy Ghost, and began to speak with other tongues, as the Spirit gave them utterance. And there were dwelling at Jerusalem Jews, devout men, out of every nation under heaven. Now when this was noised abroad, the multitude came together, and were confounded, because that every man heard them speak in his own language. And they were all amazed, and marvelled, saying one to another, Behold, are not all these which speak Galileans? And how hear we every man in our own tongue, wherein we were born? Parthians, and Medes, and Elamites, and the dwellers in Mesopotamia, and in Judea, and Cappadocia, in Pontus, and Asia, Phrygia, and Pamphylia, in Egypt, and in the parts of Libya about Cyrene, and strangers of Rome, Jews and proselytes, Cretes and Arabians, we do hear them speak in our tongues the wonderful works of God.

The Gospel. John xiv. 15.

JESUS said unto his disciples, If ye love me, keep
my commandments. And I will pray the Father,
and he shall give you another Comforter, that he may
abide with you for ever; even the Spirit of truth, whom
the world cannot receive, because it seeth him not,
neither knoweth him: but ye know him; for he dwelleth
with you, and shall be in you. I will not leave you
comfortless; I will come to you. Yet a little while, and
the world seeth me no more; but ye see me: because I
live, ye shall live also. At that day ye shall know that I
am in my Father, and you in me, and I in you. He
that hath my commandments, and keepeth them, he it
is that loveth me; and he that loveth me shall be loved
of my Father, and I will love him, and will manifest
myself to him. Judas saith unto him, (not Iscariot,)
Lord, how is it that thou wilt manifest thyself unto us,
and not unto the world? Jesus answered and said unto
him, If a man love me, he will keep my words; and my
Father will love him, and we will come unto him, and
make our abode with him. He that loveth me not,
keepeth not my sayings; and the word which ye hear is
not mine, but the Father's which sent me. These things
have I spoken unto you, being yet present with you.
But the Comforter, who is the Holy Ghost, whom the
Father will send in my name, he shall teach you all
things, and bring all things to your remembrance, whatsoever I have said unto you. Peace I leave with you,
my peace I give unto you: not as the world giveth,
give I unto you. Let not your heart be troubled, neither let it be afraid. Ye have heard how I said unto
you, I go away, and come again unto you. If ye loved
me, ye would rejoice, because I said, I go unto the
Father: for my Father is greater than I. And now I
have told you before it come to pass, that when it is
come to pass, ye might believe. Hereafter I will not

talk much with you : for the prince of this world cometh, and hath nothing in me. But that the world may know that I love the Father; and as the Father gave me commandment, even so I do.

TRINITY-SUNDAY.

The Collect.

ALMIGHTY and everlasting God, who hast given unto us thy servants grace by the confession of a true faith to acknowledge the glory of the eternal Trinity, and in the power of the Divine Majesty to worship the Unity; We beseech thee, that thou wouldest keep us steadfast in this faith, and evermore defend us from all adversities, who livest and reignest one God, world without end. *Amen.*

For the Epistle. Rev. iv. 1.

AFTER this I looked, and, behold, a door was opened in heaven : and the first voice which I heard was as it were of a trumpet talking with me; which said, Come up hither, and I will show thee things which must be hereafter. And immediately I was in the Spirit : and, behold, a throne was set in heaven, and one sat on the throne : and he that sat was to look upon like a jasper and a sardine stone: and there was a rainbow round about the throne, in sight like unto an emerald. And round about the throne there were four and twenty seats : and upon the seats I saw four and twenty elders sitting, clothed in white raiment; and they had on their heads crowns of gold : and out of the throne proceeded lightnings, and thunderings, and voices. And there were seven lamps of fire burning before the throne, which are the seven spirits of God. And before the throne there was a sea of glass, like unto crystal: and in the midst of the throne, and round about the throne, were four beasts, full of eyes before and behind. And the first beast was like a lion, and the second beast like a calf, and the third beast had a face as a man, and the fourth beast was like a flying eagle. And the four beasts had each of them six wings about him; and they were full of eyes within: and they rest not day and night, saying, Holy, holy, holy, Lord God Almighty, who was, and is, and is to come. And when those beasts give glory, and honour, and thanks, to him that sat on the throne, who liveth for ever and ever, the four and twenty elders fall down before him that sat on the throne, and worship him that liveth for ever and ever, and cast their crowns before the throne, saying, Thou art worthy, O Lord, to receive glory, and honour, and power; for thou hast created all things, and for thy pleasure they are and were created.

The Gospel. John iii. 1.

THERE was a man of the Pharisees, named Nicodemus, a ruler of the Jews: the same came to Jesus by night, and said unto him, Rabbi, we know that thou art a teacher come from God : for no man can do these miracles that thou doest, except God be with him. Jesus answered and said unto him, Verily, verily, I say unto thee, Except a man be born again, he cannot see the kingdom of God. Nicodemus saith unto him, How can a man be born when he is old? can he enter the second time into his mother's womb, and be born ? Jesus answered, Verily, verily, I say unto thee, Except a man be born of water and of the Spirit, he cannot enter into the kingdom of God. That which is born of the flesh is flesh; and that which is born of the Spirit is spirit. Marvel not that I said unto thee, Ye must be born again. The wind bloweth where it listeth, and thou

hearest the sound thereof, but canst not tell whence it
cometh, and whither it goeth ; so is every one that is
born of the Spirit. Nicodemus answered and said unto
him, How can these things be ? Jesus answered and
said unto him, Art thou a master of Israel, and knowest
not these things ? Verily, verily, I say unto thee, We
speak that we do know, and testify that we have seen ;
and ye receive not our witness. If I have told you
earthly things, and ye believe not ; how shall ye believe,
if I tell you of heavenly things ? And no man hath
ascended up to heaven, but he that came down from
heaven, even the Son of Man, who is in heaven. And
as Moses lifted up the serpent in the wilderness, even
so must the Son of Man be lifted up : that whosoevei
believeth in him should not perish, but have eternal life

THE FIRST SUNDAY AFTER TRINITY.

The Collect.

O GOD, the strength of all them that put their trust
in thee, mercifully accept our prayers ; and because, through the weakness of our mortal nature, we
can do no good thing without thee, grant us the help of
thy grace, that in keeping thy commandments, we may
please thee both in will and deed ; through Jesus Christ
our Lord. *Amen.*

The Epistle. 1 John iv. 7.

BELOVED, let us love one another ; for love is of
God ; and every one that loveth is born of God,
and knoweth God. He that loveth not knoweth not
God ; for God is love. In this was manifested the love
of God towards us, because that God sent his only begotten Son into the world, that we might live through
him. Herein is love, not that we loved God, but that

he loved us, and sent his Son to be the propitiation for
our sins.   Beloved, if God so loved us, we ought also
to love one another.   No man hath seen God at any
time.   If we love one another, God dwelleth in us, and
his love is perfected in us.   Hereby know we that we
dwell in him, and he in us ; because he hath given us of
his Spirit.   And we have seen and do testify, that the
Father sent the Son to be the Saviour of the world.
Whosoever shall confess that Jesus is the Son of God,
God dwelleth in him, and he in God.   And we have
known and believed the love that God hath to us.   God
is love, and he that dwelleth in love dwelleth in God,
and God in him.   Herein is our love made perfect, that
we may have boldness in the day of judgment ; because
as he is, so are we in this world.   There is no fear in
love ; but perfect love casteth out fear, because fear
hath torment.   He that feareth is not made perfect in
love. We love him, because he first loved us.   If a man
say, I love God, and hateth his brother, he is a liar ;
for he that loveth not his brother, whom he hath seen,
how can he love God, whom he hath not seen ?   And
this commandment have we from him, That he who
loveth God love his brother also.

The Gospel.   Luke xvi. 19.

THERE was a certain rich man, who was clothed
in purple and fine linen, and fared sumptuously
every day.   And there was a certain beggar, named
Lazarus, who was laid at his gate full of sores, and desiring to be fed with the crumbs which fell from the
rich man's table : moreover the dogs came and licked
his sores.   And it came to pass, that the beggar died,
and was carried by the angels into Abraham's bosom.
The rich man also died, and was buried ; and in hell he
lifted up his eyes, being in torments, and seeth Abraham
afar off, and Lazarus in his bosom.   And he cried, and

said, Father Abraham, have mercy on me, and send
Lazarus, that he may dip the tip of his finger in water,
and cool my tongue; for I am tormented in this flame.
But Abraham said, Son, remember that thou in thy life-
time receivedst thy good things, and likewise Lazarus
evil things; but now he is comforted, and thou art tormented. And, beside all this, between us and you
there is a great gulf fixed, so that they who would pass
from hence to you cannot; neither can they pass to us
that would come from thence. Then he said, I pray
thee therefore, father, that thou wouldest send him to
my father's house: for I have five brethren; that he
may testify unto them, lest they also come into this
place of torment. Abraham saith unto him, They have
Moses and the prophets; let them hear them. And he
said, Nay, father Abraham: but if one went unto them
from the dead, they will repent. And he said unto him,
If they hear not Moses and the prophets, neither will
they be persuaded, though one rose from the dead.

THE SECOND SUNDAY AFTER TRINITY.

The Collect.

O LORD, who never failest to help and govern them
whom thou dost bring up in thy steadfast fear and
love; Keep us, we beseech thee, under the protection
of thy good providence, and make us to have a perpetual
fear and love of thy holy name; through Jesus Christ
our Lord. *Amen.*

The Epistle. 1 John iii. 13.

MARVEL not, my brethren, if the world hate you.
We know that we have passed from death unto
life, because we love the brethren. He that loveth not

his brother abideth in death. Whosoever hateth his brother is a murderer : and ye know that no murderer hath eternal life abiding in him. Hereby perceive we the love of God, because he laid down his life for us : and we ought to lay down our lives for the brethren. But whoso hath this world's good, and seeth his brother have need, and shutteth up his bowels of compassion from him; how dwelleth the love of God in him ? My little children, let us not love in word, neither in tongue, but in deed, and in truth. And hereby we know that we are of the truth, and shall assure our hearts before him. For if our heart condemn us, God is greater than our heart, and knoweth all things. Beloved, if our heart condemn us not, then have we confidence toward God : and whatsoever we ask, we receive of him, because we keep his commandments, and do those things that are pleasing in his sight. And this is his commandment, That we should believe on the name of his Son Jesus Christ, and love one another, as he gave us command- ment. And he that keepeth his commandments dwelleth in him, and he in him : and hereby we know that he abideth in us, by the Spirit which he hath given us.

The Gospel.   Luke xiv. 16.

A CERTAIN man made a great supper, and bade many : and sent his servants at supper-time to say to them that were bidden, Come ; for all things are now ready. And they all with one consent began to make excuse. The first said unto him, I have bought a piece of ground, and I must needs go and see it : I pray thee have me excused. And another said, I have bought five yoke of oxen, and I go to prove them : I pray thee have me excused. And another said, I have married a wife, and therefore I cannot come. So that servant came, and showed his lord these things. Then the master of the house, being angry, said to his servant,

Go out quickly into the streets and lanes of the city, and bring in hither the poor, and the maimed, and the halt, and the blind. And the servant said, Lord, it is done as thou hast commanded, and yet there is room. And the lord said unto the servant, Go out into the highways and hedges, and compel them to come in, that my house may be filled. For I say unto you, That none of those men who were bidden shall taste of my supper.

THE THIRD SUNDAY AFTER TRINITY.

The Collect.

O LORD, we beseech thee mercifully to hear us; and grant that we, to whom thou hast given an hearty desire to pray, may by thy mighty aid be defended and comforted in all dangers and adversities; through Jesus Christ our Lord. *Amen.*

The Epistle. 1 Peter v. 5.

A LL of you be subject one to another, and be clothed with humility: for God resisteth the proud, and giveth grace to the humble. Humble yourselves therefore under the mighty hand of God, that he may exalt you in due time: casting all your care upon him; for he careth for you. Be sober, be vigilant; because your adversary the devil, as a roaring lion, walketh about, seeking whom he may devour: whom resist steadfast in the faith, knowing that the same afflictions are accomplished in your brethren that are in the world. But the God of all grace, who hath called us unto his eternal glory by Christ Jesus, after that ye have suffered a while, make you perfect, stablish, strengthen, settle you. To him be glory and dominion for ever and ever. *Amen.*

E

The Gospel. Luke xv. 1.

THEN drew near unto him all the publicans and sinners for to hear him. And the Pharisees and Scribes murmured, saying, This man receiveth sinners, and eateth with them. And he spake this parable unto them, saying, What man of you, having an hundred sheep, if he lose one of them, doth not leave the ninety and nine in the wilderness, and go after that which is lost, until he find it? And when he hath found it, he layeth it on his shoulders, rejoicing. And when he cometh home, he calleth together his friends and neighbours, saying unto them, Rejoice with me; for I have found my sheep which was lost. I say unto you, That likewise joy shall be in heaven over one sinner that repenteth, more than over ninety and nine just persons who need no repentance. Either what woman having ten pieces of silver, if she lose one piece, doth not light a candle, and sweep the house, and seek diligently till she find it? And when she hath found it, she calleth her friends and her neighbours together, saying, Rejoice with me; for I have found the piece which I had lost. Likewise I say unto you, There is joy in the presence of the angels of God over one sinner that repenteth.

THE FOURTH SUNDAY AFTER TRINITY.

The Collect.

O GOD, the protector of all that trust in thee, without whom nothing is strong, nothing is holy; Increase and multiply upon us thy mercy; that thou being our ruler and guide, we may so pass through things temporal, that we finally lose not the things eternal: Grant this, O heavenly Father, for Jesus Christ's sake our Lord. *Amen.*

The Epistle. Rom. viii. 18.

I RECKON that the sufferings of this present time are not worthy to be compared with the glory which shall be revealed in us.   For the earnest expectation of the creature waiteth for the manifestation of the sons of God.   For the creature was made subject to vanity, not willingly, but by reason of him who hath subjected the same in hope : because the creature itself also shall be delivered from the bondage of corruption, into the glorious liberty of the children of God.   For we know that the whole creation groaneth and travaileth in pain together until now.   And not only they, but ourselves also, who have the first-fruits of the Spirit, even we ourselves groan within ourselves, waiting for the adoption, to wit, the redemption of our body.

The Gospel. Luke vi. 36.

BE ye therefore merciful, as your Father also is merciful.   Judge not, and ye shall not be judged : condemn not, and ye shall not be condemned : forgive, and ye shall be forgiven : give, and it shall be given unto you ; good measure, pressed down, and shaken together, and running over, shall men give into your bosom.   For with the same measure that ye meet withal it shall be measured to you again.   And he spake a parable unto them, Can the blind lead the blind ? shall they not both fall into the ditch ?   The disciple is not above his master : but every one that is perfect shall be as his master.   And why beholdest thou the mote that is in thy brother's eye, but perceivest not the beam that is in thine own eye ?   Either how canst thou say to thy brother, Brother, let me pull out the mote that is in thine eye, when thou thyself beholdest not the beam that is in thine own eye ?   Thou hypocrite, cast

E 2

out first the beam out of thine own eye, and then shalt thou see clearly to pull out the mote that is in thy brother's eye.

THE FIFTH SUNDAY AFTER TRINITY.

The Collect.

GRANT, O Lord, we beseech thee, that the course of this world may be so peaceably ordered by thy governance, that thy church may joyfully serve thee in all godly quietness; through Jesus Christ our Lord. *Amen.*

The Epistle. 1 Peter iii. 8.

BE ye all of one mind, having compassion one of another; love as brethren, be pitiful, be courteous: not rendering evil for evil, or railing for railing: but contrariwise, blessing; knowing that ye are thereunto called, that ye should inherit a blessing. For he that will love life, and see good days, let him refrain his tongue from evil, and his lips that they speak no guile : let him eschew evil, and do good ; let him seek peace, and ensue it. For the eyes of the Lord are over the righteous, and his ears are open unto their prayers : but the face of the Lord is against them that do evil. And who is he that will harm you, if ye be followers of that which is good ? But and if ye suffer for righteousness' sake, happy are ye: and be not afraid of their terror, neither be troubled ; but sanctify the Lord God in your hearts.

The Gospel. Luke v. 1.

IT came to pass, that as the people pressed upon him to hear the word of God, he stood by the lake of

Gennesaret, and saw two ships standing by the lake : but the fishermen were gone out of them, and were washing their nets. And he entered into one of the ships, which was Simon's, and prayed him that he would thrust out a little from the land. And he sat down, and taught the people out of the ship. Now when he had left speaking, he said unto Simon, Launch out into the deep, and let down your nets for a draught. And Simon answering said unto him, Master, we have toiled all the night, and have taken nothing : nevertheless at thy word I will let down the net. And when they had this done, they enclosed a great multitude of fishes : and their net brake. And they beckoned unto their partners, who were in the other ship, that they should come and help them. And they came, and filled both the ships, so that they began to sink. When Simon Peter saw it, he fell down at Jesus' knees, saying, Depart from me ; for I am a sinful man, O Lord. For he was astonished, and all that were with him, at the draught of the fishes which they had taken : and so was also James and John, the sons of Zebedee, who were partners with Simon. And Jesus said unto Simon, Fear not ; from henceforth thou shalt catch men. And when they had brought their ships to land, they forsook all, and followed him.

THE SIXTH SUNDAY AFTER TRINITY.

The Collect,

O GOD, who hast prepared for them that love thee such good things as pass man's understanding; Pour into our hearts such love toward thee, that we, loving thee above all things, may obtain thy promises, which exceed all that we can desire ; through Jesus Christ our Lord. *Amen.*

The Epistle. Rom. vi. 3.

KNOW ye not, that so many of us as were baptized into Jesus Christ, were baptized into his death? Therefore we are buried with him by baptism into his death: that like as Christ was raised up from the dead by the glory of the Father, even so we also should walk in newness of life. For if we have been planted together in the likeness of his death, we shall be also in the likeness of his resurrection: knowing this, that our old man is crucified with him, that the body of sin might be destroyed, that henceforth we should not serve sin. For he that is dead is freed from sin. Now if we be dead with Christ, we believe that we shall also live with him: knowing that Christ being raised from the dead dieth no more; death hath no more dominion over him. For in that he died, he died unto sin once: but in that he liveth, he liveth unto God. Likewise reckon ye also yourselves to be dead indeed unto sin, but alive unto God through Jesus Christ our Lord.

The Gospel. Matt. v. 20.

JESUS said unto his disciples, Except your righteousness shall exceed the righteousness of the Scribes and Pharisees, ye shall in no case enter into the kingdom of heaven. Ye have heard that it was said by them of old time, Thou shalt not kill; and whosoever shall kill shall be in danger of the judgment: but I say unto you, That whosoever is angry with his brother without a cause shall be in danger of the judgment: and whosoever shall say to his brother, Raca, shall be in danger of the council: but whosoever shall say, Thou fool, shall be in danger of hell fire. Therefore if thou bring thy gift to the altar, and there rememberest that thy brother hath aught against thee; leave there thy gift before the altar, and go thy way; first be reconciled to thy brother, and then come and offer thy gift.   Agree with thine adversary quickly, whiles thou art in the way with him ; lest at any time the adversary deliver thee to the judge, and the judge deliver thee to the officer, and thou be cast into prison.   Verily I say unto thee, Thou shalt by no means come out thence, till thou hast paid the uttermost farthing.

THE SEVENTH SUNDAY AFTER TRINITY.

The Collect.

LORD of all power and might, who art the author and giver of all good things ; Graft in our hearts the love of thy Name, increase in us true religion, nourish us with all goodness, and of thy great mercy keep us in the same ; through Jesus Christ our Lord. *Amen.*

The Epistle.   Rom. vi. 19.

I SPEAK after the manner of men, because of the infirmity of your flesh : for as ye have yielded your members servants to uncleanness, and to iniquity unto iniquity ; even so now yield your members servants to righteousness unto holiness.   For when ye were the servants of sin, ye were free from righteousness.   What fruit had ye then in those things whereof ye are now ashamed ? for the end of those things is death.   But now being made free from sin, and become servants to God, ye have your fruit unto holiness, and the end everlasting life.   For the wages of sin is death ; but the gift of God is eternal life through Jesus Christ our Lord.

The Gospel.   Mark viii. 1.

IN those days the multitude being very great, and having nothing to eat, Jesus called his disciples unto

him, and saith unto them, I have compassion on the
multitude, because they have now been with me three
days and have nothing to eat: and if I send them away
fasting to their own houses, they will faint by the way:
for divers of them came from far.   And his disciples
answered him, From whence can a man satisfy these
men with bread here in the wilderness?   And he asked
them, How many loaves have ye?   And they said,
Seven.   And he commanded the people to sit down on
the ground: and he took the seven loaves, and gave
thanks, and brake, and gave to his disciples to set before
them ; and they did set them before the people.   And
they had a few small fishes : and he blessed, and commanded to set them also before them.   So they did eat,
and were filled.   And they took up of the broken meat
that was left seven baskets.   And they that had eaten
were about four thousand : and he sent them away.

THE EIGHTH SUNDAY AFTER TRINITY.

The Collect.

O GOD, whose never-failing providence ordereth
all things both in heaven and earth ; We humbly
beseech thee to put away from us all hurtful things,
and to give us those things which are profitable for us ;
through Jesus Christ our Lord.   *Amen.*

The Epistle.   Rom. viii. 12.

B RETHREN, we are debtors, not to the flesh, to
live after the flesh.   For if ye live after the flesh,
ye shall die ; but if ye, through the Spirit, do mortify
the deeds of the body, ye shall live.   For as many as
are led by the Spirit of God, they are the sons of God.
For ye have not received the Spirit of bondage again
to fear ; but ye have received the Spirit of adoption,

whereby we cry, Abba, Father. The Spirit itself beareth witness with our spirit, that we are the children of God: and if children, then heirs; heirs of God, and joint-heirs with Christ; if so be that we suffer with him, that we may be also glorified together.

The Gospel. Matt. vii. 15.

BEWARE of false prophets, who come unto you in sheep's clothing, but inwardly they are ravening wolves. Ye shall know them by their fruits. Do men gather grapes of thorns, or figs of thistles? Even so every good tree bringeth forth good fruit; but a corrupt tree bringeth forth evil fruit. A good tree cannot bring forth evil fruit, neither can a corrupt tree bring forth good fruit. Every tree that bringeth not forth good fruit is hewn down, and cast into the fire. Wherefore by their fruits ye shall know them. Not every one that saith unto me, Lord, Lord, shall enter into the kingdom of heaven; but he that doeth the will of my Father who is in heaven.

THE NINTH SUNDAY AFTER TRINITY.

The Collect.

GRANT to us, Lord, we beseech thee, the spirit to think and do always such things as are rightful; that we, who cannot do any thing that is good without thee, may by thee be enabled to live according to thy will; through Jesus Christ our Lord. *Amen.*

The Epistle. 1 Cor. x. 1.

BRETHREN, I would not that ye should be ignorant how that all our fathers were under the cloud, and all passed through the sea; and were all baptized

unto Moses, in the cloud, and in the sea; and did all
eat the same spiritual meat; and did all drink the same
spiritual drink.   For they drank of that spiritual Rock
that followed them; and that Rock was Christ.   But
with many of them God was not well pleased; for they
were overthrown in the wilderness.   Now these things
were our examples, to the intent we should not lust
after evil things, as they also lusted.   Neither be ye
idolaters, as were some of them ; as it is written, The
people sat down to eat and drink, and rose up to play.
Neither let us commit fornication, as some of them committed, and fell in one day three and twenty thousand.
Neither let us tempt Christ, as some of them also
tempted, and were destroyed of serpents.   Neither
murmur ye, as some of them also murmured, and were
destroyed of the destroyer.   Now all these things hap-
pened unto them for ensamples ; and they are written
for our admonition, upon whom the ends of the world
are come.   Wherefore let him that thinketh he standeth
take heed lest he fall.   There hath no temptation taken
you but such as is common to man; but God is faithful,
who will not suffer you to be tempted above that ye are
able; but will with the temptation also make a way to
escape, that ye may be able to bear it.

The Gospel.   Luke xvi. 1.

JESUS said unto his disciples, There was a certain
rich man who had a steward ; and the same was
accused unto him that he had wasted his goods.   And
he called him, and said unto him, How is it that I hear
this of thee ? Give an account of thy stewardship; for
thou mayest be no longer steward.   Then the steward
said within himself, What shall I do? for my lord taketh
away from me the stewardship.   I cannot dig: to beg
I am ashamed.   I am resolved what to do, that when I
am put out of the stewardship, they may receive me

into their houses. So he called every one of his lord's debtors unto him, and said unto the first, How much owest thou to my lord? And he said, An hundred measures of oil. And he said unto him, Take thy bill, and sit down quickly, and write fifty. Then said he to another, And how much owest thou? And he said, An hundred measures of wheat. And he said unto him, Take thy bill, and write fourscore. And the lord commended the unjust steward, because he had done wisely : for the children of this world are in their generation wiser than the children of light. And I say unto you, Make to yourselves friends of the mammon of unrighteousness ; that, when ye fail, they may receive you into everlasting habitations.

THE TENTH SUNDAY AFTER TRINITY.

The Collect.

LET thy merciful ears, O Lord, be open to the prayers of thy humble servants ; and that they may obtain their petitions, make them to ask such things as shall please thee ; through Jesus Christ our Lord. *Amen.*

The Epistle. 1 Cor. xii. 1.

CONCERNING spiritual gifts, brethren, I would not have you ignorant. Ye know that ye were Gentiles, carried away unto these dumb idols, even as ye were led. Wherefore, I give you to understand that no man, speaking by the Spirit of God, calleth Jesus accursed ; and that no man can say that Jesus is the Lord, but by the Holy Ghost. Now there are diversities of gifts, but the same Spirit. And there are differences of administrations, but the same Lord. And there are diversities of operations, but it is the same God who worketh all in all. But the manifestation of the Spirit is given to every man to profit withal. For to one is given by the Spirit the word of wisdom; to another the word of knowledge by the same Spirit; to another faith by the same Spirit; to another the gifts of healing by the same Spirit; to another the working of miracles; to another prophecy; to another discerning of spirits; to another divers kinds of tongues; to another interpretation of tongues: but all these worketh that one and the selfsame Spirit, dividing to every man severally as he will.

The Gospel.   Luke xix. 41.

AND when he was come near, he beheld the city, and wept over it, saying, If thou hadst known, even thou, at least in this thy day, the things which belong unto thy peace! but now they are hid from thine eyes. For the days shall come upon thee, that thine enemies shall cast a trench about thee, and compass thee round, and keep thee in on every side, and shall lay thee even with the ground, and thy children within thee; and they shall not leave in thee one stone upon another; because thou knewest not the time of thy visitation. And he went into the temple, and began to cast out them that sold therein, and them that bought; saying unto them, It is written, My house is the house of prayer; but ye have made it a den of thieves. And he taught daily in the temple.

THE ELEVENTH SUNDAY AFTER TRINITY.

The Collect.

O GOD, who declarest thy almighty power most chiefly in showing mercy and pity; Mercifully grant unto us such a measure of thy grace, that we, running the way of thy commandments, may obtain thy gracious promises, and be made partakers of thy heavenly treasure; through Jesus Christ our Lord. *Amen.*

The Epistle.   1 Cor. xv. 1.

BRETHREN, I declare unto you the Gospel which I have preached unto you, which also ye have received, and wherein ye stand; by which also ye are saved, if ye keep in memory what I have preached unto you, unless ye have believed in vain.   For I delivered unto you first of all that which I also received, how that Christ died for our sins, according to the Scriptures; and that he was buried; and that he rose again the third day, according to the Scriptures; and that he was seen of Cephas, then of the twelve.   After that he was seen of above five hundred brethren at once; of whom the greater part remain unto this present; but some are fallen asleep.   After that he was seen of James; then of all the apostles.   And last of all he was seen of me also, as of one born out of due time : for I am the least of the apostles, that am not meet to be called an apostle, because I persecuted the church of God.   But by the grace of God I am what I am: and his grace which was bestowed upon me was not in vain; but I laboured more abundantly than they all; yet not I, but the grace of God which was with me.   Therefore, whether it were I or they, so we preach, and so ye believed.

The Gospel.   Luke xviii. 9.

JESUS spake this parable unto certain who trusted in themselves that they were righteous, and despised others: Two men went up into the temple to pray; the one a Pharisee, and the other a publican.   The Pharisee stood and prayed thus with himself; God, I thank thee, that I am not as other men are, extortioners, unjust, adulterers, or even as this publican: I fast twice in the week, I give tithes of all that I possess. And the publican, standing afar off, would not lift up so much as his eyes unto heaven, but smote upon his breast, saying, God be merciful to me a sinner. I tell you, this man went down to his house justified rather than the other: for every one that exalteth himself shall be abased; and he that humbleth himself shall be exalted.

THE TWELFTH SUNDAY AFTER TRINITY.

The Collect.

ALMIGHTY and everlasting God, who art always more ready to hear than we to pray, and art wont to give more than either we desire or deserve; Pour down upon us the abundance of thy mercy; forgiving us those things whereof our conscience is afraid, and giving us those good things which we are not worthy to ask, but through the merits and mediation of Jesus Christ, thy Son, our Lord. *Amen.*

The Epistle.   2 Cor. iii. 4.

SUCH trust have we through Christ to God-ward: not that we are sufficient of ourselves to think any thing as of ourselves; but our sufficiency is of God, who also hath made us able ministers of the New Testament; not of the letter, but of the spirit: for the letter killeth, but the spirit giveth life. But if the ministration of death, written and engraven in stones, was glorious, so that the children of Israel could not steadfastly behold the face of Moses for the glory of his countenance; which glory was to be done away: how shall not the ministration of the Spirit be rather glorious? For if the ministration of condemnation be glory, much more doth the ministration of righteousness exceed in glory.

The Gospel.   Mark vii. 31.

JESUS, departing from the coasts of Tyre and Sidon, came unto the sea of Galilee, through the midst of the coasts of Decapolis.   And they bring unto him one that was deaf, and had an impediment in his speech; and they beseech him to put his hand upon him.   And he took him aside from the multitude, and put his fingers into his ears, and he spit, and touched his tongue; and looking up to heaven, he sighed, and saith unto him, *Ephphatha,* that is, Be opened. And straightway his ears were opened, and the string of his tongue was loosed, and he spake plain.   And he charged them that they should tell no man : but the more he charged them, so much the more a great deal they published it; and were beyond measure astonished, saying, He hath done all things well; he maketh both the deaf to hear, and the dumb to speak.

THE THIRTEENTH SUNDAY AFTER TRINITY.

The Collect.

ALMIGHTY and merciful God, of whose only gift it cometh that thy faithful people do unto thee true and laudable service; Grant, we beseech thee, that we may so faithfully serve thee in this life, that we fail not finally to attain thy heavenly promises; through the merits of Jesus Christ our Lord.   *Amen.*

The Epistle. Gal. iii. 16.

TO Abraham and his seed were the promises made. He saith not, And to seeds, as of many ; but as of one ; And to thy seed, which is Christ. And this I say, that the covenant that was confirmed before of God in Christ, the law, which was four hundred and thirty years after, cannot disannul, that it should make the promise of none effect. For if the inheritance be of the law, it is no more of promise ; but God gave it to Abraham by promise. Wherefore then serveth the law ? It was added because of transgressions, till the seed should come, to whom the promise was made ; and it was ordained by angels in the hand of a mediator. Now a mediator is not a mediator of one, but God is one. Is the law then against the promises of God ? God forbid : for if there had been a law given which could have given life, verily righteousness should have been by the law. But the Scripture hath concluded all under sin, that the promise by faith of Jesus Christ might be given to them that believe.

The Gospel. Luke x. 23.

BLESSED are the eyes which see the things that ye see. For I tell you, that many prophets and kings have desired to see those things which ye see, and have not seen them ; and to hear those things which ye hear, and have not heard them. And, behold, a certain lawyer stood up, and tempted him, saying, Master, what shall I do to inherit eternal life ? He said unto him, What is written in the law ? how readest thou ? And he answering said, Thou shalt love the Lord thy God with all thy heart, and with all thy soul, and with all thy strength, and with all thy mind ; and thy neighbour as thyself. And he said unto him, Thou hast answered right : this do, and thou shalt live. But he, willing to justify himself, said unto Jesus, And who

.s my neighbour? And Jesus answered and said, A certain man went down from Jerusalem to Jericho, and fell among thieves, who stripped him of his raiment, and wounded him, and departed, leaving him half dead. And by chance there came down a certain priest that way: and when he saw him, he passed by on the other side. And likewise a Levite, when he was at the place, came and looked on him, and passed by on the other side. But a certain Samaritan, as he journeyed, came where he was: and when he saw him, he had compassion on him, and went to him, and bound up his wounds, pouring in oil and wine, and set him on his own beast, and brought him to an inn, and took care of him. And on the morrow, when he departed, he took out two pence, and gave them to the host, and said unto him, Take care of him; and whatsoever thou spendest more, when I come again, I will repay thee. Which now of these three, thinkest thou, was neighbour unto him that fell among the thieves? And he said, He that showed mercy on him. Then said Jesus unto him, Go, and do thou likewise.

THE FOURTEENTH SUNDAY AFTER TRINITY.

The Collect.

ALMIGHTY and everlasting God, give unto us the increase of faith, hope, and love; and, that we may obtain that which thou dost promise, make us to love that which thou dost command; through Jesus Christ our Lord. *Amen.*

The Epistle. Gal. v. 16.

I SAY then, Walk in the Spirit, and ye shall not fulfil the lust of the flesh. For the flesh lusteth

against the Spirit, and the Spirit against the flesh : and
these are contrary the one to the other: so that ye may
not do the things that ye would.   But if ye be led by
the Spirit, ye are not under the law.   Now the works
of the flesh are manifest, which are these ; Adultery,
fornication, uncleanness, lasciviousness, idolatry, witch-
craft, hatred, variance, emulations, wrath, strife, seditions,
heresies, envyings, murders, drunkenness, revellings, and
such like: of which I tell you before, as I have also told
you in time past, that they who do such things shall not
inherit the kingdom of God.   But the fruit of the Spirit
is love, joy, peace, long-suffering, gentleness, goodness,
faith, meekness, temperance : against such there is no
law.   And they that are Christ's have crucified the flesh
with the affections and lusts.

The Gospel.   Luke xvii. 11.

AND it came to pass, as Jesus went to Jerusalem,
that he passed through the midst of Samaria and
Galilee.   And as he entered into a certain village, there
met him ten men that were lepers, who stood afar off:
and they lifted up their voices, and said, Jesus, Master,
have mercy on us.   And when he saw them, he said
unto them, Go show yourselves unto the priests.   And
it came to pass, that, as they went, they were cleansed.
And one of them, when he saw that he was healed,
turned back, and with a loud voice glorified God, and
fell down on his face at his feet, giving him thanks:
and he was a Samaritan.   And Jesus answering said,
Were there not ten cleansed ? but where are the nine ?
There are not found that returned to give glory to God,
save this stranger.   And he said unto him, Arise, go
thy way : thy faith hath made thee whole.

THE FIFTEENTH SUNDAY AFTER TRINITY.

The Collect.

KEEP, we beseech thee, O Lord, thy church with thy perpetual mercy ; and because the frailty of man without thee cannot but fall, keep us ever by thy help from all things hurtful, and lead us to all things profitable to our salvation ; through Jesus Christ our Lord. *Amen.*

The Epistle. Gal. vi. 11.

YE see how large a letter I have written unto you with mine own hand. As many as desire to make a fair show in the flesh, they constrain you to be circumcised ; only lest they should suffer persecution for the cross of Christ. For neither they themselves who are circumcised keep the law ; but desire to have you circumcised, that they may glory in your flesh. But God forbid that I should glory, save in the cross of our Lord Jesus Christ, by whom the world is crucified unto me, and I unto the world. For in Christ Jesus neither circumcision availeth any thing, nor uncircumcision, but a new creature. And as many as walk according to this rule, peace be on them, and mercy, and upon the Israel of God. From henceforth let no man trouble me ; for I bear in my body the marks of the Lord Jesus. Brethren, the grace of our Lord Jesus Christ be with your spirit. Amen.

The Gospel. Matt. vi. 24.

NO man can serve two masters : for either he will hate the one, and love the other ; or else he will hold to the one, and despise the other. Ye cannot serve

God and mammon.   Therefore I say unto you, Take no thought for your life, what ye shall eat, or what ye shall drink; nor yet for your body, what ye shall put on.   Is not the life more than meat, and the body than raiment? Behold the fowls of the air: for they sow not, neither do they reap, nor gather into barns; yet your heavenly Father feedeth them.   Are ye not much better than they?   Which of you by taking thought can add one cubit unto his stature?   And why take ye thought for raiment?   Consider the lilies of the field how they grow; they toil not, neither do they spin: and yet I say unto you, That even Solomon in all his glory was not arrayed like one of these.   Wherefore, if God so clothe the grass of the field, which to-day is, and to-morrow is cast into the oven, shall he not much more clothe you, O ye of little faith?   Therefore take no thought, saying, What shall we eat? or, What shall we drink? or, Wherewithal shall we be clothed? (for after all these things do the Gentiles seek:) for your heavenly Father knoweth that ye have need of all these things.   But seek ye first the kingdom of God, and his righteousness; and all these things shall be added unto you.   Take therefore no thought for the morrow: for the morrow shall take thought for the things of itself. Sufficient unto the day is the evil thereof.

THE SIXTEENTH SUNDAY AFTER TRINITY.

The Collect.

O LORD, we beseech thee, let thy continual pity cleanse and defend thy church; and because it cannot continue in safety without thy succour, preserve it evermore by thy help and goodness; through Jesus Christ our Lord. *Amen.*

The Epistle. Ephes. iii. 13.

I DESIRE that ye faint not at my tribulations for you, which is your glory. For this cause I bow my knees unto the Father of our Lord Jesus Christ, of whom the whole family in heaven and earth is named, that he would grant you, according to the riches of his glory, to be strengthened with might by his Spirit in the inner man, that Christ may dwell in your hearts by faith; that ye, being rooted and grounded in love, may be able to comprehend with all saints what is the breadth, and length, and depth, and height; and to know the love of Christ, which passeth knowledge, that ye might be filled with all the fulness of God. Now unto him that is able to do exceeding abundantly above all that we ask or think, according to the power that worketh in us, unto him be glory in the church by Christ Jesus, throughout all ages, world without end. *Amen.*

The Gospel. Luke vii. 11.

AND it came to pass the day after, that Jesus went into a city called Nain; and many of his disciples went with him, and much people. Now when he came nigh to the gate of the city, behold, there was a dead man carried out, the only son of his mother, and she was a widow; and much people of the city was with her. And when the Lord saw her, he had compassion on her, and said unto her, Weep not. And he came and touched the bier: and they that bare him stood still. And he said, Young man, I say unto thee, Arise. And he that was dead sat up, and began to speak. And he delivered him to his mother. And there came a fear on all; and they glorified God, saying, That a great prophet is risen up among us; and, That God hath visited his people. And this rumour of him went forth throughout all Judea, and throughout all the region round about.

THE SEVENTEENTH SUNDAY AFTER TRINITY.

The Collect.

LORD, we pray thee, that thy grace may always prevent and follow us, and make us continually to be given to all good works; through Jesus Christ our Lord. *Amen.*

The Epistle. Ephes. iv. 1.

I THEREFORE, the prisoner of the Lord, beseech you that ye walk worthy of the vocation wherewith ye are called, with all lowliness and meekness, with long-suffering, forbearing one another in love; endeavouring to keep the unity of the Spirit in the bond of peace. There is one body, and one Spirit, even as ye are called in one hope of your calling; one Lord, one faith, one baptism, one God and Father of all, who is above all, and through all, and in you all.

The Gospel. Luke xiv. 1.

IT came to pass, as Jesus went into the house of one of the chief Pharisees to eat bread on the sabbath-day, that they watched him. And, behold, there was a certain man before him who had the dropsy. And Jesus answering spake unto the lawyers and Pharisees, saying, Is it lawful to heal on the sabbath-day? And they held their peace. And he took him, and healed him, and let him go; and answered them, saying, Which of you shall have an ass or an ox fallen into a pit, and will not straightway pull him out on the Sabbath-day? And they could not answer him again to these things. And he put forth a parable to those that were bidden, when he marked how they chose out the chief rooms, saying unto them, When thou art bidden of any man to a wedding, sit not down in the highest room; lest a more honourable man than thou be bidden of him; and he that bade thee and him come and say to thee, Give this man place; and thou begin with shame to take the lowest room. But when thou art bidden, go and sit down in the lowest room; that when he that bade thee cometh, he may say unto thee, Friend, go up higher. Then shalt thou have honour in the presence of them that sit at meat with thee. For whosoever exalteth himself shall be abased; and he that humbleth himself shall be exalted.

THE EIGHTEENTH SUNDAY AFTER TRINITY.

The Collect.

LORD, we beseech thee, grant thy people grace to withstand the temptations of the world, the flesh, and the devil; and with pure hearts and minds to follow thee, the only God; through Jesus Christ our Lord. *Amen.*

The Epistle. 1 Cor. i. 4.

I THANK my God always on your behalf, for the grace of God which is given you by Jesus Christ; that in every thing ye are enriched by him in all utterance, and in all knowledge; even as the testimony of Christ was confirmed in you: so that ye come behind in no gift; waiting for the coming of our Lord Jesus Christ, who shall also confirm you unto the end, that ye may be blameless in the day of our Lord Jesus Christ.

The Gospel. Matt. xxii. 34.

WHEN the Pharisees had heard that Jesus had put the Sadducees to silence, they were gathered together. Then one of them, who was a lawyer, asked him a question, tempting him, and saying, Master, which is the great commandment in the law? Jesus said unto him, Thou shalt love the Lord thy God with all thy heart, and with all thy soul, and with all thy mind. This is the first and great commandment. And the second is like unto it, Thou shalt love thy neighbour as thyself. On these two commandments hang all the law and the prophets. While the Pharisees were gathered together, Jesus asked them, saying, What think ye of Christ? whose son is he? They say unto him, The son of David. He saith unto them, How then doth David in spirit call him Lord, saying, The Lord said unto my Lord, Sit thou on my right hand, till I make thine enemies thy footstool? If David then call him Lord, how is he his son? And no man was able to answer him a word; neither durst any man from that day forth ask him any more questions.

THE NINETEENTH SUNDAY AFTER TRINITY.

The Collect.

O GOD, forasmuch as without thee we are not able to please thee; Mercifully grant that thy Holy Spirit may in all things direct and rule our hearts; through Jesus Christ our Lord. *Amen.*

The Epistle. Ephes. iv. 17.

THIS I say therefore, and testify in the Lord, that ye henceforth walk not as other Gentiles walk, in the vanity of their mind, having the understanding darkened, being alienated from the life of God through the ignorance that is in them, because of the blindness of their heart : who, being past feeling, have given themselves over unto lasciviousness, to work all uncleanness with greediness. But ye have not so learned Christ ; if so be that ye have heard him, and have been taught by him, as the truth is in Jesus : That ye put off, concerning the former conversation the old man, which is corrupt according to the deceitful lusts ; and be renewed in the spirit of your mind ; and that ye put on the new man, which after God is created in righteousness and true holiness. Wherefore putting away lying, speak every man truth with his neighbour : for we are members one of another. Be ye angry, and sin not: let not the sun go down upon your wrath : neither give place to the devil. Let him that stole, steal no more ; but rather let him labour, working with his hands the thing which is good, that he may have to give to him that needeth. Let no corrupt communication proceed out of your mouth, but that which is good, to the use of edifying, that it may minister grace unto the hearers. And grieve not the Holy Spirit of God, whereby ye are sealed unto the day of redemption. Let all bitterness, and wrath, and anger, and clamour, and evil-speaking, be put away from you, with all malice : and be ye kind one to another, tender-hearted, forgiving one another, even as God for Christ's sake hath forgiven you.

The Gospel. Matt. ix. 1.

JESUS entered into a ship, and passed over, and came into his own city. And, behold, they brought to him a man sick of the palsy, lying on a bed. And Jesus, seeing their faith, said unto the sick of the palsy, Son, be of good cheer ; thy sins are forgiven thee. And, behold, certain of the Scribes said within themselves, This man blasphemeth. And Jesus knowing

F

their thoughts said, Wherefore think ye evil in your hearts? For whether is easier to say, Thy sins are forgiven thee; or to say, Arise, and walk? But that ye may know that the Son of man hath power on earth to forgive sins, (then saith he to the sick of the palsy,) Arise, take up thy bed, and go unto thine house. And he arose, and departed to his house. But when the multitude saw it, they marvelled, and glorified God, who had given such power unto men.

THE TWENTIETH SUNDAY AFTER TRINITY.

The Collect.

O ALMIGHTY and most merciful God, of thy bountiful goodness keep us, we beseech thee, from all things that may hurt us; that we, being ready both in body and soul, may cheerfully accomplish those things that thou wouldest have done; through Jesus Christ our Lord. *Amen.*

The Epistle. Ephes. v. 15.

SEE then that ye walk circumspectly, not as fools, but as wise, redeeming the time, because the days are evil. Wherefore be ye not unwise, but understanding what the will of the Lord is. And be not drunk with wine, wherein is excess; but be filled with the Spirit; speaking to yourselves in psalms and hymns and spiritual songs, singing and making melody in your heart to the Lord; giving thanks always for all things unto God and the Father in the name of our Lord Jesus Christ; submitting yourselves one to another in the fear of God.

The Gospel. Matt. xxii. 1.

JESUS said, The kingdom of heaven is like unto a certain king who made a marriage for his son, and sent forth his servants to call them that were bidden to the wedding : and they would not come. Again, he sent forth other servants, saying, Tell them that are bidden, Behold, I have prepared my dinner : my oxen and my fatlings are killed, and all things are ready : come unto the marriage. But they made light of it, and went their ways, one to his farm, another to his merchandise ; and the remnant took his servants, and entreated them spitefully, and slew them. But when the king heard thereof, he was wroth : and he sent forth his armies, and destroyed those murderers, and burned up their city. Then saith he to his servants, The wedding is ready, but they who were bidden were not worthy. Go ye therefore into the highways, and as many as ye shall find, bid to the marriage. So those servants went out into the highways, and gathered together all as many as they found, both bad and good : and the wedding was furnished with guests. And when the king came in to see the guests, he saw there a man who had not on a wedding garment : and he saith unto him, Friend, how camest thou in hither not having on a wedding garment ? And he was speechless. Then said the king to the servants, Bind him hand and foot, and take him away, and cast him into outer darkness : there shall be weeping and gnashing of teeth. For many are called, but few are chosen.

THE TWENTY-FIRST SUNDAY AFTER TRINITY.

The Collect.

GRANT, we beseech thee, merciful Lord, to thy faithful people, pardon and peace ; that they may be cleansed from all their sins, and serve thee with a quiet mind; through Jesus Christ our Lord. *Amen.*

The Epistle. Ephes. vi. 10.

MY brethren, be strong in the Lord, and in the power of his might. Put on the whole armour of God, that ye may be able to stand against the wiles of the devil. For we wrestle not against flesh and blood, but against principalities, against powers, against the rulers of the darkness of this world, against spiritual wickedness in high places. Wherefore take unto you the whole armour of God, that ye may be able to withstand in the evil day, and having done all, to stand. Stand therefore, having your loins girt about with truth, and having on the breast-plate of righteousness; and your feet shod with the preparation of the Gospel of peace; above all, taking the shield of faith, wherewith ye shall be able to quench all the fiery darts of the wicked. And take the helmet of salvation, and the sword of the Spirit, which is the word of God: praying always with all prayer and supplication in the Spirit, and watching thereunto with all perseverance and supplication for all saints; and for me, that utterance may be given unto me, that I may open my mouth boldly, to make known the mystery of the Gospel, for which I am an ambassador in bonds: that therein I may speak boldly, as I ought to speak.

The Gospel. John iv. 46.

THERE was a certain nobleman, whose son was sick at Capernaum. When he heard that Jesus was come out of Judea into Galilee, he went unto him, and besought him that he would come down, and heal his son: for he was at the point of death. Then said Jesus unto him, Except ye see signs and wonders, ye will not believe. The nobleman saith unto him, Sir, come down ere my child die. Jesus saith unto him, Go thy way; thy son liveth. And the man believed the word that Jesus had spoken unto him, and he went his way. And as he was now going down, his servants met him, and told him, saying, Thy son liveth. Then inquired he of them the hour when he began to amend: and they said unto him, Yesterday at the seventh hour the fever left him. So the father knew that it was at the same hour in which Jesus said unto him, Thy son liveth; and himself believed, and his whole house. This is again the second miracle that Jesus did, when he was come out of Judea into Galilee.

THE TWENTY-SECOND SUNDAY AFTER TRINITY.

The Collect.

LORD, we beseech thee to keep thy household the church in continual godliness; that through thy protection it may be free from all adversities, and devoutly given to serve thee in good works, to the glory of thy name; through Jesus Christ our Lord. *Amen.*

The Epistle. Phil. i. 3.

I THANK my God upon every remembrance of you, (always in every prayer of mine for you all making request with joy,) for your fellowship in the Gospel from the first day, until now; being confident of this very thing, that he who hath begun a good work in you, will perform it until the day of Jesus Christ: even as it is meet for me to think this of you all, because I have you in my heart, inasmuch as both in my bonds, and in the defence and confirmation of the Gospel, ye are all partakers of my grace. For God is my record, how greatly I long after you all in the bowels of Jesus Christ. And this I pray, that your love may abound yet more and more in knowledge, and in all judgment; that ye may approve things that are excellent; that ye may be sincere and without offence till the day of Christ; being filled with the fruits of righteousness, which are by Jesus Christ, unto the glory and praise of God.

The Gospel. Matt. xviii. 21.

PETER said unto Jesus, Lord, how oft shall my brother sin against me, and I forgive him? till seven times? Jesus saith unto him, I say not unto thee, Until seven times; but, Until seventy times seven. Therefore is the kingdom of heaven likened unto a certain king, who would take account of his servants. And when he had begun to reckon, one was brought unto him who owed him ten thousand talents. But forasmuch as he had not to pay, his lord commanded him to be sold, and his wife and children, and all that he had, and payment to be made. The servant therefore fell down and worshipped him, saying, Lord, have patience with me, and I will pay thee all. Then the lord of that servant was moved with compassion, and loosed him, and forgave him the debt. But the same servant went out, and found one of his fellow-servants, who owed him an hundred pence: and he laid hands on him, and took him by the throat, saying, Pay me that thou owest. And his fellow-servant fell down at his feet, and besought him, saying, Have patience with me, and I will pay thee all. And he would not: but went and cast him into prison, till he should pay the debt. So when his fellow-servants saw what was done, they were very sorry, and came and told unto their lord all that was done. Then his lord, after that he had called him, said unto him, O thou wicked servant, I forgave thee all that debt, because thou desiredst me : shouldest not thou also have had compassion on thy fellow-servant, even as I had pity on thee ?   And his lord was wroth, and delivered him to the tormentors, till he should pay all that was due unto him.   So likewise shall my heavenly Father do also unto you, if ye from your hearts forgive not every one his brother their trespasses.

THE TWENTY-THIRD SUNDAY AFTER TRINITY.

The Collect.

O GOD, our refuge and strength, who art the author of all godliness ; Be ready, we beseech thee, to hear the devout prayers of thy church ; and grant that those things which we ask faithfully, we may obtain effectually ; through Jesus Christ our Lord.   *Amen.*

The Epistle.   Phil. iii. 17.

BRETHREN, be followers together of me, and mark them who walk so as ye have us for an ensample.   (For many walk, of whom I have told you often, and now tell you even weeping, that they are the enemies of the cross of Christ: whose end is destruction, whose god is their belly, and whose glory is in their shame, who mind earthly things.)   For our conversation is in heaven ; from whence also we look for the Saviour, the Lord Jesus Christ ; who shall change our vile body, that it may be fashioned like unto his glorious body, according to the working whereby he is able even to subdue all things unto himself.

The Gospel. Matt. xxii. 15.

THEN went the Pharisees, and took counsel how they might entangle him in his talk. And they sent unto him their disciples, with the Herodians, saying, Master, we know that thou art true, and teachest the way of God in truth, neither carest thou for any man: for thou regardest not the person of men. Tell us, therefore, What thinkest thou? Is it lawful to give tribute unto Cæsar, or not? But Jesus perceived their wickedness, and said, Why tempt ye me, ye hypocrites? Show me the tribute-money. And they brought unto him a penny. And he saith unto them, Whose is this image and superscription? They say unto him, Cæsar's. Then saith he unto them, Render therefore unto Cæsar the things which are Cæsar's; and unto God the things that are God's. When they had heard these words, they marvelled, and left him, and went their way.

THE TWENTY-FOURTH SUNDAY AFTER TRINITY.

The Collect.

O LORD, we beseech thee, absolve thy people from their offences; that through thy bountiful goodness we may all be delivered from the bands of those sins, which by our frailty we have committed. Grant this, O heavenly Father, for Jesus Christ's sake, our blessed Lord and Saviour. *Amen.*

The Epistle. Col. i. 3.

WE give thanks to God and the Father of our Lord Jesus Christ, praying always for you, since we heard of your faith in Christ Jesus, and of the love which ye have to all the saints, for the hope which is

laid up for you in heaven, whereof ye heard before in
the word of the truth of the Gospel; which is come
unto you, as it is in all the world; and bringeth forth
fruit, as it doth also in you, since the day ye heard of
it, and knew the grace of God in truth: as ye also
learned of Epaphras, our dear fellow-servant, who is for
you a faithful minister of Christ; who also declared
unto us your love in the Spirit. For this cause we
also, since the day we heard it, do not cease to pray for
you, and to desire that ye might be filled with the
knowledge of his will in all wisdom and spiritual understanding; that ye might walk worthy of the Lord unto
all pleasing, being fruitful in every good work, and
increasing in the knowledge of God; strengthened
with all might, according to his glorious power, unto
all patience and long-suffering with joyfulness; giving
thanks unto the Father, who hath made us meet to be
partakers of the inheritance of the saints in light.

The Gospel. Matt. ix. 18.

WHILE Jesus spake these things unto John's
disciples, behold, there came a certain ruler, and
worshipped him, saying, My daughter is even now
dead; but come and lay thy hand upon her, and she
shall live. And Jesus arose, and followed him, and so
did his disciples. And, behold, a woman who was
diseased with an issue of blood twelve years, came
behind him, and touched the hem of his garment: for
she said within herself, If I may but touch his garment,
I shall be whole. But Jesus turned him about; and
when he saw her, he said, Daughter, be of good comfort; thy faith hath made thee whole. And the woman
was made whole from that hour. And when Jesus came
into the ruler's house, and saw the minstrels and the
people making a noise, he said unto them, Give place:
for the maid is not dead, but sleepeth. And they

laughed him to scorn. But when the people were put forth, he went in, and took her by the hand, and the maid arose. And the fame hereof went abroad into all that land.

THE TWENTY-FIFTH SUNDAY AFTER TRINITY.

The Collect.

STIR up, we beseech thee, O Lord, the wills of thy faithful people, that they, plenteously bringing forth the fruit of good works, may of thee be plenteously rewarded; through Jesus Christ our Lord. *Amen.*

For the Epistle. Jer. xxiii. 5.

BEHOLD, the days come, saith the Lord, that I will raise unto David a righteous Branch, and a King shall reign and prosper, and shall execute judgment and justice on the earth. In his days Judah shall be saved; and Israel shall dwell safely: and this is his name whereby he shall be called, THE LORD OUR RIGHTEOUSNESS. Therefore, behold, the days come, saith the Lord, that they shall no more say, The Lord liveth, who brought up the children of Israel out of the land of Egypt; but, The Lord liveth, who brought up and who led the seed of the house of Israel out of the north country, and from all countries whither I had driven them; and they shall dwell in their own land.

The Gospel. John vi. 5.

WHEN Jesus then lifted up his eyes, and saw a great company come unto him, he saith unto Philip, Whence shall we buy bread, that these may eat?

And this he said to prove him; for he himself knew what he would do. Philip answered him, Two hundred penny-worth of bread is not sufficient for them, that every one of them may take a little. One of his disciples, Andrew, Simon Peter's brother, saith unto him, There is a lad here, who hath five barley loaves, and two small fishes: but what are they among so many? And Jesus said, Make the men sit down. Now there was much grass in the place. So the men sat down, in number about five thousand. And Jesus took the loaves; and when he had given thanks, he distributed to the disciples, and the disciples to them that were set down; and likewise of the fishes as much as they would. When they were filled, he said unto his disciples, Gather up the fragments that remain, that nothing be lost. Therefore they gathered them together, and filled twelve baskets with the fragments of the five barley loaves, which remained over and above unto them that had eaten. Then those men, when they had seen the miracle that Jesus did, said, This is of a truth that Prophet that should come into the world.

THE

ORDER FOR THE ADMINISTRATION

OF THE

LORD'S SUPPER.

The table at the Communion-time, having a fair white linen cloth upon it, shall stand in some convenient place. And the Elder, standing at the table, shall say the Lord's Prayer, with the Collect following, the people kneeling.

OUR Father, who art in heaven, Hallowed be thy Name. Thy kingdom come. Thy will be done in earth, As it is in heaven. Give us this day our daily bread. And forgive us our trespasses, As we forgive them that trespass against us. And lead us not into temptation ; But deliver us from evil. *Amen.*

The Collect.

ALMIGHTY God, unto whom all hearts be open, all desires known, and from whom no secrets are hid ; Cleanse the thoughts of our hearts by the inspiration of thy Holy Spirit, that we may perfectly love thee, and worthily magnify thy holy Name ; through Christ our Lord. *Amen.*

Then shall the Elder, turning to the people, rehearse distinctly all the TEN COMMANDMENTS: and the people still kneeling, shall, after every Commandment, ask God mercy for their transgression thereof for the time past, and grace to keep the same for the time to come, as followeth:

Minister.

GOD spake these words, and said; I am the Lord thy God: Thou shalt have none other gods but me.

People. *Lord, have mercy upon us, and incline our hearts to keep this law.*

Minist. Thou shalt not make to thyself any graven image, nor the likeness of any thing that is in heaven above, or in the earth beneath, or in the water under the earth. Thou shalt not bow down to them, nor worship them: for I the Lord thy God am a jealous God, and visit the sins of the fathers upon the children, unto the third and fourth generation of them that hate me, and show mercy unto thousands in them that love me, and keep my commandments.

People. *Lord, have mercy upon us, and incline our hearts to keep this law.*

Minist. Thou shalt not take the name of the Lord thy God in vain: for the Lord will not hold him guiltless that taketh his name in vain.

People. *Lord, have mercy upon us, and incline our hearts to keep this law.*

Minist. Remember that thou keep holy the Sabbath-day. Six days shalt thou labour, and do all that thou hast to do; but the seventh day is the Sabbath of the Lord thy God. In it thou shalt do no manner of work, thou, and thy son, and thy daughter, thy man-servant, and thy maid-servant, thy cattle, and the stranger that is within thy gates. For in six days the Lord made heaven and earth, the sea, and all that in them is, and rested the seventh day: wherefore the Lord blessed the seventh day, and hallowed it.

People. Lord, have mercy upon us, and incline our hearts to keep this law.

Minist. Honour thy father and thy mother ; that thy days may be long in the land, which the Lord thy God giveth thee.

People. Lord, have mercy upon us, and incline our hearts to keep this law.

Minist. Thou shalt do no murder.

People. Lord, have mercy upon us, and incline our hearts to keep this law.

Minist. Thou shalt not commit adultery.

People. Lord, have mercy upon us, and incline our hearts to keep this law.

Minist. Thou shalt not steal.

People. Lord, have mercy upon us, and incline our hearts to keep this law.

Minist. Thou shalt not bear false witness against thy neighbour.

People. Lord, have mercy upon us, and incline our hearts to keep this law.

Minist. Thou shalt not covet thy neighbour's house, thou shalt not covet thy neighbour's wife, nor his servant, nor his maid, nor his ox, nor his ass, nor any thing that is his.

People. Lord, have mercy upon us, and write all these thy laws in our hearts, we beseech thee.

Then shall follow this Collect.

A LMIGHTY and everlasting God, we are taught by thy holy word, that the hearts of Kings are in thy rule and governance, and that thou dost dispose and turn them as it seemeth best to thy godly wisdom ; We humbly beseech thee so to dispose and govern the heart of VICTORIA thy servant, our Queen and Governor, that in all her thoughts, words, and works, she may ever seek thy honour and glory, and study to preserve thy people committed to her charge, in wealth, peace, and godliness: Grant this, O merciful Father, for thy dear Son's sake, Jesus Christ our Lord. *Amen.*

Then shall be said the Collect of the day. And immediately after the Collect, the Elder shall read the Epistle, saying, The Epistle [or, The portion of Scripture appointed for the Epistle] is written in the ———— chapter of ————, beginning at the ———— verse. And the Epistle ended, he shall say, Here endeth the Epistle. Then shall he read the Gospel, (the People all standing up,) saying, The holy Gospel is written in the ———— chapter of ————, beginning at the ———— verse.

Then shall follow the Sermon.

Then shall the Elder say one or more of these Sentences.

LET your light so shine before men, that they may see your good works, and glorify your Father who is in heaven. *Matt.* v. 16.

Lay not up for yourselves treasures upon earth, where moth and rust do corrupt, and where thieves break through and steal; but lay up for yourselves treasures in heaven, where neither moth nor rust doth corrupt, and where thieves do not break through nor steal. *Matt.* vi. 19, 20.

He that soweth little shall reap little; and he that soweth plenteously shall reap plenteously. Let every man do according as he is disposed in his heart, not grudgingly, or of necessity; for God loveth a cheerful giver. 2 *Cor.* ix. 6, 7.

Be merciful after thy power. If thou hast much, give plenteously: if thou hast little, do thy diligence gladly to give of that little: for so gatherest thou thyself a good reward in the day of necessity. *Tob.* iv. 8, 9.

God is not unrighteous, that he will forget your works, and labour that proceedeth of love; which love ye have showed for his Name's sake, who have ministered unto the saints, and yet do minister. *Heb.* vi. 10.

Zaccheus stood forth, and said unto the Lord, Behold, Lord, the half of my goods I give to the poor ; and if I have done any wrong to any man, I restore him four-fold. *Luke* xix. 8.

Whatsoever ye would that men should do unto you, even so do unto them; for this is the law and the prophets. *Matt.* vii. 12.

Not every one that saith unto me, Lord, Lord, shall enter into the kingdom of heaven ; but he that doeth the will of my Father who is in heaven. *Matt.* vii. 21.

Who goeth a warfare at any time at his own cost? who planteth a vineyard, and eateth not of the fruit thereof? or who feedeth a flock, and eateth not of the milk of the flock ?   1 *Cor.* ix. 7.

If we have sown unto you spiritual things, is it a great matter if we shall reap your worldly things ? 1 *Cor.* ix. 11.

Do ye not know, that they who minister about holy things live of the sacrifice; and they who wait at the altar are partakers with the altar?   Even so hath the Lord also ordained, that they who preach the Gospel should live of the Gospel.   1 *Cor.* ix. 13, 14.

Let him that is taught in the word minister unto him that teacheth, in all good things. Be not deceived, God is not mocked : for whatsoever a man soweth, that shall he reap.   *Gal.* vi. 6, 7.

As we have opportunity, let us do good unto all men, and especially unto them that are of the household of faith.   *Gal.* vi. 10.

Godliness with contentment is great gain : for we brought nothing into the world, and it is certain we can carry nothing out.   1 *Tim.* vi. 6, 7.

Charge them who are rich in this world, that they be ready to give, and glad to distribute ; laying up in store for themselves a good foundation against the time to come, that they may attain eternal life. 1 *Tim.* vi. 17—19.

To do good, and to distribute, forget not; for with such sacrifices God is well pleased. *Heb*. xiii. 16.

Whoso hath this world's good, and seeth his brother have need, and shutteth up his compassion from him, how dwelleth the love of God in him? 1 *John* iii. 17.

He that hath pity upon the poor lendeth unto the Lord: and look, what he layeth out, it shall be paid him again. *Prov*. xix. 17.

Blessed is the man that provideth for the sick and needy: the Lord shall deliver him in time of trouble. *Psalm* xli. 1.

While these sentences are in reading, some fit person, appointed for that purpose, shall receive the alms for the poor, and other devotions of the people, in a decent basin, to be provided for that purpose; and then bring it to the Elder, who shall place it upon the table.

After which done, the Elder shall say,

Let us pray for the whole state of Christ's church militant here on earth.

ALMIGHTY and everliving God, who by thy holy Apostle hast taught us to make prayers and supplications, and to give thanks, for all men; We humbly beseech thee most mercifully [*to accept our alms and oblations, and*] to receive these our prayers, which we offer unto thy Divine Majesty; beseeching thee to inspire continually the universal church with the spirit of truth, unity, and concord: and grant that all they that do confess thy holy Name, may agree in the truth of thy holy word, and live in unity and godly love. We beseech thee also to save and defend all Christian Kings, Princes, and Governors; and especially thy servant VICTORIA our Queen; that under her we may be godly and quietly governed: And grant unto all that are put in authority under her, that they may truly and

> * If there be no alms or oblations, then shall the words [*of accepting our alms and oblations*] be left unsaid.

indifferently minister justice, to the punishment of wickedness and vice, and to the maintenance of thy true
religion and virtue.   Give grace, O heavenly Father, to
all the Ministers of thy Gospel, that they may, both by
their life and doctrine, set forth thy true and lively word,
and rightly and duly administer thy holy Sacraments :
And to all thy people give thy heavenly grace ; and
especially to this congregation here present ; that, with
meek heart and due reverence, they may hear and
receive thy holy word ; truly serving thee in holiness
and righteousness all the days of their life.   And we
most humbly beseech thee of thy goodness, O Lord, to
comfort and succour all them, who in this transitory
life are in trouble, sorrow, need, sickness, or any other
adversity.   And we also bless thy holy Name for all
thy servants departed this life in thy faith and fear ;
beseeching thee to give us grace so to follow their good
examples, that with them we may be partakers of thy
heavenly kingdom : Grant this, O Father, for Jesus
Christ's sake, our only Mediator and Advocate. *Amen.*

Then shall the Elder say to them that come to receive the
Holy Communion,

YE that do truly and earnestly repent of your sins,
   and are in love and charity with your neighbours,
and intend to lead a new life, following the commandments of God, and walking from henceforth in his holy
ways ; Draw near with faith, and take this holy Sacrament to your comfort; and make your humble confession
to Almighty God, meekly kneeling upon your knees.

Then shall this general Confession be made by the Minister in the
  name of those that are minded to receive the holy Communion,
  both he and all the people kneeling humbly upon their knees,
  and saying,

ALMIGHTY God, Father of our Lord Jesus Christ,
   Maker of all things, Judge of all men ; We acknow-

ledge and bewail our manifold sins and wickedness, Which we from time to time most grievously have committed, By thought, word, and deed, Against thy divine Majesty, Provoking most justly thy wrath and indignation against us. We do earnestly repent, And are heartily sorry for these our misdoings; The remembrance of them is grievous unto us. Have mercy upon us, Have mercy upon us, most merciful Father; For thy Son our Lord Jesus Christ's sake, Forgive us all that is past; And grant that we may ever hereafter serve and please thee in newness of life, To the honour and glory of thy Name; Through Jesus Christ our Lord. *Amen.*

Then shall the Elder say,

O ALMIGHTY God, our heavenly Father, who of thy great mercy hast promised forgiveness of sins to all them that with hearty repentance and true faith turn unto thee; Have mercy upon us; pardon and deliver us from all our sins, confirm and strengthen us in all goodness, and bring us to everlasting life; through Jesus Christ our Lord. *Amen.*

Then all standing, the Elder shall say,

Hear what comfortable words our Saviour Christ saith unto all that truly turn to him:

COME unto me, all ye that are burdened and heavy laden, and I will refresh you. *Matt.* xi. 28.

So God loved the world, that he gave his only-begotten Son, to the end that all that believe in him should not perish, but have everlasting life. *John* iii. 16.

Hear also what St. Paul saith:

This is a true saying, and worthy of all men to be received, That Christ Jesus came into the world to save sinners. 1 *Tim.* i. 15.

Hear also what St. John saith:

If any man sin, we have an Advocate with the Father, Jesus Christ the righteous: and he is the propitiation for our sins.   1 *John* ii. 1, 2.

After which the Elder shall proceed, saying,

Lift up your hearts.

Answ. *We lift them up unto the Lord.*

Elder. Let us give thanks unto our Lord God.

Answ. *It is meet and right so to do.*

Then shall the Elder say,

IT is very meet, right, and our bounden duty, that we should at all times, and in all places, give thanks unto thee, O Lord, Holy Father,* Almighty, Everlasting God.

Here shall follow the proper Preface, according to the time, if there be any especially appointed ; or else immediately shall follow,

THEREFORE with Angels and Archangels, and with all the company of heaven, we laud and magnify thy glorious Name ; evermore praising thee, and saying, Holy, holy, holy, Lord God of Hosts, heaven and earth are full of thy glory: Glory be to thee, O Lord most high.   *Amen.*

PROPER PREFACES.

Upon Christmas-Day.

BECAUSE thou didst give Jesus Christ, thine only Son, to be born as at this time for us ; who, by the operation of the Holy Ghost, was made very man, and that without spot of sin, to make us clean from all sin.   Therefore with Angels, &c.

---

* These words [Holy Father] must be omitted on Trinity Sunday.

Upon Easter-Day.

BUT chiefly we are bound to praise thee for the glorious Resurrection of thy Son Jesus Christ our Lord : for he is the very Paschal Lamb, which was offered for us, and hath taken away the sin of the world ; who by his death hath destroyed death, and by his rising to life again hath restored to us everlasting life.   Therefore with Angels, &c.

Upon Ascension-Day.

THROUGH thy most dearly beloved Son Jesus Christ our Lord ; who after his most glorious Resurrection manifestly appeared to all his Apostles, and in their sight ascended up into heaven, to prepare a place for us ; that where he is, thither we might also ascend, and reign with him in glory.   Therefore with Angels, &c.

Upon Whit-Sunday.

THROUGH Jesus Christ our Lord ; according to whose most true promise the Holy Ghost came down as at this time from heaven with a sudden great sound, as it had been a mighty wind, in the likeness of fiery tongues, lighting upon the Apostles, to teach them, and to lead them into all truth ; giving them both the gift of divers languages, and also boldness, with fervent zeal, constantly to preach the Gospel unto all nations, whereby we have been brought out of darkness and error into the clear light and true knowledge of thee, and of thy Son Jesus Christ. Therefore with Angels, &c.

Upon the Feast of Trinity.

WHO art one God, one Lord; not one only Person, but three Persons in one substance. For that which we believe of the glory of the Father, the same we believe of the Son, and of the Holy Ghost, without any inequality. Therefore with Angels, &c.

After each of which Prefaces shall immediately be said,

THEREFORE with Angels and Archangels, and with all the company of heaven, we laud and magnify thy glorious Name; evermore praising thee, and saying, Holy, holy, holy, Lord God of hosts, heaven and earth are full of thy glory: Glory be to thee, O Lord most high. *Amen.*

Then shall the Elder, kneeling down at the table, say in the name of all them that shall receive the Communion this prayer following; the People also kneeling.

WE do not presume to come to this thy table, O merciful Lord, trusting in our own righteousness, but in thy manifold and great mercies. We are not worthy so much as to gather up the crumbs under thy table. But thou art the same Lord, whose property is always to have mercy: Grant us therefore, gracious Lord, so to eat the flesh of thy dear Son Jesus Christ, and to drink his blood, that our sinful bodies may be made clean by his body, and our souls washed through his most precious blood, and that we may evermore dwell in him, and he in us. *Amen.*

Then the Elder shall say the Prayer of Consecration, as followeth.

ALMIGHTY God, our heavenly Father, who of thy tender mercy didst give thine only Son Jesus Christ to suffer death upon the cross for our redemption; who made there (by his oblation of himself once offered) a full, perfect, and sufficient sacrifice, oblation, and satisfaction for the sins of the whole world; and did institute, and in his holy Gospel command us to continue, a perpetual memory of that his precious death, until his coming again; Hear us, O merciful Father, we most humbly beseech thee; and grant that we receiving these thy creatures of bread and wine, according to thy Son our Saviour Jesus Christ's holy institution, in remembrance of his death and passion, may be partakers of his most blessed Body and Blood: who in the same night that he was betrayed took bread (a); and when he had given thanks, he brake it (b), and gave it to his disciples, saying, Take, eat; this (c) is my Body which is given for you: Do this in remembrance of me. Likewise, after supper, he took (d) the Cup; and when he had given thanks, he gave it to them, saying, Drink ye all of this; for this (e) is my Blood of the New Testament, which is shed for you and for many, for the remission of sins: Do this, as oft as ye shall drink it, in remembrance of me. *Amen.*

(a) Here the Elder is to take the Paten into his hands:

(b) And here to break the Bread:

(c) And here to lay his hand upon all the Bread.

(d) Here he is to take the Cup in his hand:

(e) And here to lay his hand upon the cup.

Then shall the Elder first receive the Communion in both kinds himself, and then proceed to deliver the same to the other Ministers in like manner, (if any be present,) and after that to the People also, in order, into their hands. And when he delivereth the Bread to any one, he shall say,

THE Body of our Lord Jesus Christ, which was given for thee, preserve thy body and soul unto everlasting life. Take and eat this in remembrance that Christ died for thee, and feed on him in thy heart by faith with thanksgiving.

And the Minister that delivereth the Cup to any one shall say,

THE Blood of our Lord Jesus Christ, which was shed for thee, preserve thy body and soul unto everlasting life. Drink this in remembrance that Christ's Blood was shed for thee, and be thankful.

If the consecrated Bread or Wine be all used before all have communicated, the Elder is to consecrate more, according to the form before prescribed; beginning at (Our Saviour Christ, in the same night, &c.) for the blessing of the Bread; and at (Likewise after supper, &c.) for the blessing of the Cup.

When all have communicated, the Minister shall return to the Lord's Table, and place upon it what remaineth of the consecrated Elements, covering the same with a fair linen cloth.

Then shall the Elder say the Lord's Prayer, the People repeating after him every Petition.

OUR Father, who art in heaven, Hallowed be thy Name. Thy kingdom come. Thy will be done on earth, As it is in heaven. Give us this day our daily bread. And forgive us our trespasses, As we forgive them that trespass against us. And lead us not into temptation; But deliver us from evil: For thine is the kingdom, and the power, and the glory, For ever and ever. *Amen.*

After which shall be said as followeth.

O LORD and heavenly Father, we thy humble servants desire thy fatherly goodness mercifully to accept this our sacrifice of praise and thanksgiving; most humbly beseeching thee to grant, that by the merits and death of thy Son Jesus Christ, and through faith in his blood, we and all thy whole church may obtain remission of our sins, and all other benefits of his passion. And here we offer and present unto thee, O Lord, ourselves, our souls and bodies, to be a reasonable, holy, and lively sacrifice unto thee; humbly beseeching thee that all we who are partakers of this holy Communion, may be filled with thy grace and heavenly benediction. And although we be unworthy, through our manifold sins, to offer unto thee any sacrifice, yet we beseech thee to accept this our bounden duty and service; not weighing our merits, but pardoning our offences, through Jesus Christ our Lord; by whom, and with whom, in the unity of the Holy Ghost, all honour and glory be unto thee, O Father Almighty, world without end. *Amen.*

Then shall be said,

GLORY be to God on high, and on earth peace, goodwill towards men. We praise thee, we bless thee, we worship thee, we glorify thee, we give thanks to thee for thy great glory, O Lord God, heavenly King, God the Father Almighty.

O Lord, the only-begotten Son Jesus Christ; O Lord God, Lamb of God, Son of the Father, that takest away the sins of the world, have mercy upon us. Thou that takest away the sins of the world, have mercy upon us. Thou that takest away the sins of the world, receive our prayer. Thou that sittest at the right hand of God the Father, have mercy upon us.

For thou only art holy, thou only art the Lord; thou only, O Christ, with the Holy Ghost, art most high in the glory of God the Father. *Amen.*

Then the Elder, if he see it expedient, may put up a prayer extempore; and afterwards shall let the people depart with this blessing.

MAY the peace of God, which passeth all understanding, keep your hearts and minds in the knowledge and love of God, and of his Son Jesus Christ our Lord; and may the blessing of God Almighty, the Father, the Son, and the Holy Ghost, be amongst you, and remain with you always. *Amen.*

G

THE MINISTRATION

OF

BAPTISM OF INFANTS.

The Minister coming to the Font, which is to be filled with pure Water, shall say,

DEARLY beloved, forasmuch as all men are conceived and born in sin, and that our Saviour Christ
saith, None can enter into the kingdom of God, except he
be regenerate and born anew of water and of the Holy
Ghost; I beseech you to call upon God the Father,
through our Lord Jesus Christ, that of his bounteous
mercy he will grant to *this Child* that which by nature
he cannot have; that *he* may be baptized not only with
water, but also with the Holy Ghost, and received into
Christ's holy church, and be made *a lively member* of the
same.

Hear for your encouragement in this service the words
of the Gospel written by St. Mark, in the tenth chapter,
at the thirteenth verse.

THEY brought young children to Christ, that he
should touch them. And his disciples rebuked
those that brought them: but when Jesus saw it, he was
much displeased, and said unto them, Suffer the little
children to come unto me, and forbid them not; for of
such is the kingdom of God. Verily I say unto you,
Whosoever shall not receive the kingdom of God as a
little child, he shall not enter therein. And he took them
up in his arms, put his hands upon them, and blessed them.

After the Gospel is read, the Minister shall make this brief
Exhortation upon the words of the Gospel:

BELOVED, ye hear in this Gospel the words of our
Saviour Christ, that he commanded the children
to be brought unto him; how he blamed those that

would have kept them from him ; how he exhorteth all men to follow their innocency. Ye perceive how by his outward gesture and deed he declared his good will toward them : for he embraced them in his arms, he laid his hands upon them, and blessed them. Doubt ye not therefore, but earnestly believe, that he will likewise favourably receive *this* present *Infant ;* that he will embrace *him* with the arms of his mercy ; that he will give unto *him* the blessing of eternal life, and make *him partaker* of his everlasting kingdom. Wherefore we being thus persuaded of the good will of our heavenly Father towards *this Infant,* declared by his Son Jesus Christ ; and nothing doubting but that he favourably alloweth this godly work of ours in bringing *this Infant* to his holy Baptism ; let us faithfully and devoutly give thanks unto him, and say,

A LMIGHTY and everlasting God, heavenly Father, we give thee humble thanks, for that thou hast vouchsafed to call us to the knowledge of thy grace, and faith in thee : Increase this knowledge, and confirm this faith in us evermore. Give thy Holy Spirit to *this Infant,* that *he* may be born again, and be made *an heir* of everlasting salvation ; through our Lord Jesus Christ, who liveth and reigneth with thee and the Holy Spirit, now and for ever. *Amen.*

Then the following Prayers shall be used.

A LMIGHTY and everlasting God, who of thy great mercy didst save Noah and his family in the ark from perishing by water ; and also didst safely lead the children of Israel thy people through the Red Sea, figuring thereby thy holy Baptism ; and by the Baptism of thy well-beloved Son Jesus Christ in the river Jordan, didst sanctify water for this holy Sacrament ; We beseech thee, for thine infinite mercies, that thou wilt look upon *this Child ;* wash *him* and sanctify *him* with the Holy Ghost ; that *he,* being delivered from thy wrath, may be received into the ark of Christ's church; and being steadfast in faith, joyful through hope, and rooted in love, may so pass the waves of this troublesome world, that finally *he* may come to the land of everlasting life, there to reign with thee, world without end; through Jesus Christ our Lord. *Amen.*

ALMIGHTY and immortal God, the aid of all that need, the helper of all that flee to thee for succour, the life of them that believe, and the resurrection of the dead; We call upon thee for *this Infant*, that *he*, coming to thy holy Baptism, may receive the inward and spiritual grace which is thereby signified. Receive *him*, O Lord, as thou hast promised by thy well-beloved Son, saying, Ask, and ye shall have; seek, and ye shall find; knock, and it shall be opened unto you: So give now unto us that ask; let us that seek find; open the gate unto us that knock; that *this Infant* may enjoy the everlasting benediction of thy heavenly washing, and may come to the eternal kingdom which thou hast promised by Christ our Lord. *Amen.*

ALMIGHTY, everliving God, whose most dearly beloved Son Jesus Christ, for the forgiveness of our sins, did shed out of his most precious side both water and blood: and gave commandment to his disciples, that they should go teach all nations, and baptize them in the Name of the Father, and of the Son, and of the Holy Ghost; Regard, we beseech thee, the supplications of this congregation; and grant that *this Child*, now to be baptized, may receive the fulness of thy grace, and be found at last in the number of thy faithful and elect children; through Jesus Christ our Lord. *Amen.*

Then the Congregation rising up, the Minister shall say as follows:

O MERCIFUL God, grant that the old Adam in *this Child* may be so buried, that the new man may be raised up in *him*. *Amen.*

Grant that all carnal affections may die in *him*, and that all things belonging to the Spirit may live and grow in *him*. *Amen.*

Grant that *he* may have power and strength to have victory, and to triumph against the devil, the world, and the flesh. *Amen.*

Grant that whosoever is here dedicated to thee by our office and ministry may also be endued with heavenly virtues, and everlastingly rewarded, through thy mercy, O blessed Lord God, who dost live, and govern all things, world without end. *Amen.*

At the close of each of these Petitions, the Congregation shall devoutly say *Amen.*

Then the Minister shall say to the Parents or Friends, taking the Child into his arms,

Name this Child.

And naming it after them, he shall dip it in the Water, or pour Water upon it, or sprinkle it therewith, saying,

N. I baptize thee In the Name of the Father, and of the Son, and of the Holy Ghost. *Amen.*

The Minister, if he see it expedient, may here address a brief exhortation to Parents, and the young people then present, and shall conclude with prayer.

THE MINISTRATION OF BAPTISM

TO SUCH AS ARE OF RIPER YEARS.

The Minister shall say,

DEARLY beloved, forasmuch as all men are conceived and born in sin, (and that which is born of the flesh is flesh,) and they that are in the flesh cannot please God, but live in sin, committing many

actual transgressions; and that our Saviour Christ
saith, None can enter into the kingdom of God, except
he be regenerate and born anew of water and of the
Holy Ghost; I beseech you to call upon God the
Father, through our Lord Jesus Christ, that of his
bounteous goodness he will grant to *these persons* that
which by nature *they* cannot have; that *they* may be
baptized, not only with water, but also with the Holy
Ghost, and received into Christ's holy church, and be
made lively *members* of the same.

Then shall the Minister use as many of the following Prayers as
the time will permit, saying,

Let us pray.

(And here all the Congregation shall kneel.)

ALMIGHTY and everlasting God, who of thy great
mercy didst save Noah and his family in the ark
from perishing by water; and also didst safely lead the
children of Israel thy people through the Red Sea,
figuring thereby thy holy Baptism; and by the
Baptism of thy well-beloved Son Jesus Christ in the
river Jordan, didst sanctify the element of water for
this holy Sacrament; We beseech thee, for thine infinite mercies, that thou wilt mercifully look upon *these*
thy *servants*; wash *them*, and sanctify *them* with the
Holy Ghost; that *they*, being delivered from thy wrath,
may be received into the ark of Christ's church; and
being steadfast in faith, joyful through hope, and rooted
in love, may so pass the waves of this troublesome
world, that finally *they* may come to the land of everlasting life, there to reign with thee world without end;
through Jesus Christ our Lord. *Amen.*

ALMIGHTY and immortal God, the aid of all that
need, the helper of all that flee to thee for
succour, the life of them that believe, and the resurrection
of the dead; We call upon thee for *these persons*; that

they, coming to thy holy Baptism, may receive remission of *their* sins, and the grace of regeneration. Receive *them*, O Lord, as thou hast promised, by thy well-beloved Son, saying, Ask, and ye shall receive; seek, and ye shall find; knock, and it shall be opened unto you: So give now unto us that ask; let us that seek find; open the gate unto us that knock; that *these persons* may enjoy the everlasting benediction of thy heavenly washing, and may come to the eternal kingdom which thou hast promised by Christ our Lord. *Amen.*

Then shall the People stand up, and the Minister shall say,

Hear the words of the Gospel written by St. John, in the third chapter, beginning at the first verse.

THERE was a man of the Pharisees, named Nicodemus, a ruler of the Jews. The same came to Jesus by night, and said unto him, Rabbi, we know that thou art a teacher come from God; for no man can do these miracles that thou doest, except God be with him. Jesus answered and said unto him, Verily, verily, I say unto thee, Except a man be born again, he cannot see the kingdom of God. Nicodemus saith unto him, How can a man be born when he is old? Can he enter the second time into his mother's womb, and be born? Jesus answered, Verily, verily, I say unto thee, Except a man be born of water, and of the Spirit, he cannot enter into the kingdom of God. That which is born of the flesh is flesh; and that which is born of the Spirit is spirit. Marvel not that I said unto you, Ye must be born again. The wind bloweth where it listeth, and thou hearest the sound thereof; but canst not tell whence it cometh, and whither it goeth: so is every one that is born of the Spirit.

Then the Minister shall speak to the Persons to be baptized, on this wise:

WELL-beloved, who *are* come hither, desiring to receive holy Baptism, *ye* have heard how the congregation hath prayed, that our Lord Jesus Christ would vouchsafe to receive you and bless you, to release you of your sins, to give you the kingdom of heaven, and everlasting life. And our Lord Jesus Christ hath promised in his holy word to grant all those things that we have prayed for; which promise he for his part will most surely keep and perform.

Wherefore, after this promise made by Christ, *ye* must also faithfully for your part promise, in the presence of the whole congregation, that *ye* will renounce the devil and all his works, and constantly believe God's holy word, and obediently keep his commandments.

Then shall the Minister demand of the persons to be baptized,

Quest. DOST thou renounce the devil and all his works, the vain pomp and glory of the world, with all covetous desires of the same, and the carnal desires of the flesh, so that thou wilt not follow, nor be led by, them?

Answ. *I renounce them all.*

Quest. DOST thou believe in God the Father Almighty, Maker of heaven and earth? And in Jesus Christ, his only-begotten Son our Lord? And that he was conceived by the Holy Ghost; born of the Virgin Mary; that he suffered under Pontius Pilate; was crucified, dead, and buried; that he went down into hell, and also did rise again the third day; that he ascended into heaven, and sitteth at the right hand of God the Father Almighty; and from thence he shall come again, at the end of the world, to judge the quick and the dead?

And dost thou believe in the Holy Ghost; the holy Catholic Church; the Communion of Saints; the Remission of Sins; the Resurrection of the Body; and everlasting life after death?

Answ. *All this I steadfastly believe.*

Quest. WILT thou be baptized in this faith ?
Answ. *This is my desire.*

Quest. WILT thou then obediently keep God's holy will and commandments, and walk in the same all the days of thy life?
Answ. *I will endeavour so to do, God being my helper.*

Then shall the Minister say,

O MERCIFUL God, grant that the old Adam in *these persons* may be so buried, that the new man may be raised up in *them. Amen.*

Grant that all carnal affections may die in *them*, and that all things belonging to the Spirit may live and grow in *them. Amen.*

Grant that *they* may have power and strength to have victory, and to triumph against the devil, the world, and the flesh. *Amen.*

Grant that *they*, being here dedicated to thee by our office and ministry, may also be endued with heavenly virtues, and everlastingly rewarded, through thy mercy, O blessed Lord God, who dost live and govern all things, world without end. *Amen.*

ALMIGHTY, ever-living God, whose most dearly beloved Son Jesus Christ, for the forgiveness of our sins, did shed out of his most precious side both water and blood ; and gave commandment to his disciples, that they should go teach all nations, and baptize them, in the name of the Father, and of the Son, and of the Holy Ghost ; Regard, we beseech thee, the supplications of this congregation ; and grant that the *persons* now to be baptized may receive the fulness of thy grace, and ever remain in the number of thy faithful and elect children ; through Jesus Christ our Lord. *Amen.*

The Congregation may here sing a hymn suitable to the occasion.

Then shall the Minister take each person to be baptized by the right hand; and placing him conveniently by the Font, according to his discretion, shall ask the Name; and then shall dip him in the Water, or pour Water upon him, or sprinkle him therewith, saying,

N. I baptize thee In the Name of the Father, and of the Son, and of the Holy Ghost. *Amen.*

Then shall the Minister say,

SEEING now, dearly beloved brethren, that *these persons are* admitted into the visible body of Christ's church; let us give thanks unto Almighty God for this benefit, and with one accord make our prayers unto him, that *they* may lead the rest of *their* lives according to this beginning.

Then shall be said the Lord's Prayer, all kneeling.

OUR Father, which art in heaven, Hallowed be thy Name. Thy kingdom come. Thy will be done on earth, As it is in heaven. Give us this day our daily bread. And forgive us our trespasses, As we forgive them that trespass against us. And lead us not into temptation; but deliver us from evil. *Amen.*

WE yield thee hearty thanks, most merciful Father, that it hath pleased thee to admit *these persons* into thy holy church. And humbly we beseech thee to grant, that *they* being dead unto sin, and living unto righteousness, and being buried with Christ in his death, may crucify the old man, and utterly abolish the whole body of sin; and that being made *partakers* of the death of thy Son, *they* may also be *partakers* of his resurrection; so that finally, with the residue of thy holy church, *they* may be *inheritors* of thine everlasting kingdom, through Jesus Christ our Lord. *Amen.*

The Minister, if he deem it expedient, may conclude the service with an extemporary prayer.

THE FORM OF SOLEMNIZATION

MATRIMONY.

At the day and time appointed for solemnization of Matrimony, the persons to be married standing together, the Man on the right hand and the Woman on the left, the Minister shall say,

DEARLY beloved, we are gathered together here in the sight of God, and in the face of this Congregation, to join together this Man and this Woman in holy Matrimony; which is an honourable estate, instituted of God in the time of man's innocency, signifying unto us the mystical union that is between Christ and his church: which holy estate Christ sanctioned and adorned with his presence, and first miracle that he wrought in Cana of Galilee; and is commended of St. Paul to be honourable among all men, and therefore is not by any to be enterprised, or taken in hand, unadvisedly, lightly, or wantonly; but reverently, discreetly, advisedly, soberly, and in the fear of God; duly considering the causes for which Matrimony was ordained.

It was ordained for the purpose of perpetuating the human race, and that children might be brought up in the fear and nurture of the Lord, and to the praise of his holy name.

It was also ordained for the mutual society, help, and comfort, that the one ought to have of the other, both in prosperity and adversity.

Into this holy estate these two persons present come now to be joined. Therefore, if any man can show any just cause why they may not lawfully be joined together, let him now speak, or else hereafter for ever hold his peace.

And also, speaking unto the persons that are to be married, he shall say,

I REQUIRE and charge you both, (as you will answer at the dreadful day of judgment, when the secrets of all hearts shall be disclosed,) that if either of you know any impediment why you may not be lawfully joined together in Matrimony, you do now confess it. For be ye well assured, that so many as are coupled together otherwise than God's word doth allow, are not joined together by God ; neither is their Matrimony lawful.

The Man shall then say, in the presence of the Registrar and two Witnesses,

I *Do solemnly declare, that I know not of any lawful impediment, why I,* A. B.,* *may not* • The Man. *be joined in Matrimony to* C. D.† † The Woman.

In like manner the Woman shall say, in the presence of the same persons,

I *Do solemnly declare, that I know not of any lawful impediment, why I,* C. D.,* *may not* * The Woman. *be joined in Matrimony to* A. B.† † The Man.

N.B. The names of the persons to be married must be repeated as they stand upon the Licence or Certificate.

If no impediment be alleged, then shall the Minister say unto the Man,

A. B. WILT thou have this Woman to thy wedded Wife, to live together after God's ordinance in the holy estate of Matrimony ? Wilt thou love her, comfort her, honour and keep her, in sickness and in health ; and, forsaking all other, keep thee only unto her, so long as ye both shall live ?

The Man shall answer,

I WILL.

Then shall the Minister say unto the Woman,

C. D. WILT thou have this Man to thy wedded Husband, to live together after God's ordinance in the holy estate of Matrimony? Wilt thou obey him, serve him, love, honour, and keep him, in sickness and in health; and, forsaking all other, keep thee only unto him, so long as ye both shall live?

The Woman shall answer,

I WILL.

Then the Minister shall cause the Man with his right hand to take the Woman by her right hand, and to say after him as followeth:

I *A. B.* take thee *C. D.* to be my wedded Wife, to have and to hold from this day forward, for better for worse, for richer for poorer, in sickness and in health, to love and to cherish, till death us do part, according to God's holy ordinance; and thereto I plight thee my faith.

Then shall they loose their hands; and the Woman, with her right hand taking the Man by his right hand, shall likewise say after the Minister,

I *C. D.* take thee *A. B.* to be my wedded Husband, to have and to hold from this day forward, for better for worse, for richer for poorer, in sickness and in health, to love, cherish, and to obey, till death us do part, according to God's holy ordinance; and thereto I give thee my faith.

Then the Minister shall cause the Man with his right hand to take the Woman by her right hand, and to say after him as follows:

I *Call upon these persons here present to witness, that I, A. B.,* do take thee, C. D.,†* to be my lawful wedded Wife.

* The Man.
† The Woman.

Then shall they loose their hands, and the Woman, with her right hand taking the Man by his right hand, shall say after the Minister,

I *Call upon these persons here present to witness, that I, C. D.,* do take thee, A. B.,†* to be my lawful wedded Husband.

* The Woman.
† The Man.

Then shall they again loose their hands; and the Man shall give unto the Woman a Ring, laying the same upon the book. And the Minister, taking the Ring, shall deliver it unto the Man, to put it upon the fourth finger of the Woman's left hand. And the Man holding the Ring there, and taught by the Minister, shall say,

WITH this Ring, a token and pledge of the Vow and Covenant now made betwixt me and thee, I thee wed, in the name of the Father, and of the Son, and of the Holy Ghost.

Then the Man leaving the ring upon the fourth finger of the Woman's left hand, they shall both kneel down; and the Minister shall say,

Let us pray.

O ETERNAL God, Creator and Preserver of all mankind, Giver of all spiritual grace, the Author of everlasting life ; Send thy blessing upon these thy servants, this Man and this Woman, whom we bless in thy Name ; that, as Isaac and Rebecca lived faithfully together, so these persons may surely perform and keep the vow and covenant betwixt them made, (whereof this Ring given and received is a token and pledge,) and may ever remain in perfect love and peace together, and live according to thy laws; through Jesus Christ our Lord. *Amen.*

Then shall the Minister join their right hands together, and say,

Those whom God hath joined together, let no man put asunder.

Then shall the Minister speak unto the People :

FORASMUCH as *A. B.* and *C. D.* have consented together in holy wedlock, and have witnessed the same before God and this company, and thereto have pledged their faith either to other, and have declared the same by giving and receiving of a Ring, and by joining of hands ; I pronounce that they be Man and Wife together, In the Name of the Father, and of the Son, and of the Holy Ghost. *Amen.*

And the Minister shall add this blessing:

GOD the Father, God the Son, God the Holy Ghost, bless, preserve, and keep you; the Lord mercifully with his favour look upon you; and so fill you with all spiritual benediction and grace, that ye may so live together in this life that in the world to come ye may have life everlasting. *Amen.*

Then shall the Minister read one or both of the following Psalms.

Beati Omnes. Psalm cxxviii.

BLESSED *is* every one that feareth the Lord; that walketh in his ways.

For thou shalt eat the labour of thine hands : happy *shalt* thou *be*, and *it shall be* well with thee.

Thy wife *shall be* as a fruitful vine by the sides of thine house : thy children like olive plants round about thy table.

Behold, that thus shall the man be blessed that feareth the Lord.

The Lord shall bless thee out of Zion : and thou shalt see the good of Jerusalem all the days of thy life.

Yea, thou shalt see thy children's children, *and* peace upon Israel.

Glory be to the Father, and to the Son, and to the Holy Ghost;

As it was in the beginning, is now, and ever shall be, world without end. Amen.

Deus misereatur. Psalm lxvii.

GOD be merciful unto us, and bless us; *and* cause his face to shine upon us. Selah.

That thy way may be known upon earth, thy saving health among all nations.

Let the people praise thee, O God; let all the people praise thee.

O let the nations be glad and sing for joy : for thou

shalt judge the people righteously, and govern the nations upon earth.   Selah.

Let the people praise thee, O God ; let all the people praise thee.

Then shall the earth yield her increase ; *and* God, *even* our own God, shall bless us.

God shall bless us ; and all the ends of the earth shall fear him.

Glory be to the Father, and to the Son, and to the Holy Ghost ;

As it was in the beginning, is now, and ever shall be, world without end.   Amen.

Then, all present kneeling, the Minister shall say,

Lord, have mercy upon us.

Answer. *Christ, have mercy upon us.*

Minister. Lord, have mercy upon us.

OUR Father, which art in heaven, Hallowed be thy Name.   Thy kingdom come.   Thy Will be done in earth, As it is in heaven.   Give us this day our daily bread.   And forgive us our trespasses, As we forgive them that trespass against us.   And lead us not into temptation ; But deliver us from evil.   For thine is the kingdom, the power, and the glory, for ever and ever.   *Amen.*

Minister. O Lord, save thy servant and thy handmaid ;

Answer. *And let them put their trust in thee.*

Minister. O Lord, send them help from thy holy place ;

Answer. *And evermore defend them.*

Minister. Be unto them a tower of strength,

Answer. *From the face of their enemy.*

Minister. O Lord, hear our prayer ;

Answer. *And let our cry come unto thee.*

Minister.

O GOD of Abraham, God of Isaac, God of Jacob, bless these thy servants, and sow the seed of eternal life in their hearts, that whatsoever in thy holy Word they shall profitably learn, they may in deed fulfil the same. Look, O Lord, mercifully upon them from heaven, and bless them. And as thou didst send thy blessing upon Abraham and Sarah, to their great comfort ; so vouchsafe to send thy blessing upon these thy servants ; that they, obeying thy will, and always being in safety under thy protection, may abide in thy love unto their lives' end ; through Jesus Christ our Lord. *Amen.*

O GOD, who by thy mighty power hast made all things of nothing, who also (after other things set in order) didst appoint that out of man (created after thine own image and similitude) woman should take her beginning ; and, knitting them together, didst teach that it should never be lawful to put asunder those whom thou by Matrimony hadst made one : O God, who hast consecrated the state of Matrimony to such an excellent mystery, that in it is signified and represented the spiritual marriage and unity between Christ and his church ; Look mercifully upon these thy servants, that both this man may love his wife, according to thy word ; (as Christ did love his spouse the Church, who gave himself for it, loving and cherishing it, even as his own flesh ;) and also that this woman may be loving and amiable, faithful and obedient to her husband ; and in all quietness, sobriety, and peace, be a follower of holy and godly matrons. O Lord, bless them both, and grant them to inherit thy everlasting kingdom, through Jesus Christ our Lord. *Amen.*

Then shall the Minister say,

A LMIGHTY God, who at the beginning did create our first parents, Adam and Eve, and did sanctify and join them together in marriage ; pour upon you the riches of his grace, sanctify, and bless you, that you may

please him both in body and soul, and live together in
holy love unto your lives' end.   *Amen.*

After which the Minister shall read as followeth :

ALL ye that are married, or that intend to take the
holy estate of Matrimony upon you, hear what
the Holy Scripture doth say, as touching the duty of
husbands towards their wives, and wives towards their
husbands.

St. Paul, in his Epistle to the Ephesians, the fifth
chapter, doth give this commandment to all married
men ; Husbands, love your wives, even as Christ also
loved the Church, and gave himself for it ; that he
might sanctify and cleanse it with the washing of water,
by the Word ; that he might present it to himself a
glorious Church, not having spot, or wrinkle, or any
such thing ; but that it should be holy and without
blemish.   So ought men to love their wives as their
own bodies.   He that loveth his wife, loveth himself.
For no man ever yet hated his own flesh, but nourisheth
and cherisheth it, even as the Lord the Church : for we
are members of his body, of his flesh, and of his bones.
For this cause shall a man leave his father and mother,
and shall be joined unto his wife, and they two shall be
one flesh.   This is a great mystery : but I speak concerning Christ and the Church.   Nevertheless, let every
one of you in particular so love his wife even as himself.
—*Ephes.* v. 25.

Likewise the same St. Paul, writing to the Colossians,
speaketh thus to all men that are married ; Husbands,
love your wives, and be not bitter against them.—
Col. iii. 19.

Hear also what St. Peter, an Apostle of Christ, who
was himself a married man, saith unto them that are
married ; Ye husbands, dwell with your wives according
to knowledge ; giving honour unto the wife, as unto
the weaker vessel, and as being heirs together of

the grace of life ; that your prayers be not hindered.—
1 *Peter* iii. 7.

Hitherto ye have heard the duty of the husband
toward the wife. Now likewise, ye wives, hear and
learn your duties toward your husbands, even as they
are plainly set forth in Holy Scripture.

St. Paul, in the aforenamed Epistle to the Ephesians,
teacheth you thus ; Wives, submit yourselves unto your
own husbands, as unto the Lord. For the husband is
the head of the wife, even as Christ is the head of the
Church, and he is the Saviour of the body. Therefore
as the Church is subject unto Christ, so let the wives be
to their own husbands in every thing. And again he
saith, Let the wife see that she reverence her husband.
—*Ephes.* v. 22.

And in his Epistle to the Colossians, Saint Paul giveth
you this short lesson ; Wives, submit yourselves unto
your own husbands, as it is fit in the Lord.— *Col.* iii. 18.

St. Peter also doth instruct you, thus saying ; Ye
wives, be in subjection to your own husbands; that if
any obey not the word, they also may without the
word be won by the conversation of the wives, while
they behold your chaste conversation coupled with fear.
Whose adorning, let it not be that outward adorning of
plaiting the hair, and of wearing of gold, or of putting
on of apparel ; but let it be the hidden man of the heart,
in that which is not corruptible, even the ornament of a
meek and quiet spirit, which is in the sight of God of great
price. For after this manner in the old time the holy
women also, who trusted in God, adorned themselves,
being in subjection unto their own husbands ; even as
Sarah obeyed Abraham, calling him lord ; whose
daughters ye are as long as ye do well, and are not
afraid with any amazement.—1 *Peter* iii. 1.

THE grace of the Lord Jesus Christ, and the love of
God, and the communion of the Holy Ghost, be
with you all. *Amen.*—2 *Cor.* xiii. 14.

THE ORDER

FOR

THE BURIAL OF THE DEAD.

―――

The Minister meeting the Corpse, and going before it, shall say,

I AM the resurrection and the life, saith the Lord. He that believeth on me, though he were dead, yet shall he live : and whosoever liveth and believeth on me shall never die.—*John* xi. 25, 26.

I KNOW that my Redeemer liveth, and that he shall stand at the latter day upon the earth. And though after my skin worms destroy this body, yet in my flesh shall I see God : whom I shall see for myself, and mine eyes shall behold, and not another.—*Job* xix. 25—27.

WE brought nothing into this world, and it is certain we can carry nothing out. The Lord gave, and the Lord hath taken away. Blessed be the name of the Lord.—1 *Tim.* vi. 7 ; *Job* i. 21.

Then shall be read Psalm xc.

LORD, thou hast been our refuge : from one generation to another.

Before the mountains were brought forth, or ever the earth and the world were made : thou art God from everlasting, and world without end.

Thou turnest man to destruction : again thou sayest, Come again, ye children of men.

For a thousand years in thy sight are but as yesterday : seeing that is past as a watch in the night.

As soon as thou scatterest them, they are even as a sleep : and fade away suddenly like the grass.

In the morning it is green, and groweth up : but in the evening it is cut down, dried up, and withered.

For we consume away in thy displeasure : and are afraid at thy wrathful indignation.

Thou hast set our misdeeds before thee : and our secret sins in the light of thy countenance.

For when thou art angry, all our days are gone : we bring our years to an end, as it were a tale that is told.

The days of our age are threescore years and ten ; and though men be so strong, that they come to fourscore years : yet is their strength then but labour and sorrow ; so soon passeth it away, and we are gone.

But who regardeth the power of thy wrath : for even according to thy fear, so is thy displeasure.

So teach us to number our days : that we may apply our hearts unto wisdom.

Turn thee again, O Lord, at the last : and be gracious unto thy servants.

O satisfy us with thy mercy, and that soon : so shall we rejoice and be glad all the days of our life.

Comfort us again now after the time that thou hast plagued us : and for the years wherein we have suffered adversity.

Show thy servants thy work : and their children thy glory.

And the glorious Majesty of the Lord our God be upon us : prosper thou the work of our hands upon us, O prosper thou our handy work.

Glory be to the Father, and to the Son, and to the Holy Ghost.

As it was in the beginning, is now, and ever shall be, world without end.   Amen.

Then shall follow the Lesson taken out of the fifteenth Chapter of the first Epistle of St. Paul to the Corinthians.

1 *Cor.* xv. 20.

NOW is Christ risen from the dead, and become the first-fruits of them that slept. For since by

man came death, by man came also the resurrection of
the dead.　For as in Adam all die, even so in Christ
shall all be made alive.　But every man in his own
order : Christ the first-fruits ; afterward they that are
Christ's at his coming.　Then cometh the end, when
he shall have delivered up the kingdom to God, even
the Father ; when he shall have put down all rule, and
all authority and power.　For he must reign, till he hath
put all enemies under his feet.　The last enemy that
shall be destroyed is death.　For he hath put all
things under his feet.　But when he saith, All
things are put under him, it is manifest that He is
excepted who did put all things under him.　And when
all things shall be subdued unto him, then shall the
Son also himself be subject unto Him that put all
things under him, that God may be all in all.　Else
what shall they do who are baptized for the dead, if
the dead rise not at all ?　Why are they then baptized
for the dead ? and why stand we in jeopardy every
hour ?　I protest by your rejoicing, which I have in
Christ Jesus our Lord, I die daily.　If after the
manner of men I have fought with beasts at Ephesus,
what advantageth it me, if the dead rise not ?　Let
us eat and drink ; for to-morrow we die.　Be not
deceived : evil communications corrupt good manners.
Awake to righteousness, and sin not : for some have
not the knowledge of God.　I speak this to your
shame.　But some man will say, How are the dead
raised up ? and with what body do they come ?　Thou
fool, that which thou sowest is not quickened, except it
die.　And that which thou sowest, thou sowest not
that body that shall be, but bare grain, it may chance
of wheat, or of some other grain : but God giveth it a
body as it hath pleased him ; and to every seed his
own body.　All flesh is not the same flesh : but there is
one kind of flesh of men, another flesh of beasts, another
of fishes, and another of birds.　There are also celestial

bodies, and bodies terrestrial: but the glory of the celestial is one, and the glory of the terrestrial is another. There is one glory of the sun, and another glory of the moon, and another glory of the stars: for one star differeth from another star in glory. So also is the resurrection of the dead. It is sown in corruption ; it is raised in incorruption : it is sown in dishonour ; it is raised in glory : it is sown in weakness ; it is raised in power : it is sown a natural body ; it is raised a spiritual body. There is a natural body, and there is a spiritual body. And so it is written, The first man Adam was made a living soul ; the last Adam was made a quickening spirit. Howbeit, that was not first which is spiritual, but that which is natural ; and afterward that which is spiritual. The first man is of the earth, earthy : the second man is the Lord from heaven. As is the earthy, such are they that are earthy : and as is the heavenly, such are they also that are heavenly. And as we have borne the image of the earthy, we shall also bear the image of the heavenly. Now this I say, brethren, that flesh and blood cannot inherit the kingdom of God ; neither doth corruption inherit incorruption. Behold, I show you a mystery ; We shall not all sleep, but we shall all be changed, in a moment, in the twinkling of an eye, at the last trump : for the trumpet shall sound, and the dead shall be raised incorruptible, and we shall be changed. For this corruptible must put on in- corruption, and this mortal must put on immortality. So when this corruptible shall have put on incorruption, and this mortal shall have put on immortality, then shall be brought to pass the saying that is written, Death is swallowed up in victory. O death, where is thy sting ? O grave, where is thy victory ? The sting of death is sin, and the strength of sin is the law. But thanks be to God, which giveth us the victory through our Lord Jesus Christ. Therefore, my be- loved brethren, be ye steadfast, unmoveable, always abounding in the work of the Lord, forasmuch as ye know that your labour is not in vain in the Lord.

MAN that is born of a woman hath but a short time to live, and is full of misery. He cometh up, and is cut down like a flower; he fleeth as it were a shadow, and never continueth in one stay.

In the midst of life we are in death : of whom may we seek for succour, but of thee, O Lord, who for our sins art justly displeased ?

Yet, O Lord God most holy, O Lord most mighty, O holy and most merciful Saviour, deliver us not into the bitter pains of eternal death.

Thou knowest, Lord, the secrets of our hearts : shut not thy merciful ears to our prayers ; but spare us, Lord most holy, O God most mighty, O holy and merciful Saviour, thou most worthy Judge eternal, suffer us not at our last hour for any pains of death to fall from thee.

I HEARD a voice from heaven, saying unto me, Write; From henceforth, blessed are the dead which die in the Lord : even so, saith the Spirit; for they rest from their labours.

Lord, have mercy upon us.
Christ, have mercy upon us.
Lord, have mercy upon us.

OUR Father, which art in heaven, Hallowed be thy Name. Thy kingdom come. Thy Will be done in earth, As it is in heaven. Give us this day our daily bread. And forgive us our trespasses, As we forgive them that trespass against us. And lead us not into temptation ; But deliver us from evil. *Amen.*

The Collect.

O MERCIFUL God, the Father of our Lord Jesus Christ, who is the resurrection and the life ; in whom whosoever believeth shall live, though he die ; and whosoever liveth and believeth in him, shall not die eternally ; We meekly beseech thee, O Father, to raise us from the death of sin unto the life of righteousness ; that when we shall depart this life, we may rest in him; and at the general resurrection on the last day, may be found acceptable in thy sight, and receive that blessing which thy well-beloved Son shall then pronounce to all that love and fear thee, saying, Come, ye blessed children of my Father, receive the kingdom prepared for you from the beginning of the world. Grant this, we beseech thee, O merciful Father, through Jesus Christ, our Mediator and Redeemer. *Amen.*

THE grace of our Lord Jesus Christ, and the love of God, and the fellowship of the Holy Ghost, be with you all evermore. *Amen.*—2 *Cor.* xiii. 14.

SELECT PSALMS.

MORNING PRAYER.

PSALM I.

BLESSED is the man that hath not walked in the counsel of the ungodly, nor stood in the way of sinners: and hath not sat in the seat of the scornful.

2 But his delight is in the law of the Lord: and in his law will he exercise himself day and night.

3 He shall be like a tree planted by the water-side: that will bring forth his fruit in due season.

4 His leaf also shall not wither: and look, whatsoever he doeth, it shall prosper.

5 As for the ungodly, it is not so with them: but they are like the chaff which the wind scattereth away from the face of the earth.

6 Therefore the ungodly shall not be able to stand in the judgment: neither the sinners in the congregation of the righteous.

7 But the Lord knoweth the way of the righteous: and the way of the ungodly shall perish.

PSALM II.

WHY do the heathen so furiously rage together: and why do the people imagine a vain thing?

2 The kings of the earth stand up, and the rulers

take counsel together : against the Lord, and against his Anointed.

3 Let us break their bonds asunder : and cast away their cords from us.

4 He that dwelleth in heaven shall laugh them to scorn : the Lord shall have them in derision.

5 Then shall he speak unto them in his wrath : and vex them in his sore displeasure.

6 Yet have I set my King: upon my holy hill of Sion.

7 I will declare the decree ; the Lord hath said unto me : Thou art my Son, this day have I begotten thee.

8 Desire of me, and I shall give thee the heathen for thine inheritance : and the uttermost parts of the earth for thy possession.

9 Thou shalt bruise them with a rod of iron : and break them to pieces like a potter's vessel.

10 Be wise now, therefore, O ye kings : be learned, ye that are judges of the earth.

11 Serve the Lord in fear : and rejoice unto him with reverence.

12 Kiss the Son, lest he be angry, and so ye perish from the right way : when his wrath is kindled but a little.   Blessed are all they that put their trust in him.

EVENING PRAYER.

PSALM III.

LORD, how are they increased that trouble me : many are they that rise against me.

2 Many are they that say of my soul : There is no help for him in his God.

3 But thou, O Lord, art my defender : thou art my glory, and the lifter up of my head.

4 I did call upon the Lord with my voice: and he heard me out of his holy hill.

5 I laid me down and slept, and rose up again: for the Lord sustained me.

6 I will not be afraid for ten thousands of the people: that have set themselves against me round about.

7 Up, Lord, and help me, O my God: for thou smitest all mine enemies upon the cheek-bone; thou hast broken the teeth of the ungodly.

8 Salvation belongeth unto the Lord: and thy blessing is upon thy people.

PSALM IV.

HEAR me when I call, O God of my righteousness: thou hast set me at liberty when I was in trouble; have mercy upon me, and hearken unto my prayer.

2 O ye sons of men, how long will ye blaspheme mine honour: and have such pleasure in vanity, and seek after lying?

3 Know this also, that the Lord hath chosen to himself the man that is godly: when I call upon the Lord, he will hear me.

4 Stand in awe, and sin not: commune with your own heart, and in your chamber, and be still.

5 Offer the sacrifice of righteousness: and put your trust in the Lord.

6 There are many that say: Who will show us any good?

7 Lord, lift thou up: the light of thy countenance upon us.

8 Thou hast put gladness in my heart: more than in the time that their corn and their wine increased.

9 I will lay me down in peace, and take my rest: for it is thou, Lord, only that makest me dwell in safety.

PSALM V.

PONDER my words, O Lord: consider my meditation.

2 O hearken thou unto the voice of my calling, my King and my God: for unto thee will I make my prayer.

3 My voice shalt thou hear betimes, O Lord: early in the morning will I direct my prayer unto thee, and will look up.

4 For thou art the God that hast no pleasure in wickedness: neither shall any evil dwell with thee.

5 Such as be foolish shall not stand in thy sight: for thou hatest all them that work vanity.

6 Thou shalt destroy them that speak lies: the Lord will abhor both the blood-thirsty and deceitful man.

7 But as for me, I will come into thine house, even upon the multitude of thy mercy: and in thy fear will I worship toward thy holy temple.

8 Lead me, O Lord, in thy righteousness, because of mine enemies: make thy way plain before my face.

9 And let all them that put their trust in thee rejoice: they shall ever be giving of thanks, because thou defendest them; they that love thy name shall be joyful in thee.

10 For thou, Lord, wilt give thy blessing unto the righteous: and with thy favourable kindness wilt thou defend him, as with a shield.

MORNING PRAYER.

PSALM VI.

O LORD, rebuke me not in thine indignation: neither chasten me in thy displeasure.

2 Have mercy upon me, O Lord, for I am weak: O Lord, heal me; for my bones are vexed.

3 My soul also is sore troubled : but, Lord, how long wilt thou punish me?

4 Turn thee, O Lord, and deliver my soul : O save me, for thy mercy's sake.

5 For in death no man remembereth thee : and who will give thee thanks in the pit?

6 I am weary of my groaning : every night wash I my bed, and water my couch with my tears.

7 My beauty is gone for very trouble : and worn away because of all mine enemies.

8 Away from me, all ye that work vanity : for the Lord hath heard the voice of my weeping.

9 The Lord hath heard my petition : the Lord will receive my prayer.

10 All mine enemies shall be confounded, and sore vexed : they shall be turned back, and put to shame suddenly.

PSALM VII.

O LORD, my God, in thee have I put my trust : save me from all them that persecute me, and deliver me ;

2 Lest he devour my soul like a lion : and tear it in pieces while there is none to help. .

3 O Lord, my God, if I have done any such thing : or if there be any wickedness in my hands ;

4 If I have rewarded evil unto him that dealt friendly with me : (yea, I have delivered him that without any cause is mine enemy ;)

5 Then let mine enemy persecute my soul, and take me : yea, let him tread my life down upon the earth, and lay mine honour in the dust.

6 Stand up, O Lord, and lift up thyself because of the indignation of mine enemies : arise up for me to the judgment that thou hast commanded.

7 And so shall the congregation of the people come about thee : for their sakes therefore lift up thyself again.

8 The Lord shall judge the people ; give sentence with me, O Lord : according to my righteousness, and according to the innocency that is in me.

9 O let the wickedness of the ungodly come to an end : but guide thou the just.

10 For the righteous God : trieth the very hearts and reins.

11 My help cometh of God : who preserveth them that are true of heart.

12 God is a righteous Judge, strong and patient : and God is provoked every day.

13 If a man will not turn, he will whet his sword : he hath bent his bow, and made it ready.

14 He hath prepared for him the instruments of death : he ordaineth his arrows against the persecutors.

15 Behold, he travaileth with mischief : he hath conceived sorrow, and brought forth ungodliness.

16 He hath graven and digged up a pit : and is fallen himself into the destruction that he made for others.

17 I will give thanks unto the Lord, according to his righteousness : and I will praise the name of the Lord most high.

EVENING PRAYER.

PSALM VIII.

O LORD our Governor, how excellent is thy name in all the world : thou that hast set thy glory above the heavens !

2 Out of the mouths of very babes and sucklings hast thou ordained strength, because of thine enemies : that thou mightest still the enemy and the avenger.

3 I will consider thy heavens, even the works of thy fingers : the moon and the stars which thou hast ordained.

4 What is man, that thou art mindful of him: and the son of man, that thou visitest him?

5 Thou madest him a little lower than the angels: to crown him with glory and honour.

6 Thou makest him to have dominion over the works of thy hands: and thou hast put all things in subjection under his feet;

7 All sheep and oxen: yea, and the beasts of the field;

8 The fowls of the air, and the fishes of the sea: and whatsoever passeth through the paths of the seas.

9 O Lord our Governor: how excellent is thy name in all the world!

PSALM IX.

I WILL give thanks unto thee, O Lord, with my whole heart: I will speak of all thy marvellous works.

2 I will be glad and rejoice in thee: yea, my songs will I make of thy name, O thou most Highest.

3 When mine enemies are driven back: they shall fall and perish at thy presence.

4 For thou hast maintained my right and my cause: thou art set in the throne judging right.

5 Thou hast rebuked the heathen, and destroyed the ungodly: thou hast put out their name for ever and ever.

6 O thou enemy, destructions are come to a perpetual end: even as the cities which thou hast destroyed; their memorial is perished with them.

7 But the Lord shall endure for ever: he hath also prepared his seat for judgment.

8 For he shall judge the world in righteousness: and minister true judgment unto the people.

9 The Lord will also be a defence for the oppressed: even a refuge in times of trouble.

10 And they that know thy name will put their trust in thee: for thou, Lord, hast never failed them that seek thee.

11 O praise the Lord, who dwelleth in Sion: show the people his doings.

12 For when he maketh inquisition for blood, he remembereth them: and forgetteth not the complaint of the humble.

13 Have mercy upon me, O Lord; consider the trouble which I suffer of them that hate me: thou that liftest me up from the gates of death.

14 That I may show all thy praises within the gates of the daughter of Sion: I will rejoice in thy salvation.

15 The heathen are sunk down in the pit that they made: in the same net which they hid privily is their foot taken.

16 The Lord is known to execute judgment: the ungodly is trapped in the work of his own hands.

17 The wicked shall be turned into hell: and all the people that forget God.

18 For the poor shall not alway be forgotten: the patient abiding of the meek shall not perish for ever.

19 Up, Lord, and let not man have the upper hand: let the heathen be judged in thy sight.

20 Put them in fear, O Lord: that the heathen may know themselves to be but men.

MORNING PRAYER.

PSALM X.

WHY standest thou so far off, O Lord: and hidest thy face in the needful time of trouble?

2 The ungodly, for his own lust, doth persecute the poor: they shall be taken in the crafty wiliness that they have imagined.

3 For the ungodly hath made boast of his own heart's desire : and speaketh good of the covetous, whom God abhorreth.

4 The ungodly is so proud, that he careth not for God : neither is God in all his thoughts.

5 His ways are always grievous : thy judgments are far above out of his sight, and therefore defieth he all his enemies.

6 Arise, O Lord God, and lift up thine hand : forget not the poor.

7 Wherefore should the wicked blaspheme God : while he doth say in his heart, Tush, thou God carest not for it ?

8 Surely thou hast seen it : for thou beholdest ungodliness and wrong.

9 That thou mayest take the matter into thy hand : the poor committeth himself unto thee ; for thou art the helper of the friendless.

10 Break thou the power of the ungodly and malicious : seek out his wickedness till thou find none.

11 The Lord is King for ever and ever : and the heathen are perished out of the land.

12 Lord, thou hast heard the desire of the poor : thou preparest their heart, and thine ear hearkeneth thereto ;

13 To help the fatherless and poor unto their right : that the man of the earth be no more exalted against them.

PSALM XI.

IN the Lord I put my trust : how say ye then to my soul, that she should flee as a bird unto the hill ?

2 For, lo, the ungodly bend their bow, and make ready their arrows within the quiver : that they may privily shoot at them who are true of heart.

3 If the foundations be destroyed : what can the righteous do ?

4 The Lord is in his holy temple : the Lord's seat is in heaven.

5 His eyes consider the poor : and his eyelids try the children of men.

6 The Lord trieth the righteous : but the ungodly, and him that delighteth in wickedness, doth his soul abhor.

7 Upon the ungodly he shall rain snares, fire and brimstone, storm and tempest : this shall be their portion to drink.

8 For the righteous Lord loveth righteousness : his countenance will behold the thing that is just.

PSALM XII.

HELP me, Lord : for the faithful are minished from among the children of men.

2 They talk of vanity every one with his neighbour : they do but flatter with their lips, and dissemble in their double heart.

3 The Lord shall root out all deceitful lips : and the tongue that speaketh proud things ;

4 Which have said, With our tongue will we prevail : we are they that ought to speak ; who is Lord over us ?

5 Now, for the comfortless troubles' sake of the needy : and because of the deep sighing of the poor ;

6 I will up, saith the Lord : and will help every one from him that swelleth against him, and will set him at rest.

7 The words of the Lord are pure words : even as the silver, which from the earth is tried, and purified seven times in the fire.

8 Thou shalt keep them, O Lord : thou shalt preserve them from this generation for ever.

9 The ungodly walk on every side : when they are exalted, the children of men are put to rebuke.

EVENING PRAYER.

PSALM XIII.

HOW long wilt thou forget me, O Lord? For ever? How long wilt thou hide thy face from me?

2 How long shall I seek counsel in my soul, and be so vexed in my heart? How long shall mine enemies triumph over me?

3 Consider, and hear me, O Lord, my God: lighten mine eyes, that I sleep not in death:

4 Lest mine enemy say, I have prevailed against him: for if I be cast down, they that trouble me will rejoice at it.

5 But my trust is in thy mercy: and my heart is joyful in thy salvation.

6 I will sing of the Lord, because he hath dealt so lovingly with me: yea, I will praise the Name of the Lord most Highest.

PSALM XV.

LORD, who shall dwell in thy tabernacle: or who shall rest upon thy holy hill?

2 Even he that leadeth an uncorrupt life: and doeth the thing which is right, and speaketh the truth from his heart;

3 He that hath used no deceit with his tongue, nor done evil to his neighbour: and hath not slandered his neighbour.

4 He that setteth not by himself, but is lowly in his own eyes: and maketh much of them that fear the Lord.

5 He that sweareth unto his neighbour, and disappointeth him not: though it were to his own hinderance.

6 He that hath not given up his money upon usury: nor taken reward against the innocent.

7 Whoso doeth these things: shall never fall.

PSALM XVI.

PRESERVE me, O God: for in thee have I put my trust.

2 O my soul, thou hast said unto the Lord, Thou art my God : my goodness extendeth not to thee.

3 All my delight is upon the saints that are in the earth : and upon such as excel in virtue.

4 But they that run after another god : shall have great trouble.

5 Their drink-offerings of blood will I not offer : neither make mention of their names within my lips.

6 The Lord himself is the portion of mine inheritance, and of my cup: thou shalt maintain my lot.

7 The lot is fallen unto me in a fair ground : yea, I have a goodly heritage.

8 I will thank the Lord for giving me warning : my reins also chasten me in the night season.

9 I have set God always before me : for he is on my right hand, therefore I shall not fall.

10 Wherefore my heart is glad, and my glory rejoiceth : my flesh also shall rest in hope.

11 For why? thou shalt not leave my soul in hell : neither shalt thou suffer thy Holy One to see corruption.

12 Thou shalt show me the path of life ; in thy presence is the fulness of joy : and at thy right hand there is pleasure for evermore.

MORNING PRAYER.

PSALM XVII.

HEAR the right, O Lord, consider my complaint : and hearken unto my prayer, that goeth not out of feigned lips.

2 Let my sentence come forth from thy presence : and let thine eyes look upon the thing that is equal.

3 Thou hast proved, and visited mine heart in the night season ; thou hast tried me, and shalt find no wickedness in me : for I am utterly purposed that my mouth shall not offend.

4 Because of men's works that are done against the words of thy lips : I have kept me from the ways of the destroyer.

5 O hold thou up my goings in thy paths : that my footsteps slip not.

6 I have called upon thee, O God, for thou shalt hear me : incline thine ear to me, and hearken unto my words.

7 Show thy marvellous lovingkindness, O thou that savest by thy right hand them who put their trust in thee : from those that rise up against them.

8 Keep me as the apple of an eye : hide me under the shadow of thy wings.

9 Arise, O Lord, and deliver my soul from the wicked : who are thy sword :

10 From men who are thy hand, O Lord ; from men of the world : who have their portion in this life, and whose belly thou fillest with thy hid treasure.

11 They have children at their desire : and leave the rest of their substance for their babes.

12 But as for me, I will behold thy presence in righteousness : and when I awake up after thy likeness, I shall be satisfied with it.

PSALM XVIII.—Part I.

I WILL love thee, O Lord, my strength : the Lord is my stony rock and my defence ; my Saviour, my God, and my might, in whom I will trust ; my buckler, the horn also of my salvation, and my refuge.

2 I will call upon the Lord, who is worthy to be praised : so shall I be safe from mine enemies.

3 The sorrows of death compassed me : and the overflowings of ungodliness made me afraid.

4 The pains of hell came about me : the snares of death overtook me.

5 In my trouble I will call upon the Lord : and complain unto my God.

6 So shall he hear my voice out of his holy temple : and my complaint shall come before him ; it shall enter even into his ears.

7 The earth trembled and quaked : the very foundations also of the hills shook, and were removed, because he was wroth.

8 There went a smoke out in his presence, and a consuming fire out of his mouth : so that coals were kindled at it.

9 He bowed the heavens also, and came down : and it was dark under his feet.

10 He rode upon the cherubim, and did fly : he came flying upon the wings of the wind.

11 He made darkness his secret place : his pavilion round about him with dark water, and thick clouds to cover him.

12 At the brightness of his presence his clouds removed : hail-stones, and coals of fire.

13 The Lord also thundered out of heaven, and the Highest gave his voice : hail-stones, and coals of fire.

14 He sent out his arrows, and scattered them : he cast forth lightnings, and destroyed them.

15 The springs of water were seen, and the foundations of the round world were discovered at thy chiding, O Lord : at the blasting of the breath of thy displeasure.

16 He shall send down from on high to fetch me : and shall take me out of many waters.

17 He shall deliver me from my strongest enemy, and from them who hate me : for they are too mighty for me.

18 They prevented me in the day of my trouble : but the Lord was my upholder.

19 He brought me forth also into a place of liberty : he brought me forth, even because he had a favour unto me.

20 The Lord shall reward me after my righteous dealing : according to the cleanness of my hands shall he recompense me.

21 Because I have kept the ways of the Lord : and have not forsaken my God, as the wicked doth.

22 For I have an eye unto all his laws : and will not cast his commandments from me.

23 I was also uncorrupt before him : and kept myself from mine own iniquity.

24 Therefore shall the Lord reward me after my righteous dealing : and according unto the cleanness of mine hands in his eye-sight.

EVENING PRAYER.

PSALM XVIII.—Part II.

THOU shalt light my candle : the Lord my God shall make my darkness to be light.

2 The way of God is an undefiled way : the word of the Lord is also tried in the fire ; he is the defender of all them that put their trust in him.

3 For who is God but the Lord : or who hath any strength except our God ?

4 It is God that girdeth me with strength of war : and maketh my way perfect.

5 He maketh my feet like harts' feet : and setteth me up on high.

6 He teacheth mine hands to fight : and mine arms shall break even a bow of steel.

7 Thou hast given me the defence of thy salvation : thy right hand also shall hold me up, and thy loving correction shall make me great.

8 Thou shalt make room enough under me to go: that my footsteps shall not slide.

9 The Lord liveth; and blessed be my strong Helper: and praised be the God of my salvation.

10 It is he that delivereth me from my cruel enemies, and setteth me up above mine adversaries: thou shalt deliver me from the wicked man.

11 For this cause will I give thanks unto thee, O Lord, among the Gentiles: and sing praises unto thy Name.

PSALM XIX.

THE heavens declare the glory of God, and the firmament showeth his handy work.

2 One day telleth another: and one night certifieth another.

3 There is neither speech nor language: but their voices are heard among them.

4 Their sound is gone out into all lands: and their words unto the ends of the world.

5 In them hath he set a tabernacle for the sun: which cometh forth as a bridegroom out of his chamber, and rejoiceth as a giant to run his course.

6 It goeth forth from the uttermost part of the heaven, and runneth about unto the end of it again: and there is nothing hid from the heat thereof.

7 The law of the Lord is an undefiled law, converting the soul: the testimony of the Lord is sure, and giveth wisdom unto the simple.

8 The statutes of the Lord are right, and rejoice the heart: the commandment of the Lord is pure, and giveth light unto the eyes.

9 The fear of the Lord is clean, and endureth for ever: the judgments of the Lord are true and righteous altogether.

10 More to be desired are they than gold, yea, than

much fine gold : sweeter also than honey and the honey-comb.

11 Moreover by them is thy servant taught : and in keeping of them there is great reward.

12 Who can tell how oft he offendeth ? O cleanse thou me from my secret faults.

13 Keep thy servant from all presumptuous sins, lest they get the dominion over me : so shall I be undefiled, and innocent from the great offence.

14 Let the words of my mouth, and the meditation of my heart, be always acceptable in thy sight,

15 O Lord, my Strength and my Redeemer.

MORNING PRAYER.

PSALM XX.

THE Lord hear thee in the day of trouble : the Name of the God of Jacob defend thee :

2 Send thee help from the sanctuary : and strengthen thee out of Sion.

3 We will rejoice in thy salvation, and triumph in the Name of the Lord our God : the Lord perform all thy petitions.

4 Now know I that the Lord helpeth his Anointed, and will hear him from his holy heaven : even with the wholesome strength of his right hand.

5 Some put their trust in chariots, and some in horses : but we will remember the Name of the Lord our God.

6 They are brought down, and fallen : but we are risen, and stand upright.

7 Save, Lord, and hear us, O King of heaven : when we call upon thee.

PSALM XXII.—Part I.

MY God, my God, look upon me : why hast thou forsaken me ; and art so far from helping me and from the words of my complaint?

2 O my God, I cry in the daytime, but thou hearest not : and in the night season also I take no rest.

3 But thou continuest holy : O thou Worship of Israel.

4 Our fathers hoped in thee : they trusted in thee, and thou didst deliver them.

5 They called upon thee, and were holpen : they put their trust in thee, and were not confounded.

6 But as for me, I am a worm, and no man : a very scorn of men, and the outcast of the people.

7 All they that see me, laugh me to scorn : they shoot out their lips, and shake their heads, saying,

8 He trusted in God, that he would deliver him : let him deliver him, if he will have him.

9 But thou art he that took me out of my mother's womb : thou wast my hope when I hanged yet upon my mother's breasts.

10 I have been left unto thee ever since I was born : thou art my God, even from my mother's womb.

11 O go not from me, for trouble is hard at hand : and there is none to help me.

12 I am poured out like water, and all my bones are out of joint : my heart also in the midst of my body is like melting wax.

13 My strength is dried up like a potsherd, and my tongue cleaveth to my gums : and thou hast brought me into the dust of death.

14 They pierced my hands and my feet ; I may tell all my bones : they stand staring and looking upon me.

15 They part my garments among them : and cast lots upon my vesture.

16 But be not thou far from me, O Lord : thou art my succour ; haste thee to help me.

17 Deliver my soul from the sword : my darling from the power of the dog.

18 Save me from the lion's mouth : thou hast heard me also from among the horns of the unicorns.

EVENING PRAYER.

PSALM XXII.—Part II.

I WILL declare thy name unto my brethren : in the midst of the congregation will I praise thee.

2 O praise the Lord, ye that fear him : magnify him, all ye of the seed of Jacob ; and fear him, all ye seed of Israel.

3 For he hath not despised, nor abhorred the low estate of the poor : he hath not hid his face from him ; but when he called unto him, he heard him.

4 My praise is of thee in the great congregation : my vows will I perform in the sight of them that fear him.

5 The poor shall eat and be satisfied : they that seek the Lord shall praise him ; your heart shall live for ever.

6 All the ends of the world shall remember themselves, and be turned unto the Lord : and all the kindreds of the nations shall worship before him.

7 For the kingdom is the Lord's : and he is the Governor among the people.

8 All they that go down into the dust shall bow before him : and none can keep alive his own soul.

9 A seed shall serve him : they shall be accounted to the Lord for a generation.

10 They shall come, and the heavens shall declare nis righteousness : unto a people that shall be born, whom the Lord hath made.

PSALM XXIII.

THE Lord is my shepherd: therefore can I lack
nothing.

2 He shall feed me in a green pasture: and lead me
forth beside the waters of comfort.

3 He shall convert my soul: and bring me forth in
the paths of righteousness, for his Name's sake.

4 Yea, though I walk through the valley of the
shadow of death, I will fear no evil: for thou art with
me ; thy rod and thy staff comfort me.

5 Thou shalt prepare a table before me in the presence of them that trouble me: thou hast anointed my
head with oil, and my cup shall be full.

6 Surely thy lovingkindness and mercy shall follow
me all the days of my life: and I will dwell in the
house of the Lord for ever.

PSALM XXIV.

THE earth is the Lord's, and all that therein is: the
compass of the world, and they that dwell therein.

2 For he hath founded it upon the seas: and prepared it upon the floods.

3 Who shall ascend into the hill of the Lord: or who
shall rise up in his holy place?

4 Even he that hath clean hands and a pure heart:
and that hath not lifted up his mind unto vanity, nor
sworn to deceive his neighbour.

5 He shall receive the blessing from the Lord: and
righteousness from the God of his salvation.

6 This is the generation of them that seek him: even
of them that seek thy face, O Jacob.

7 Lift up your heads, O ye gates, and be ye lifted
up, ye everlasting doors: and the King of glory shall
come in.

8 Who is the King of glory? It is the Lord, strong
and mighty, even the Lord mighty in battle.

9 Lift up your heads, O ye gates, and be ye lifted up, ye everlasting doors : and the King of glory shall come in.

10 Who is the King of glory? Even the Lord of hosts, he is the King of glory.

MORNING PRAYER.

PSALM XXV.

UNTO thee, O Lord, will I lift up my soul; my God, I have put my trust in thee : O let me not be confounded, neither let mine enemies triumph over me.

2 For all they that hope in thee shall not be ashamed : but such as transgress without a cause shall be put to confusion.

3 Show me thy ways, O Lord : and teach me thy paths.

4 Lead me forth in thy truth, and teach me : for thou art the God of my salvation ; in thee hath been my hope all the day long.

5 Call to remembrance, O Lord, thy tender mercies : and thy lovingkindnesses, which have been ever of old.

6 O remember not the sins and offences of my youth : but according to thy mercy, think thou upon me, O Lord, for thy goodness.

7 Gracious and righteous is the Lord : therefore will he teach sinners in the way.

8 Them that are meek shall he guide in judgment : and such as are gentle, them shall he teach his way.

9 All the paths of the Lord are mercy and truth : unto such as keep his covenant and his testimonies.

10 For thy Name's sake, O Lord : be merciful unto my sin ; for it is great.

11 What man is he that feareth the Lord? him shall he teach in the way that he shall choose.

12 His soul shall dwell at ease: and his seed shall inherit the land.

13 The secret of the Lord is among them that fear him : and he will show them his covenant.

14 Mine eyes are ever looking unto the Lord: for he shall pluck my feet out of the net.

15 Turn thee unto me, and have mercy upon me: for I am desolate and in misery.

16 The sorrows of my heart are enlarged : O bring thou me out of my troubles.

17 Look upon my adversity and misery: and forgive me all my sin.

18 O keep my soul, and deliver me : let me not be confounded, for I have put my trust in thee.

19 Let perfectness and righteous dealing wait upon me : for my hope hath been in thee.

20 Deliver Israel, O God : out of all his troubles.

PSALM XXVI.

BE thou my Judge, O Lord, for I have walked innocently: my trust hath been also in the Lord, therefore shall I not fall.

2 Examine me, O Lord, and prove me : try my reins, and my heart.

3 For thy lovingkindness is ever before mine eyes: and I will walk in thy truth.

4 I have not dealt with vain persons : neither will I have fellowship with the deceitful.

5 I have hated the congregation of the wicked : and will not sit among the ungodly.

6 I will wash my hands in innocency, O Lord : and so will I go to thine altar.

7 That I may show the voice of thanksgiving : and tell of all thy wondrous works.

8 Lord, I have loved the habitation of thy house: and the place where thine honour dwelleth.

9 O shut not up my soul with the sinners: nor my life with the blood-thirsty.

10 As for me, I will walk innocently: O deliver me, and be merciful unto me.

11 My foot standeth right: I will praise the Lord in the congregation.

EVENING PRAYER.

PSALM XXVII.

THE Lord is my light and my salvation; whom then shall I fear? the Lord is the strength of my life; of whom then shall I be afraid?

2 When the wicked, even mine enemies and my foes, came upon me to eat up my flesh: they stumbled and fell.

3 Though an host of men were encamped against me, yet shall not my heart be afraid: and though there rose up war against me, yet will I put my trust in him.

4 One thing have I desired of the Lord, which I will require: even that I may dwell in the house of the Lord all the days of my life, to behold the fair beauty of the Lord, and visit his temple.

5 For in the time of trouble he shall hide me in his tabernacle: yea, in the secret place of his dwelling shall he hide me, and set me upon a rock of stone.

6 And now shall he lift up mine head: above mine enemies round about me.

7 Therefore will I offer in his dwelling an oblation with great gladness: I will sing, and speak praises unto the Lord.

8 Hearken unto my voice, O Lord, when I cry unto thee: have mercy upon me, and hear me.

9 When thou saidst, Seek ye my face : my heart said unto thee, Thy face, Lord, will I seek.

10 O hide not thou thy face from me : nor cast thy servant away in displeasure.

11 Thou hast been my succour : leave me not, neither forsake me, O God of my salvation.

12 When my father and my mother forsake me : the Lord taketh me up.

13 Teach me thy way, O Lord : and lead me in the right way, because of mine enemies.

14 Deliver me not over unto the will of mine adversaries : for there are false witnesses risen up against me, and such as speak wrong.

15 I should utterly have fainted : but that I believe verily to see the goodness of the Lord in the land of the living.

16 O tarry thou the Lord's leisure : be strong, and he shall comfort thine heart, and put thou thy trust in the Lord.

PSALM XXVIII.

UNTO thee will I cry, O Lord, my strength : think no scorn of me ; lest if thou make as though thou hearest not, I become like them that go down into the pit.

2 Hear the voice of my humble petitions, when I cry unto thee : when I hold up my hands towards the mercy-seat of thy holy temple.

3 O pluck me not away, neither destroy me with the ungodly and wicked doers : who speak friendly to their neighbours, but imagine mischief in their hearts.

4 Praised be the Lord : for he hath heard the voice of my humble petitions.

5 The Lord is my strength and my shield ; my heart hath trusted in him, and I am helped : therefore my heart danceth for joy, and in my song will I praise him.

I

6 The Lord is my strength: and he is the wholesome defence of his Anointed.

7 O save thy people, and give thy blessing unto thine inheritance: feed them, and set them up for ever.

MORNING PRAYER.

PSALM XXIX.

ASCRIBE unto the Lord, O ye mighty: ascribe unto the Lord glory and strength.

2 Give the Lord the honour due unto his name: worship the Lord with holy worship.

3 It is the Lord that commandeth the waters: it is the glorious God that maketh the thunder.

4 It is the Lord that ruleth the sea: the voice of the Lord is mighty in operation; the voice of the Lord is a glorious voice.

5 The voice of the Lord breaketh the cedar-trees: yea, the Lord breaketh the cedars of Libanus.

6 He maketh them also to skip like a calf: Libanus also, and Sirion, like a young unicorn.

7 The voice of the Lord divideth the flames of fire: the voice of the Lord shaketh the wilderness; yea, the Lord shaketh the wilderness of Kadesh.

8 The voice of the Lord maketh the hinds to bring forth young, and discovereth the thick bushes: in his temple doth every man speak of his honour.

9 The Lord sitteth above the water-flood: and the Lord remaineth a King for ever.

10 The Lord shall give strength unto his people: the Lord shall give his people the blessing of peace.

PSALM XXX.

I WILL magnify thee, O Lord; for thou hast set me up: and not made my foes to triumph over me.

2 O Lord my God, I cried unto thee: and thou hast healed me.

3 Thou, Lord, hast brought my soul out of hell: thou hast kept me alive, that I should not go down to the pit.

4 Sing praises unto the Lord, O ye saints of his: and give thanks unto him for a remembrance of his holiness.

5 For his wrath endureth but the twinkling of an eye, and in his pleasure is life: heaviness may endure for a night, but joy cometh in the morning.

6 And in my prosperity I said, I shall never be removed: thou, Lord, of thy goodness hadst made my hill so strong.

7 Thou didst turn thy face from me: and I was troubled.

8 Then cried I unto thee, O Lord: and gat me to my Lord right humbly.

9 What profit is there in my blood: when I go down to the pit?

10 Shall the dust give thanks unto thee: or shall it declare thy truth?

11 Hear, O Lord, and have mercy upon me: Lord, be thou my helper.

12 Thou hast turned my heaviness into joy: thou hast put off my sackcloth, and girded me with gladness.

13 Therefore shall every good man sing of thy praise without ceasing: O my God, I will give thanks unto thee for ever.

EVENING PRAYER.

PSALM XXXI.

IN thee, O Lord, have I put my trust: let me never be put to confusion; deliver me in thy righteousness.

2 Bow down thine ear to me: make haste to deliver me.

3 And be thou my strong rock and house of defence : that thou mayest save me.

4 For thou art my strong rock and my castle : be thou also my guide, and lead me for thy Name's sake.

5 Draw me out of the net that they have laid privily for me : for thou art my strength.

6 Into thy hands I commend my spirit: for thou hast redeemed me, O Lord, thou God of truth.

7 I will be glad and rejoice in thy mercy : for thou hast considered my trouble, and hast known my soul in adversities.

8 Thou hast not shut me up into the hand of the enemy : but hast set my feet in a large room.

9 My hope hath been in thee, O Lord : I have said, Thou art my God.

10 My time is in thy hand : deliver me from the hand of mine enemies, and from them that persecute me.

11 Show thy servant the light of thy countenance : and save me for thy mercies' sake.

12 O how plentiful is thy goodness, which thou hast laid up for them that fear thee : and which thou hast prepared for them that put their trust in thee, even before the sons of men !

13 Thou shalt hide them privily by thine own presence from the provoking of all men : thou shalt keep them secret in thy tabernacle from the strife of tongues.

14 O love the Lord, all ye his saints : for the Lord

preserveth them that are faithful; and plenteously rewardeth the proud doer.

15 Be strong, and he shall establish your heart: all ye that put your trust in the Lord.

PSALM XXXII.

BLESSED is he whose unrighteousness is forgiven: and whose sin is covered.

2 Blessed is the man unto whom the Lord imputeth no sin : and in whose spirit there is no guile.

3 While I held my tongue, my bones consumed away through my daily complaining.

4 For thy hand was heavy upon me, day and night : and my moisture is like the drought in summer.

5 I acknowledge my sin unto thee : and mine unrighteousness have I not hid.

6 I said, I will confess my sins unto the Lord · and so thou forgavest the wickedness of my sin.

7 For this shall every one that is godly make his prayer unto thee, in a time when thou mayest be found : but in the great waterfloods they shall not come nigh him.

8 Thou art a place to hide me in, thou shalt preserve me from trouble : thou shalt compass me about with songs of deliverance.

9 I will inform thee, and teach thee in the way wherein thou shalt go : and I will guide thee with mine eye.

10 Be ye not like to horse and mule, which have no understanding : whose mouths must be held with bit and bridle, lest they fall upon thee.

11 Great plagues remain for the ungodly : but whoso putteth his trust in the Lord, mercy embraceth him on every side.

12 Be glad, O ye righteous, and rejoice in the Lord : and be joyful, all ye that are true of heart.

MORNING PRAYER.

PSALM XXXIII.

R EJOICE in the Lord, O ye righteous : for it becometh well the just to be thankful.

2 Sing unto the Lord a new song : sing praises lustily unto him with a good courage.

3 For the word of the Lord is true : and all his works are faithful.

4 He loveth righteousness and judgment : the earth is full of the goodness of the Lord.

5 By the word of the Lord were the heavens made : and all the hosts of them by the breath of his mouth.

6 He gathereth the waters of the sea together, as it were upon an heap : and layeth up the deep as in a treasure-house.

7 Let all the earth fear the Lord : stand in awe of him, all ye that dwell in the world.

8 For he spake, and it was done : he commanded, and it stood fast.

9 The Lord bringeth the counsel of the heathen to nought : and maketh the devices of the people to be of none effect, and casteth out the counsels of princes.

10 The counsel of the Lord shall endure for ever : and the thoughts of his heart from generation to generation.

11 Blessed are the people whose God is the Lord Jehovah : and blessed are the folk that he hath chosen to him to be his inheritance.

12 The Lord looketh down from heaven, and beholdeth all the children of men : from the habitation of his dwelling he considereth all them that dwell on the earth.

13 He fashioneth all the hearts of them : and understandeth all their works.

14 There is no king that can be saved by the multi-

tude of an host : neither is any mighty man delivered by much strength.

15 A horse is counted but a vain thing to save a man : neither shall he deliver any man by his great strength.

16 Behold, the eye of the Lord is upon them that fear him : and upon them that put their trust in his mercy ;

17 To deliver their soul from death : and to feed them in the time of dearth.

18 Our soul hath patiently tarried for the Lord : for he is our help and our shield.

19 For our heart shall rejoice in him : because we have hoped in his holy Name.

20 Let thy merciful kindness, O Lord, be upon us : like as we do put our trust in thee.

EVENING PRAYER.

PSALM XXXIV.

I WILL alway give thanks unto the Lord : his praise shall ever be in my mouth.

2 My soul shall make her boast in the Lord : the humble shall hear thereof, and be glad.

3 O praise the Lord with me : and let us magnify his Name together.

4 I sought the Lord, and he heard me : yea, he delivered me out of all my fear.

5 They had an eye unto him, and were lightened : and their faces were not ashamed.

6 Lo, the poor crieth, and the Lord heareth him : yea, and saveth him out of all his troubles.

7 The angel of the Lord tarrieth round about them that fear him : and delivereth them.

8 O taste and see how gracious the Lord is : blessed is the man that trusteth in him.

9 O fear the Lord, ye that are his saints : for they that fear him lack nothing.

10 The lions do lack and suffer hunger : but they who seek the Lord shall want no manner of thing that is good.

11 Come, ye children, and hearken unto me : I will teach you the fear of the Lord.

12 What man is he that desireth to live : and would fain see good days ?

13 Keep thy tongue from evil : and thy lips that they speak no guile.

14 Eschew evil, and do good : seek peace, and ensue it.

15 The eyes of the Lord are over the righteous : and his ears are open unto their prayers.

16 The countenance of the Lord is against them that do evil : to root out the remembrance of them from the earth.

17 The righteous cry, and the Lord heareth them : and delivereth them out of all their troubles.

18 The Lord is nigh unto them that are of a contrite heart : and will save such as are of an humble spirit.

19 Great are the troubles of the righteous : but the Lord delivereth him out of all.

20 He keepeth all his bones : so that not one of them is broken.

21 But misfortune shall slay the ungodly : and they that hate the righteous shall be desolate.

22 The Lord delivereth the souls of his servants : and all they that put their trust in him shall not be destitute.

PSALM XXXV.

PLEAD thou my cause, O Lord, with them that strive with me : and fight thou against them that fight against me.

2 Lay hand upon the shield and buckler : and stand up to help me.

3 Bring forth the spear, and stop the way against them that persecute me : say unto my soul, I am thy salvation.

4 My soul, be joyful in the Lord : it shall rejoice in his salvation.

5 All my bones shall say, Lord, who is like unto thee, who deliverest the poor from him that is too strong for him : yea, the poor, and him that is in misery, from him that spoileth him?

6 I will give thee thanks in the great congregation : I will praise thee among much people.

7 Let them be glad and rejoice that favour my righteous dealing : yea, let them say alway, Blessed be the Lord, who hath pleasure in the prosperity of his servant.

8 And as for my tongue, it shall be talking of thy righteousness : and of thy praise, all the day long.

MORNING PRAYER.

PSALM XXXVI.

THY mercy, O Lord, reacheth unto the heavens : and thy faithfulness unto the clouds.

2 Thy righteousness standeth like the strong mountains : thy judgments are like the great deep.

3 Thou, Lord, preservest both man and beast. How excellent is thy mercy, O God : and the children of men shall put their trust under the shadow of thy wings.

4 They shall be satisfied with the plenteousness of thy house : and thou shalt give them drink of thy pleasures, as out of the river.

I 5

5 For with thee is the well of life : and in thy light shall we see light.

6 O continue thy lovingkindness unto them that know thee : and thy righteousness unto them that are true of heart.

7 O let not the foot of pride come against me : and let not the hand of the ungodly cast me down.

8 There are they fallen, all that work wickedness : they are cast down, and shall not be able to stand.

PSALM XXXVII.—Part I.

FRET not thyself because of the ungodly : neither be thou envious against the evil doers.

2 For they shall be soon cut down like the grass : and be withered even as the green herb.

3 Put thou thy trust in the Lord, and be doing good : dwell in the land, and verily thou shalt be fed.

4 Delight thou in the Lord : and he shall give thee thy heart's desire.

5 Commit thy way unto the Lord, and put thy trust in him : and he shall bring it to pass.

6 He shall make thy righteousness as clear as the light : and thy just dealing as the noon-day.

7 Hold thee still in the Lord, and abide patiently upon him : but grieve not thyself at him whose way doth prosper, at the man that doeth after evil counsels.

8 Cease from wrath, and let go displeasure : fret not thyself, else thou shalt be moved to do evil.

9 Wicked doers shall be rooted out : but they that patiently wait upon the Lord, those shall inherit the land.

10 Yet a little while, and the ungodly shall be clean gone: thou shalt look after his place, and he shall be away.

11 But the meek-spirited shall possess the earth : and shall be refreshed in the multitude of peace.

12 The ungodly seeketh counsel against the just: and gnasheth upon him with his teeth.

13 The Lord shall laugh him to scorn: for he seeth that his day is coming.

14 A small thing that the righteous hath: is better than great riches of the ungodly.

15 For the arms of the ungodly shall be broken: and the Lord upholdeth the righteous.

16 The Lord knoweth the days of the godly: and their inheritance shall endure for ever.

17 They shall not be confounded in the perilous time: and in the days of dearth they shall have enough.

18 As for the ungodly, they shall perish; and the enemies of the Lord shall consume as the fat of lambs: yea, even as the smoke shall they consume away.

19 The ungodly borroweth, and payeth not again: but the righteous is merciful and liberal.

20 Such as are blessed of God shall possess the land: and they that are cursed of him shall be rooted out.

EVENING PRAYER.

PSALM XXXVII.—Part II.

THE Lord ordereth a good man's going: and maketh his way acceptable to himself.

2 Though he fall, he shall not be cast away: for the Lord upholdeth him with his hand.

3 I have been young, and now am old: and yet saw I never the righteous forsaken, nor his seed begging their bread.

4 The righteous is ever merciful, and lendeth: and his seed is blessed.

5 Flee from evil, and do the thing that is good: and dwell for evermore.

6 For the Lord loveth the thing that is right: he forsaketh not his saints; but they are preserved for ever.

7 The righteous shall be punished: as for the seed of the ungodly, it shall be rooted out.

8 The righteous shall inherit the land: and dwell therein for ever.

9 The mouth of the righteous is exercised in wisdom: and his tongue will be talking of judgment.

10 The law of his God is in his heart: and his going shall not slide.

11 The ungodly seeth the righteous: and seeketh occasion to slay him.

12 The Lord will not leave him in his hand: nor condemn him when he is judged.

13 Hope thou in the Lord, and keep his way, and he shall promote thee, that thou shalt possess the land: when the ungodly shall perish, thou shalt see it.

14 I myself have seen the ungodly in great power: and flourishing like a green bay-tree.

15 I went by, and, lo, he was gone: I sought him, but his place could no where be found.

16 Keep innocency, and take heed unto the thing that is right: for that shall bring a man peace at the last.

17 As for the transgressors, they shall perish together: and the end of the ungodly is, they shall be rooted out at last.

18 But the salvation of the righteous cometh of the Lord: who is also their strength in the time of trouble.

19 And the Lord shall stand by them, and save them: he shall deliver them from the ungodly, and shall save them, because they put their trust in him.

PSALM XXXVIII.

PUT me not to rebuke, O Lord, in thine anger: neither chasten me in thy heavy displeasure.

2 For thine arrows stick fast in me: and thy hand presseth me sore.

3 There is no health in my flesh, because of thy displeasure: neither is there any rest in my bones, by reason of my sin.

4 For my wickednesses are gone over my head: and are like a sore burden, too heavy for me to bear.

5 My wounds stink, and are corrupt: through my foolishness.

6 I am brought into so great trouble and misery: that I go mourning all the day long.

7 I am feeble and sore smitten: I have roared for the very disquietness of my heart.

8 Lord, thou knowest all my desire: and my groaning is not hid from thee.

9 My heart panteth, my strength hath failed me: and the sight of mine eyes is gone from me.

10 My lovers and my neighbours did stand looking upon my trouble: and my kinsmen stood afar off.

11 In thee, O Lord, have I put my trust: thou shalt answer for me, O Lord my God.

12 I will confess my wickedness: and be sorry for my sin.

13 Forsake me not, O Lord, my God: be not thou far from me.

14 Haste thee to help me: O Lord God of my salvation.

MORNING PRAYER.

PSALM XXXIX.

I SAID, I will take heed to my ways: that I offend not with my tongue.

2 I will keep my mouth as it were with a bridle: while the ungodly is in my sight.

3 I held my tongue, and spake nothing: I kept silence, yea, even from good words; but it was pain and grief to me.

4 My heart was hot within me, and while I was thus musing, the fire kindled: and at the last I spake with my tongue.

5 Lord, let me know my end, and the number of my days: that I may be certified how long I have to live.

6 Behold, thou hast made my days as it were a span long, and mine age is even as nothing in respect of thee: and verily every man living is altogether vanity.

7 For man walketh in a vain shadow, and disquieteth himself in vain: he heapeth up riches, and cannot tell who shall gather them.

8 And now, Lord, what is my hope? truly my hope is even in thee.

9 Deliver me from all mine offences: and make me not a rebuke unto the foolish.

10 I became dumb, and opened not my mouth: for it was thy doing.

11 Take thy plague away from me: I am even consumed by the means of thy heavy hand.

12 When thou with rebukes dost chasten man for sin, thou makest his beauty to consume away, like as it were a moth fretting a garment: every man therefore is but vanity.

13 Hear my prayer, O Lord, and with thine ears consider my calling: hold not thy peace at my tears;

14 For I am a stranger with thee: and a sojourner, as all my fathers were.

15 O spare me a little, that I may recover my strength: before I go hence, and be no more seen.

PSALM XL.

I WAITED patiently for the Lord: and he inclined unto me, and heard my calling.

2 He brought me also out of the horrible pit, out of

the mire and clay: and set my feet upon the rock, and ordered my goings.

3 And he hath put a new song in my mouth: even a thanksgiving unto our God.

4 Many shall see it, and fear: and shall put their trust in the Lord.

5 Blessed is the man that hath set his hope in the Lord: and turned not unto the proud, and to such as go about with lies.

6 O Lord, my God, great are the wondrous works which thou hast done, like as are also thy thoughts, which are to us-ward: and yet there is no man that ordereth them unto thee.

7 If I should declare them, and speak of them: they would be more than I am able to express.

8 Sacrifice and meat-offering thou wouldest not: but mine ears hast thou opened.

9 Burnt-offerings and sacrifice for sin hast thou not required: then said I, Lo, I come,

10 In the volume of the book it is written of me, that I should fulfil thy will, O my God: I am content to do it; yea, thy law is within my heart.

11 I have declared thy righteousness in the great congregation: lo, I will not refrain my lips, O Lord, and that thou knowest.

12 I have not hid thy righteousness within my heart: my talk hath been of thy truth, and of thy salvation.

13 I have not kept back thy loving mercy and truth: from the great congregation.

14 Withdraw not thou thy mercy from me, O Lord: let thy loving-kindness and thy truth alway preserve me.

15 For innumerable troubles are come about me; my sins have taken such hold upon me, that I am not able to look up: yea, they are more in number than the hairs of my head, and my heart hath failed me.

16 O Lord, let it be thy pleasure to deliver me : make haste, O Lord, to help me.

17 Let all those that seek thee, be joyful and glad in thee : and let such as love thy salvation say alway, The Lord be praised.

18 As for me, I am poor and needy : but the Lord careth for me.

19 Thou art my helper and redeemer : make no long tarrying, O my God.

EVENING PRAYER.

PSALM XLI.

BLESSED is he that considereth the poor and needy : the Lord shall deliver him in the time of trouble.

2 The Lord will preserve him, and keep him alive, and he shall be blessed upon the earth : and thou wilt not deliver him unto the will of his enemies.

3 The Lord will comfort him, when he lieth sick upon his bed : thou wilt make all his bed in his sickness.

4 I said, Lord, be merciful unto me : heal my soul ; for I have sinned against thee.

5 By this I know thou favourest me : that mine enemy doth not triumph against me.

6 And when I am in my health, thou upholdest me : and shalt set me before thy face for ever.

7 Blessed be the Lord God of Israel : world without end. Amen.

PSALM XLII.

AS the hart panteth after the water-brooks : so panteth my soul after thee, O God.

2 My soul is athirst for God, yea, even for the living

God : when shall I come to appear before the presence of God ?

3 My tears have been my meat day and night: while daily they say unto me, Where is now thy God ?

4 Now when I think thereupon, I pour out my heart by myself : for I went with the multitude, and brought them forth into the house of God ;

5 In the voice of praise and thanksgiving : among such as keep holy-day.

6 Why art thou so full of heaviness, O my soul : and why art thou so disquieted within me ?

7 Put thy trust in God : for I shall yet give him thanks for the help of his countenance.

8 The Lord hath granted his lovingkindness in the day-time : and in the night season did I sing of him, and made my prayer unto the God of my life.

9 I will say unto the God of my strength, Why hast thou forgotten me: why go I thus heavily, while the enemy oppresseth me ?

10 Why art thou so vexed, O my soul: and why art thou so disquieted within me ?

11 O put thy trust in God : for I shall yet thank him, who is the help of my countenance, and my God.

PSALM XLIII.

GIVE sentence with me, O God, and defend my cause against the ungodly people : O deliver me from the deceitful and wicked man.

2 For thou art the God of my strength, why hast thou put me from thee : and why go I so heavily, while the enemy oppresseth me ?

3 O send out thy light and thy truth, that they may lead me : and bring me unto thy holy hill, and to thy dwelling.

4 Then will I go unto the altar of God : even unto God, my exceeding joy.

5 Why art thou so heavy, O my soul: and why art thou so disquieted within me?

6 O put thy trust in God: for I shall yet give him thanks, who is the help of my countenance, and my God.

MORNING PRAYER.

PSALM XLIV.

WE have heard with our ears, O God: our fathers have told us what thou hast done in their time of old.

2 How thou hast driven out the heathen with thy hand, and planted them in: how thou hast destroyed the nations, and cast them out.

3 For they gat not the land in possession through their own sword: neither was it their own arm that helped them;

4 But thy right hand, and thine arm, and the light of thy countenance: because thou hadst a favour unto them.

5 Thou art my King, O God: send help unto Jacob.

6 Through thee will we overthrow our enemies: and in thy name will we tread them under that rise up against us.

7 For I will not trust in my bow: it is not my sword that shall help me.

8 But it is thou that savest us from our enemies: and puttest them to confusion that hate us.

9 We make our boast of God all day long: and will praise thy Name for ever.

PSALM XLV.

MY heart is inditing of a good matter: I speak of the things which I have made touching the King.

2 My tongue is the pen of a ready writer.

3 Thou art fairer than the children of men : full of grace are thy lips, because God hath blessed thee for ever.

4 Gird thee with thy sword upon thy thigh, O thou most Mighty : according to thy glory and renown.

5 Good luck have thou with thine honour : ride on, because of the word of truth, of meekness, and righteousness ; and thy right hand shall teach thee terrible things.

6 Thy arrows are very sharp in the heart of the King's enemies : whereby the people shall be subdued unto thee.

7 Thy seat, O God, endureth for ever : the sceptre of thy kingdom is a right sceptre.

8 Thou hast loved righteousness, and hated iniquity : wherefore God, even thy God, hath anointed thee with the oil of gladness above thy fellows.

9 I will remember thy Name from one generation to another : therefore shall the people give thanks unto thee world without end.

PSALM XLVI.

GOD is our hope and strength : a very present help in trouble.

2 Therefore will we not fear, though the earth be moved : and though the hills be carried into the midst of the sea.

3 Though the waters thereof rage and swell : and though the mountains shake at the tempest of the same.

4 There is a river, the streams whereof shall make glad the city of God : the holy place of the tabernacle of the Most High.

5 God is in the midst of her, therefore shall she not be removed : God shall help her, and that right early.

6 The heathen make much ado, and the kingdoms are moved: but God hath showed his voice, and the earth shall melt away.

7 The Lord of hosts is with us: the God of Jacob is our refuge.

8 O come hither, and behold the works of the Lord: what destruction he hath brought upon the earth.

9 He maketh wars to cease in all the world: he breaketh the bow, and knappeth the spear in sunder, and burneth the chariots in the fire.

10 Be still, then, and know that I am God: I will be exalted among the heathen, and I will be exalted in the earth.

11 The Lord of hosts is with us: the God of Jacob is our refuge.

EVENING PRAYER.

PSALM XLVII.

O CLAP your hands together, all ye people: O sing unto God with the voice of melody.

2 For the Lord is high, and to be feared: he is the great King upon all the earth.

3 He shall subdue the people under us: and the nations under our feet.

4 He shall choose out an heritage for us: even the excellency of Jacob, whom he loved.

5 God is gone up with a merry noise: and the Lord with the sound of the trump.

6 O sing praises, sing praises unto our God: O sing praises unto our King.

7 For God is the King of all the earth: sing ye praises with understanding.

8 God reigneth over the heathen : God sitteth upon his holy seat.

9 God, who is very high exalted, doth defend the earth as it were with a shield.

PSALM XLVIII.

GREAT is the Lord, and greatly to be praised: in the city of our God, even upon his holy hill.

2 Like as we have heard, so we have seen in the city of the Lord of hosts, in the city of our God : God upholdeth the same for ever.

3 We wait for thy lovingkindness, O God : in the midst of thy temple.

4 O God, according to thy Name, so is thy praise unto the world's end : thy right hand is full of right-eousness.

5 Let the mount Sion rejoice, and the daughter of Judah be glad : because of thy judgments.

6 Walk about Sion, and go round about her : and tell the towers thereof.

7 Mark well her bulwarks, set up her palaces : that ye may tell them that come after.

8 For this God is our God for ever and ever : he shall be our guide unto death.

PSALM XLIX.

O HEAR ye this, all ye people : ponder it with your ears, all ye that dwell in the world.

2 High and low, rich and poor : one with another.

3 My mouth shall speak of wisdom : and my heart shall muse of understanding.

4 There are some that put their trust in their goods : and boast themselves in the multitude of their riches.

5 But no man may deliver his brother : or make an agreement unto God for him ;

6 For it cost more to redeem their souls : so that he must let that alone for ever ;

7 That he should still live for ever, and not see corruption.

8 For he seeth that wise men also die and perish together : as well as the ignorant and foolish, and leave their riches for other.

9 And yet they think that their houses shall continue for ever, and that their dwelling-places shall endure from one generation to another : and call the lands after their own names.

10 Nevertheless, man being in honour abideth not : he is like the beasts that perish.

11 This their way is their folly : yet their posterity approve their sayings.

12 Like sheep they are laid in the grave, death shall feed on them, and the upright shall have dominion over them in the morning : their beauty shall consume in the grave from their dwelling.

13 But God will redeem my soul from the power of the grave : for he shall receive me.

14 Be not thou afraid, when one is made rich : when the glory of his house is increased.

15 For when he dieth, he shall carry nothing away : his glory shall not descend after him.

16 Though while he lived, he blessed his soul : and men will praise thee when thou doest well to thyself.

17 He shall go to the generation of his fathers : they shall never see light.

18 Man that is in honour, and understandeth not, is like the beasts that perish.

MORNING PRAYER.

PSALM L.

THE Lord, even the most mighty God, hath spoken : and called the world, from the rising up of the sun unto the going down thereof.

2 Out of Sion hath God appeared: in perfect beauty.

3 Our God shall come, and shall not keep silence : there shall go before him a consuming fire, and a mighty tempest shall be stirred up round about him.

4 He shall call the heaven from above: and the earth, that he may judge his people.

5 Gather my saints together unto me : those that have made a covenant with me with sacrifice.

6 And the heavens shall declare his righteousness : for God is judge himself.

7 Hear, O my people, and I will speak : I myself will testify against thee, O Israel; for I am God, even thy God.

8 I will not reprove thee, because of thy sacrifices, or for thy burnt-offerings: because they were not always before me.

9 I will take no bullock out of thine house : nor he-goat out of thy folds.

10 For all the beasts of the forest are mine: and so are the cattle upon a thousand hills.

11 I know all the fowls upon the mountains : and the wild beasts of the field are in my sight.

12 If I were hungry, I would not tell thee: for the whole world is mine, and all that is therein.

13 Thinkest thou that I will eat bulls' flesh : and drink the blood of goats?

14 Offer unto God thanksgiving: and pay thy vows unto the Most High ;

15 And call upon me in the time of trouble : so will I hear thee, and thou shalt praise me.

16 But unto the ungodly said God: Why dost thou preach my laws, and takest my covenant in thy mouth ;

17 Whereas thou hatest to be reformed : and hast cast my words behind thee ?

18 O consider this, ye that forget God : lest I pluck you away, and there be none to deliver you.

19 Whoso offereth me thanks and praise, he honoureth me : and to him that ordereth his conversation aright, will I show the salvation of God.

PSALM LI.

HAVE mercy upon me, O God, after thy great goodness : according to the multitude of thy mercies do away mine offences.

2 Wash me thoroughly from my wickedness : and cleanse me from my sin.

3 For I acknowledge my faults : and my sin is ever before me.

4 Against thee only have I sinned, and done this evil in thy sight : that thou mightest be justified in thy saying, and clear when thou art judged.

5 Behold, I was shapen in wickedness : and in sin hath my mother conceived me.

6 But, lo, thou requirest truth in the inward parts : and shalt make me to understand wisdom secretly.

7 Thou shalt purge me with hyssop, and I shall be clean : thou shalt wash me, and I shall be whiter than snow.

8 Thou shalt make me hear of joy and gladness : that the bones which thou hast broken may rejoice.

9 Turn thy face from my sins : and put out all my misdeeds.

10 Make me a clean heart, O God : and renew a right spirit within me.

11 Cast me not away from thy presence : and take not thy Holy Spirit from me.

12 O give me the comfort of thy help again : and establish me with thy free Spirit.

13 Then shall I teach thy ways unto the wicked : and sinners shall be converted unto thee.

14 Deliver me from blood-guiltiness, O God, thou that art the God of my health : and my tongue shall sing of thy righteousness.

15 Thou shalt open my lips, O Lord : and my mouth shall show thy praise.

16 For thou desirest no sacrifice, else would I give it thee : but thou delightest not in burnt-offerings.

17 The sacrifice of God is a troubled spirit : a broken and a contrite heart, O God, shalt thou not despise.

EVENING PRAYER.

PSALM LV.

HEAR my prayer, O God : and hide not thyself from my petition.

2 Attend unto me, and hear me : how I mourn in my prayer, and am vexed.

3 My heart is disquieted within me : and the fear of death is fallen upon me :

4 Fearfulness and trembling are come upon me : and an horrible dread hath overwhelmed me.

5 And I said, O that I had wings like a dove : for then I would flee away, and be at rest.

6 Lo, then would I get me away far off : and remain in the wilderness.

7 I would make haste to escape : because of the stormy wind and tempest.

8 For it is not an open enemy that hath done me this dishonour : for then I could have borne it.

9 Neither was it mine adversary that did magnify himself against me : for then, peradventure, I would have hid myself from him.

K

10 But it was even thou, my companion : my guide, and mine own familiar friend.

11 We took sweet counsel together : and walked in the house of God as friends.

12 As for me, I will call upon God : and the Lord shall save me.

13 In the evening and morning, and at noon-day, will I pray, and that instantly : and he shall hear my voice.

14 It is he that hath delivered my soul in peace, from the battle that was against me : for there were many with me.

15 Yea, even God, that endureth for ever, shall hear me, and bring them down : for they will not turn, nor fear God.

16 O cast thy burden upon the Lord, and he shall nourish thee : and shall not suffer the righteous to fall for ever.

17 And as for them : thou, O God, shalt bring them into the pit of destruction.

18 The blood-thirsty and deceitful men shall not live out half their days : but my trust shall be in thee, O Lord.

PSALM LVI.

BE merciful unto me, O God, for man goeth about to devour me : he is daily fighting and troubling me.

2 Nevertheless, though I am sometimes afraid : yet put I my trust in thee.

3 I will praise God because of his word : I have put my trust in God, and will not fear what flesh can do unto me.

4 Whensoever I call upon thee, then shall mine enemies be put to flight : this I know, for God is on my side.

5 In God's word will I rejoice : in the Lord's word will I comfort me.

6 Yea, in my God have I put my trust : I will not be afraid what man can do unto me.

7 Unto thee, O God, will I pay my vows : unto thee will I give thanks.

8 For thou hast delivered my soul from death, and my feet from falling : that I may walk before God in the light of the living.

MORNING PRAYER.

PSALM LVII.

BE merciful unto me, O God, be merciful unto me, for my soul trusteth in thee : and under the shadow of thy wings shall be my refuge, until this tyranny be overpast.

2 I will call unto the most high God : even unto the God that shall perform the cause which I have in hand.

3 Set up thyself, O God, above the heavens : and thy glory above all the earth.

4 My heart is fixed, O God, my heart is fixed : I will sing and give praise.

5 I will give thanks unto thee, O Lord, among the people : and I will sing unto thee among the nations.

6 For the greatness of thy mercy reacheth unto the heavens : and thy truth unto the clouds.

7 Set up thyself, O God, above the heavens : and thy glory above all the earth.

PSALM LIX.

DELIVER me from mine enemies, O God : defend me from them that rise up against me.

2 O deliver me from the wicked doers : and save me from the blood-thirsty men.

3 My strength will I ascribe unto thee : for thou art the God of my refuge.

4 God showeth me his goodness plenteously : and God shall let me see my desire upon mine enemies.

5 As for me, I will sing of thy power, and will praise thy mercy betimes in the morning : for thou hast been my defence and refuge in the day of my trouble.

6 Unto thee, O my strength, will I sing : for thou, O God, art my refuge, and my merciful God.

PSALM LXI.

HEAR my cry, O God : give ear unto my prayer.

2 From the ends of the earth will I call upon thee : when my heart is in heaviness.

3 O set me upon the rock that is higher than I : for thou hast been my hope, and a strong tower for me against the enemy.

4 I will dwell in thy tabernacle for ever : and my trust shall be under the covering of thy wings.

5 For thou, O Lord, hast heard my desires : and hast given an heritage unto those that fear thy Name.

6 I will always sing praise unto thy Name : that I may daily perform my vows.

PSALM LXII.

MY soul truly waiteth still upon God : for of him cometh my salvation.

2 He verily is my strength and my salvation : he is my defence, so that I shall not greatly fall.

3 My soul, wait thou still upon God : for my hope is in him.

4 He truly is my strength and my salvation : he is my defence, so that I may not fall.

5 In God is my health, and my glory, the rock of my might : and in God is my trust.

6 O put your trust in him alway, ye people, pour out your hearts before him : for God is our hope.

7 As for the children of men, they are but vanity : the children of men are deceitful in the balance, they are altogether lighter than vanity itself.

8 Give not yourselves unto vanity : if riches increase, set not your heart upon them.

9 God spake once, and twice I have also heard the same : That power belongeth unto God ;

10 And that thou, Lord, art merciful : for thou rewardest every man according to his work.

EVENING PRAYER.

PSALM LXIII.

O GOD, thou art my God : early will I seek thee.

2 My soul thirsteth for thee, my flesh also longeth after thee : in a barren and dry land, where no water is.

3 Thus have I looked for thee in holiness : that I might behold thy power and glory.

4 For thy lovingkindness is better than the life itself : my lips shall praise thee.

5 As long as I live I will magnify thee on this manner : and lift up my hands in thy Name.

6 My soul shall be satisfied even as it were with marrow and fatness : when my mouth praiseth thee with joyful lips.

7 Have I not remembered thee in my bed : and thought upon thee when I was waking ?

8 Because thou hast been my helper : therefore under the shadow of thy wings will I rejoice.

9 My soul hangeth upon thee : thy right hand hath upholden me.

PSALM LXV.

THOU, O God, art praised in Sion : and unto thee shall the vow be performed in Jerusalem.

2 Thou that hearest the prayer: unto thee shall all flesh come.

3 My misdeeds prevail against me : O be thou merciful unto our sins.

4 Blessed is the man whom thou choosest, and receivest unto thee : he shall dwell in thy court, and shall be satisfied with the pleasures of thy house, even of thy holy temple.

5 Thou shalt show us wonderful things in thy righteousness, O God of our salvation : thou that art the hope of all the ends of the earth, and of them that remain in the broad sea.

6 Who in his strength setteth fast the mountains : and is girded about with power.

7 Who stilleth the raging of the sea : and the noise of his waves, and the madness of the people.

8 They also that dwell in the uttermost parts of the earth shall be afraid at thy tokens : thou that makest the outgoings of the morning and evening to praise thee.

9 Thou visitest the earth, and blessest it : thou makest it very plenteous.

10 The river of God is full of water : thou preparest their corn, for so thou providest for the earth.

11 Thou waterest her furrows, thou sendest rain into the little valleys thereof: thou makest it soft with the drops of rain, and blessest the increase of it.

12 Thou crownest the year with thy goodness: and thy clouds drop fatness.

13 They shall drop upon the dwellings of the wilderness : and the little hills shall rejoice on every side.

14 The folds shall be full of sheep: the valleys also shall stand so thick with corn, that they shall laugh and sing.

MORNING PRAYER.

PSALM LXVI.

O BE joyful in God, all ye lands: sing praises unto the honour of his Name, make his praise to be glorious.

2 Say unto God, O how wonderful art thou in thy works: through the greatness of thy power shall thine enemies submit themselves unto thee.

3 For all the world shall worship thee: sing of thee, and praise thy Name.

4 O come hither, and behold the works of God: how wonderful he is in his doing toward the children of men.

5 He turned the sea into dry land: so that they went through the water on foot; there did we rejoice in him.

6 He ruleth with his power for ever; his eyes behold the people: and such as will not believe shall not be able to exalt themselves.

7 O praise our God, ye people: and make the voice of his praise to be heard.

8 Who holdeth our soul in life: and suffereth not our feet to slip.

9 For thou, O God, hast proved us: thou also hast tried us like as silver is tried.

10 Thou broughtest us into the snare: and laidest trouble upon our loins.

11 We went through fire and water: and thou broughtest us out into a wealthy place.

12 I will pay thee my vows, which I promised with

my lips, and spake with my mouth, when I was in trouble.

13 O come hither, and hearken, all ye that fear God: and I will tell you what he hath done for my soul.

14 I called unto him with my mouth: and gave him praises with my tongue.

15 If I incline unto wickedness with mine heart: the Lord will not hear me.

16 But God hath heard me: and considered the voice of my prayer.

17 Praised be God, who hath not cast out my prayer: nor turned his mercy from me.

PSALM LXVII.

GOD be merciful unto us, and bless us: and show us the light of his countenance, and be merciful unto us;

2 That thy way may be known upon earth: thy saving health among all nations.

3 Let the people praise thee, O God: yea, let all the people praise thee.

4 O let the nations rejoice and be glad: for thou shalt judge the people righteously, and govern the nations upon earth.

5 Let the people praise thee, O God: yea, let all the people praise thee.

6 Then shall the earth bring forth her increase: and God, even our own God, shall give us his blessing.

7 God shall bless us: and all the ends of the world shall fear him.

EVENING PRAYER.

PSALM LXVIII.

L ET God arise, and let his enemies be scattered : let them also that hate him, flee before him.

2 Like as the smoke vanisheth, so shalt thou drive them away: and like as wax melteth at the fire, so let the ungodly perish at the presence of God.

3 But let the righteous be glad, and rejoice before God : let them also be merry and joyful.

4 O sing unto God, and sing praises unto his Name : magnify him that rideth upon the heavens, as it were upon a horse; praise him in his Name JAH, and rejoice before him.

5 He is a Father of the fatherless, and defendeth the cause of the widows : even God in his holy habitation.

6 He is the God that maketh men to be of one mind in an house, and bringeth the prisoners out of captivity: but letteth the rebellious continue in scarceness.

7 O God, when thou wentest forth before the people : when thou wentest through the wilderness ;

8 The earth shook, and the heavens dropped at the presence of God : even as Sinai also was moved at the presence of God, who is the God of Israel.

9 Thou, O God, sentest a gracious rain upon thine inheritance : and refreshedst it when it was weary.

10 Thy congregation shall dwell therein : for thou, O God, hast of thy goodness prepared for the poor.

11 Thou art gone up on high, thou hast led captivity captive, and received gifts for men : yea, even for thine enemies, that the Lord God might dwell among them.

12 Praised be the Lord daily : even the God who helpeth us, and poureth his benefits upon us.

13 He is our God, even the God of whom cometh salvation : God is the Lord, by whom we escape death.

14 Thy God hath sent forth strength for thee : stablish the thing, O God, that thou hast wrought in us.

15 Sing unto God, O ye kingdoms of the earth : O sing praises unto the Lord.

16 Who sitteth in the heavens over all, from the beginning : lo, he doth send out his voice, yea, and that a mighty voice.

17 Ascribe ye the power to God over Israel : his excellency and strength is in the clouds.

18 O God, wonderful art thou in thy holy places, even the God of Israel : he will give strength and power unto his people ; blessed be God.

PSALM LXIX.

SAVE me, O God : for the waters have come in even unto my soul.

2 I sink in deep mire, where there is no standing : I am come into deep waters, so that the floods run over me.

3 I am weary of crying, my throat is dry : my sight faileth me for waiting so long upon my God.

4 Let not them that trust in thee, O Lord God of hosts, be ashamed for my sake : let not those that seek thee be confounded through me, O Lord God of Israel.

5 And why? for thy sake have I suffered reproof : shame hath covered my face.

6 I am become a stranger unto my brethren : even an alien unto my mother's children.

7 For the zeal of thine house hath even eaten me : and the rebukes of them that rebuked thee are fallen upon me.

8 I wept and chastened myself with fasting : and that was turned to my reproof.

9 But, Lord, I make my prayer unto thee : in an acceptable time.

10 Hear me, O God, in the multitude of thy mercy: even in the truth of thy salvation.

11 Take me out of the mire, that I sink not: O let me be delivered from them that hate me, and out of the deep waters.

12 Let not the water-flood drown me, neither let the deep swallow me up: and let not the pit shut her mouth upon me.

13 Hear me, O Lord, for thy lovingkindness is comfortable: turn thee unto me, according to the multitude of thy mercies;

14 And hide not thy face from thy servant, for I am in trouble: O haste thee, and hear me.

15 Draw nigh unto my soul, and save it: O deliver me, because of mine enemies.

16 Thou hast known my reproof, my shame, and my dishonour: mine adversaries are all in thy sight.

17 Reproach hath broken my heart, I am full of heaviness: I looked for some to have pity on me, but there was no man, neither found I any to comfort me.

18 They gave me gall to eat: and when I was thirsty, they gave me vinegar to drink.

19 But as for me, when I am poor and in heaviness, thy help, O God, shall lift me up.

20 I will praise the name of God with a song: and magnify it with thanksgiving.

21 The humble shall consider this, and be glad: seek ye after God, and your soul shall live.

22 For the Lord heareth the poor: and despiseth not his prisoners.

23 Let heaven and earth praise him: the sea, and all that moveth therein.

MORNING PRAYER.

PSALM LXX.

HASTE thee, O God, to deliver me : make haste to help me, O Lord.

2 Let all those that seek thee be joyful and glad in thee : and let all such as delight in thy salvation, say alway, The Lord be praised.

3 As for me, I am poor and in misery : haste thou unto me, O God.

4 Thou art my Helper and my Redeemer : O make no long tarrying.

PSALM LXXI.

IN thee, O Lord, have I put my trust, let me never be put to confusion : but rid me and deliver me in thy righteousness ; incline thine ear unto me, and save me.

2 Be thou my strong hold, whereunto I may alway resort : thou hast promised to help me, for thou art my house of defence, and my castle.

3 Deliver me, O my God, out of the hand of the ungodly : out of the hand of the unrighteous and cruel man.

4 For thou, O Lord God, art the thing that I long for : thou art my hope, even from my youth.

5 Through thee have I been holden up ever since I was born : thou art he that took me out of my mother's womb ; my praise shall be always of thee.

6 I am become as it were a monster unto many : but my sure trust is in thee.

7 O let my mouth be filled with thy praise : that I may sing of thy glory and honour all the day long.

8 Cast me not away in the time of age : forsake me not when my strength faileth me.

9 Go not far from me, O God : my God, haste thee to help me.

10 As for me, I will patiently abide alway : and will praise thee more and more.

11 My mouth shall daily speak of thy righteousness and salvation : for I know no end thereof.

12 I will go forth in the strength of the Lord God : and will make mention of thy righteousness only.

13 Thou, O God, hast taught me from my youth up until now : therefore will I tell of thy wondrous works.

14 Forsake me not, O God, in mine old age, when I am grey headed : until I have showed thy strength unto this generation, and thy power to all them that are yet for to come.

15 Thy righteousness, O God, is very high : and great things are they that thou hast done ; O God, who is like unto thee ?

16 O what great troubles and adversities hast thou showed me ! and yet didst thou turn and refresh me : yea, and broughtest me from the deep of the earth again.

17 Thou hast brought me to great honour : and comforted me on every side.

18 My lips will be glad, when I sing unto thee : and so will my soul which thou hast delivered.

19 My tongue also shall talk of thy righteousness all the day long.

EVENING PRAYER.

PSALM LXXIII.

TRULY God is loving unto Israel : even unto such as are of a clean heart.

2 Nevertheless, my feet were almost gone : my treadings had well nigh slipped.

3 And why? I was grieved at the wicked : I do also see the ungodly in such prosperity.

4 Then thought I to understand this : but it was too hard for me,

5 Until I went into the sanctuary of God : then understood I the end of these men ;

6 Namely, how thou dost set them in slippery places : and castest them down, and destroyest them.

7 O how suddenly do they consume : perish, and come to a fearful end !

8 Yea, even like as a dream when one awaketh : so shalt thou make their image to vanish out of the city.

9 Thus my heart was grieved : and it went even through my reins.

10 So foolish was I and ignorant : even as it were a beast before thee.

11 Nevertheless, I am alway by thee : for thou hast holden me by my right hand.

12 Thou shalt guide me with thy counsel : and after that receive me to glory.

13 Whom have I in heaven but thee ? and there is none upon earth that I desire in comparison of thee.

14 My flesh and my heart faileth : but God is the strength of my heart, and my portion for ever.

PSALM LXXV.

UNTO thee, O God, do we give thanks : yea, unto thee do we give thanks.

2 Thy name also is so near : and that do thy wondrous works declare.

3 When I receive the congregation : I shall judge according unto right.

4 I said unto the fools, Deal not so madly : and to the ungodly, Set not up your horn.

5 Set not up your horn on high : and speak not with a stiff neck.

6 For promotion cometh neither from the east, nor from the west: nor yet from the south.

7 And why? God is the judge: he putteth down one, and setteth up another.

8 For in the hand of the Lord there is a cup, and the wine is red: it is full mixed, and he poureth out of the same.

9 As for the dregs thereof: all the ungodly of the earth shall drink them, and suck them out.

10 But I will talk of the God of Jacob: and praise him for ever.

11 All the horns of the ungodly also will I break: and the horns of the righteous shall be exalted.

MORNING PRAYER.

PSALM LXXVI.

THOU, even thou, O God, art to be feared: and who may stand in thy sight when thou art angry?

2 Thou didst cause thy judgment to be heard from heaven: the earth trembled, and was still,

3 When God arose to judgment: and to help all the meek upon earth.

4 The fierceness of man shall turn to thy praise: and the remainder of wrath shalt thou restrain.

5 Vow and pay unto the Lord your God, all ye that are round about him: bring presents unto him that ought to be feared.

6 He shall cut off the spirit of princes: and is wonderful among the kings of the earth.

PSALM LXXVII.

I WILL cry unto God with my voice: even unto God will I cry with my voice, and he shall hearken unto me.

2 In the time of my trouble I sought the Lord : my sore ran, and ceased not in the night season ; my soul refused comfort.

3 When I am in heaviness, I will think upon God : when my heart is vexed, I will complain.

4 Thou holdest mine eyes waking : I am so feeble that I cannot speak.

5 I have considered the days of old : and the years that are past.

6 I call to remembrance my song : and in the night I commune with mine own heart, and search out my spirits.

7 Will the Lord absent himself for ever ? and will he be no more entreated ?

8 Is his mercy clean gone for ever ? and is his promise come utterly to an end for evermore ?

9 Hath God forgotten to be gracious ? and will he shut up his lovingkindness in displeasure ?

10 And I said, It is mine own infirmity : but I will remember the years of the right hand of the most Highest.

11 I will remember the works of the Lord : and call to mind thy wonders of old time.

12 I will think also of all thy works : and my talking shall be of thy doings.

13 Thy way, O God, is holy : who is so great a God as our God ?

14 Thou art the God that doest wonders : and hast declared thy power among the people.

15 Thou hast mightily delivered thy people : even the sons of Jacob and Joseph.

16 The waters saw thee, O God, the waters saw thee, and were afraid : the depths also were troubled.

17 The clouds poured out water, the air thundered : and thine arrows went abroad.

18 The voice of thy thunder was heard round about : the lightning shone upon the ground ; the earth was moved, and shook withal.

19 Thy way is in the sea, and thy paths in the great waters: and thy footsteps are not known.

20 Thou leddest thy people like sheep, by the hand of Moses and Aaron.

EVENING PRAYER.

PSALM LXXXIV.

O HOW amiable are thy dwellings: thou Lord of hosts!

2 My soul hath a desire and longing to enter into the courts of the Lord: my heart and my flesh rejoice in the living God.

3 Yea, the sparrow hath found her an house; and the swallow a nest where she may lay her young: even thine altars, O Lord of hosts, my King and my God.

4 Blessed are they that dwell in thy house: they will be alway praising thee.

5 Blessed is the man whose strength is in thee: in whose heart are thy ways.

6 Who, going through the vale of misery, use it for a well: and the pools are filled with water.

7 They will go from strength to strength: and unto the God of gods appeareth every one of them in Sion.

8 O Lord God of hosts, hear my prayer: hearken, O God of Jacob.

9 Behold, O God our defender: and look upon the face of thine Anointed.

10 For one day in thy courts: is better than a thousand.

11 I had rather be a door-keeper in the house of my God: than to dwell in the tents of ungodliness.

12 For the Lord God is a light and defence, the

Lord will give grace and glory: and no good thing shall he withhold from them that live a godly life.

13 O Lord God of hosts: blessed is the man that putteth his trust in thee.

PSALM LXXXV.

LORD, thou art become gracious unto thy land: thou hast turned away the captivity of Jacob.

2 Thou hast forgiven the offence of thy people : and covered all their sins.

3 Thou hast taken away all thy displeasure : and turned thyself from thy wrathful indignation.

4 Turn us then, O God our Saviour: and let thine anger cease from us.

5 Wilt thou be displeased at us for ever : and wilt thou stretch out thy wrath from one generation to another ?

6 Wilt thou not turn again and quicken us: that thy people may rejoice in thee ?

7 Show us thy mercy, O Lord : and grant us thy salvation.

8 I will hearken what the Lord God will say concerning me : for he shall speak peace unto his people, and to his saints, that they turn not again.

9 For his salvation is nigh them that fear him : that glory may dwell in our land.

10 Mercy and truth have met together : righteousness and peace have kissed each other.

11 Truth shall flourish out of the earth: and righteousness hath looked down from heaven.

12 Yea, the Lord shall show lovingkindness : and our land shall give her increase.

13 Righteousness shall go before him : and shall direct us in the way of his steps.

MORNING PRAYER.

PSALM LXXXVI.

BOW down thine ear, O Lord, and hear me : for I am poor and in misery.

2 Preserve thou my soul, for I am holy : my God, save thy servant that putteth his trust in thee.

3 Be merciful unto me, O Lord : for I call daily upon thee.

4 Comfort the soul of thy servant : for unto thee, O Lord, do I lift up my soul.

5 For thou, Lord, art good and gracious : and of great mercy unto them that call upon thee.

6 Give ear, Lord, unto my prayer : and ponder the voice of my humble desires.

7 In the time of my trouble I will call upon thee : for thou hearest me.

8 Among the gods, there is none like unto thee, O Lord : there is none that can do as thou doest.

9 All nations whom thou hast made shall come and worship thee, O Lord : and shall glorify thy Name.

10 For thou art great, and doest wondrous things : thou art God alone.

11 Teach me thy way, O Lord, and I will walk in thy truth : O knit my heart unto thee, that I may fear thy Name.

12 I will thank thee, O Lord my God, with all my heart : and will praise thy Name for evermore.

13 For great is thy mercy toward me : and thou hast delivered my soul from the nethermost hell.

14 Thou, O Lord God, art full of compassion and mercy : long-suffering, plenteous in goodness and truth.

15 O turn thee unto me, and have mercy upon me : give thy strength unto thy servant, and help the son of thine handmaid.

16 Show some token unto me for good, that they who hate me may see it, and be ashamed : because thou, Lord, hast holpen me, and comforted me.

PSALM LXXXIX.

M Y song shall be alway of the lovingkindness of the Lord : with my mouth will I ever be showing thy truth from one generation to another.

2 For I have said, Mercy shall be set up for ever : thy truth shalt thou establish in the heavens.

3 I have made a covenant with my chosen : I have sworn unto David my servant ;

4 Thy seed will I establish for ever : and set up thy throne from one generation to another.

5 O Lord, the very heavens shall praise thy wondrous works : and thy truth in the congregation of thy saints.

6 For who is he among the clouds : that shall be compared unto the Lord?

7 And what is he among the gods : that shall be like unto the Lord?

8 God is very greatly to be feared in the council of the saints : and to be had in reverence of all them that are round about him.

9 O Lord God of hosts, who is like unto thee? thy truth, most mighty Lord, is on every side.

10 Thou rulest the raging of the sea : thou stillest the waves thereof when they arise.

11 The heavens are thine, the earth is thine : thou hast laid the foundation of the round world, and all that therein is.

12 Thou hast a mighty arm : strong is thy hand, and high is thy right hand.

13 Righteousness and equity are the habitation of thy seat : mercy shall go before thy face.

14 Blessed is the people, O Lord, that can rejoice

in thee : they shall walk in the light of thy countenance.

15 Their delight shall be daily in thy Name : and in
thy righteousness shall they make their boast.

16 For thou art the glory of their strength : and in
thy lovingkindness thou shalt lift up our horns.

17 For the Lord is our defence : the Holy One of
Israel is our King.

EVENING PRAYER.

PSALM XC.

LORD, thou hast been our refuge from one generation to another.

2 Before the mountains were brought forth, or ever
the earth and the world were made : thou art God from
everlasting, and world without end.

3 Thou turnest man to destruction : again thou
sayest, Come again, ye children of men.

4 For a thousand years in thy sight are but as yesterday : seeing that is past as a watch in the night.

5 As soon as thou scatterest them, they are even as
a sleep : and fade away suddenly like the grass.

6 In the morning it is green, and groweth up : but
in the evening it is cut down, dried up, and withered.

7 For we consume away in thy displeasure : and are
afraid at thy wrathful indignation.

8 Thou hast set our misdeeds before thee : and our
secret sins in the light of thy countenance.

9 For when thou art angry, all our days are gone :
we bring our years to an end as it were a tale that is
told.

10 The days of our age are threescore years and ten;
and though men be so strong, that they come to four-

score years, yet is their strength then but labour and sorrow : so soon passeth it away, and we are gone.

11 But who regardeth the power of thy wrath ? for even according to thy fear, so is thy displeasure.

12 So teach us to number our days : that we may apply our hearts unto wisdom.

13 Turn thee again, O Lord, at the last : and be gracious unto thy servants.

14 O satisfy us with thy mercy, and that soon : so shall we rejoice and be glad all the days of our life.

15 Comfort us again now after the time that thou hast plagued us : and for the years wherein we have suffered adversity.

16 Show thy servants thy work : and their children thy glory.

17 And the glorious majesty of the Lord our God be upon us : prosper thou the work of our hands upon us, O prosper thou our handywork.

PSALM XCI.

WHOSO dwelleth under the defence of the Most High : shall abide under the shadow of the Almighty.

2 I will say unto the Lord, Thou art my hope, and my strong hold : my God, in him will I trust.

3 Surely he shall deliver thee from the snare of the hunter : and from the noisome pestilence.

4 He shall defend thee under his wings, and thou shalt be safe under his feathers : his faithfulness and truth shall be thy shield and buckler.

5 Thou shalt not be afraid for any terror by night : nor for the arrow that flieth by day ;

6 For the pestilence that walketh in darkness : nor for the sickness that destroyeth in the noon-day.

7 A thousand shall fall beside thee, and ten thousand at thy right hand : but it shall not come nigh thee.

8 Yea, with thine eyes shalt thou behold : and see the reward of the ungodly.

9 Because thou hast made the Lord, who is my refuge : even the Most High, thy habitation ;

10 There shall no evil happen unto thee : neither shall any plague come nigh thy dwelling.

11 For he shall give his angels charge over thee : to keep thee in all thy ways.

12 They shall bear thee in their hands : that thou hurt not thy foot against a stone.

13 Thou shalt go upon the lion and adder: the young lion and the dragon shalt thou tread under thy feet.

14 Because he hath set his love upon me, therefore will I deliver him : I will set him up, because he hath known my Name.

15 He shall call upon me, and I will hear him ; yea, I am with him in trouble : I will deliver him, and bring him to honour.

16 With long life will I satisfy him : and show him my salvation.

MORNING PRAYER.

PSALM XCII.

IT is a good thing to give thanks unto the Lord : and to sing praises unto thy Name, O Most Highest.

2 To tell of thy lovingkindness early in the morning: and of thy truth in the night season.

3 For thou, Lord, hast made me glad through thy works : and I will rejoice in giving praise for the operations of thy hands.

4 O Lord, how glorious are thy works : thy thoughts are very deep.

5 An unwise man doth not well consider this : and a fool doth not understand it.

6 When the ungodly are green as the grass, and when all the workers of iniquity do flourish, then they shall be destroyed for ever : but thou, Lord, art the Most Highest for evermore.

7 For, lo, thine enemies, O Lord, lo, thine enemies shall perish : and all the workers of wickedness shall be destroyed.

8 The righteous shall flourish like a palm-tree : and shall spread abroad like a cedar of Libanus.

9 Such as are planted in the house of the Lord : shall flourish in the courts of the house of our God.

10 They also shall bring forth more fruit in their old age : and shall be fat and flourishing.

11 That they may show how true the Lord my strength is : and that there is no unrighteousness in him.

PSALM XCIII.

THE Lord is King, and hath put on glorious apparel : the Lord hath put on his apparel, and girded himself with strength.

2 He hath made the round world so sure : that it cannot be moved.

3 Thy throne hath been established of old : thou art from everlasting.

4 The floods have risen, O Lord, the floods have lift up their voice : the floods lift up their waves.

5 The waves of the sea are mighty, and rage horribly : but yet the Lord, who dwelleth on high, is mightier.

6 Thy testimonies, O Lord, are very sure : holiness becometh thine house for ever.

EVENING PRAYER.

PSALM XCV.

O COME, let us sing unto the Lord : let us heartily rejoice in the strength of our salvation.

2 Let us come before his presence with thanksgiving: and show ourselves glad in him with psalms.

3 For the Lord is a great God: and a great King above all gods.

4 In his hand are all the corners of the earth : and the strength of the hills is his also.

5 The sea is his, and he made it : and his hands prepared the dry land.

6 O come let us worship, and fall down, and kneel before the Lord our Maker.

7 For he is the Lord our God: and we are the people of his pasture, and the sheep of his hand.

8 To-day, if ye will hear his voice, harden not your hearts : as in the provocation, and as in the day of temptation in the wilderness ;

9 When your fathers tempted me, proved me, and saw my works.

10 Forty years long was I grieved with this generation : and said, It is a people that do err in their hearts; for they have not known my ways.

11 Unto whom I sware in my wrath : that they should not enter into my rest.

PSALM XCVI.

O SING unto the Lord a new song : sing unto the Lord, all the whole earth.

2 Sing unto the Lord, and praise his Name: be telling of his salvation from day to day.

3 Declare his honour unto the heathen : and his wonders unto all people.

L

4 For the Lord is great, and cannot worthily be praised : he is more to be feared than all gods.

5 As for all the gods of the heathen, they are but idols : but it is the Lord that made the heavens.

6 Glory and majesty are before him : strength and beauty are in his sanctuary.

7 Ascribe unto the Lord, O ye kindreds of the people : ascribe unto the Lord glory and power.

8 Ascribe unto the Lord the honour due unto his Name : bring presents, and come into his courts.

9 O worship the Lord in the beauty of holiness : let the whole earth stand in awe of him.

10 Tell it out among the heathen, that the Lord is King : and that it is he who hath made the round world so fast that it cannot be moved ; and that he shall judge the people righteously.

11 Let the heavens rejoice, and let the earth be glad : let the sea make a noise, and all that therein is.

12 Let the field be joyful, and all that is in it : then shall all the trees of the wood rejoice before the Lord ;

13 For he cometh, for he cometh to judge the earth : and with righteousness to judge the world, and the people with his truth.

MORNING PRAYER.

PSALM XCVII.

THE Lord is King, the earth may be glad thereof : yea, the multitude of the isles may be glad thereof.

2 Clouds and darkness are round about him : righteousness and judgment are the habitation of his throne.

3 There shall go a fire before him : and burn up his enemies on every side.

4 His lightnings enlightened the world: the earth saw it, and was afraid.

5 The hills melted like wax at the presence of the Lord: at the presence of the Lord of the whole earth.

6 The heavens have declared his righteousness: and all the people have seen his glory.

7 Thou, Lord, art higher than all that are in the earth: thou art exalted far above all gods.

8 O ye that love the Lord, see that ye hate the thing which is evil: the Lord preserveth the souls of his saints; he shall deliver them from the hand of the ungodly.

9 There is sprung up a light for the righteous: and joyful gladness for such as are true-hearted.

10 Rejoice in the Lord, ye righteous: and give thanks for a remembrance of his holiness.

PSALM XCVIII.

O SING unto the Lord a new song: for he hath done marvellous things.

2 With his own right hand, and with his holy arm: hath he gotten himself the victory.

3 The Lord declared his salvation: his righteousness hath he openly showed in the sight of the heathen.

4 He hath remembered his mercy and truth toward the house of Israel: and all the ends of the world have seen the salvation of our God.

5 Show yourselves joyful unto the Lord, all ye lands: sing, rejoice, and give thanks.

6 Let the sea make a noise, and all that therein is: the round world, and they that dwell therein.

7 Let the floods clap their hands, and let the hills be joyful together before the Lord: for he cometh to judge the earth.

8 With righteousness shall he judge the world: and the people with equity.

PSALM XCIX.

THE Lord is King, be the people never so impatient: he sitteth between the cherubim, be the earth never so unquiet.

2 The Lord is great in Sion: and high above all people.

3 They shall give thanks unto thy Name: which is great, wonderful, and holy.

4 O magnify the Lord our God: and fall down before his footstool, for he is holy.

5 O magnify the Lord our God, and worship him upon his holy hill: for the Lord our God is holy.

EVENING PRAYER.

PSALM C.

O BE be joyful in the Lord, all ye lands: serve the Lord with gladness, and come before his presence with a song.

2 Be ye sure that the Lord he is God; it is he that hath made us, and not we ourselves: we are his people, and the sheep of his pasture.

3 O go your way into his gates with thanksgiving, and into his courts with praise: be thankful unto him, and speak good of his Name.

4 For the Lord is gracious, his mercy is everlasting: and his truth endureth from generation to generation.

PSALM CII.

HEAR my prayer, O Lord: and let my cry come unto thee.

2 Hide not thy face from me in the time of my

trouble : incline thine ear unto me when I call ; O hear me, and that speedily.

3 For my days are consumed away like smoke : and my bones are burnt up as it were a fire-brand.

4 My heart is smitten down, and withered like grass : so that I forget to eat my bread.

5 For the voice of my groaning, my bones will scarce cleave to my flesh.

6 I am become like a pelican in the wilderness : and like an owl that is in the desert.

7 I have watched, and am even as it were a sparrow that sitteth alone upon the house-top.

8 Mine enemies revile me all the day long : and they that are mad upon me are sworn together against me.

9 For I have eaten ashes as it were bread : and mingled my drink with weeping ;

10 And that because of thine indignation and wrath : for thou hast taken me up, and cast me down.

11 My days are gone like a shadow : and I am withered like grass.

12 But thou, O Lord, shalt endure for ever : and thy remembrance throughout all generations.

13 Thou shalt arise, and have mercy upon Sion : for it is time that thou have mercy upon her, yea, the time is come.

14 And why ? thy servants think upon her stones : and it pitieth them to see her in the dust.

15 The heathen shall fear thy name, O Lord : and all the kings of the earth thy majesty.

16 When the Lord shall build up Sion : and when his glory shall appear ;

17 When he turneth him unto the prayer of the poor destitute : and despiseth not their desire.

18 This shall be written for those that come after : and the people that shall be born shall praise the Lord.

19 For he hath looked down from his sanctuary : out of heaven did the Lord behold the earth ;

20 That he might hear the mournings of such as are in captivity: and deliver those that are appointed unto death.

21 That they may declare the name of the Lord in Sion: and his praise in Jerusalem;

22 When the people are gathered together: and the kingdoms also, to serve the Lord.

23 He brought down my strength in my journey: and shortened my days.

24 But I said, O my God, take me not away in the midst of mine age: as for thy years, they endure throughout all generations.

25 Thou, Lord, in the beginning hast laid the foundation of the earth: and the heavens are the work of thy hands.

26 They shall perish, but thou shalt endure: they all shall wax old as doth a garment,

27 And as a vesture shalt thou change them, and they shall be changed: but thou art the same, and thy years shall not fail.

28 The children of thy servants shall continue: and their seed shall stand fast in thy sight.

MORNING PRAYER.

PSALM CIII.

PRAISE the Lord, O my soul: and all that is within me, praise his holy Name.

2 Praise the Lord, O my soul: and forget not all his benefits.

3 Who forgiveth all thy sins: and healeth all thine infirmities.

4 Who saveth thy life from destruction: and crowneth thee with mercy and lovingkindness.

5 Who satisfieth thy mouth with good things: making thee young and lusty as an eagle.

6 The Lord executeth righteousness and judgment for all them that are oppressed.

7 He showed his ways unto Moses: his works unto the children of Israel.

8 The Lord is full of compassion and mercy: long-suffering, and of great goodness.

9 He will not alway be chiding: neither keepeth he his anger for ever.

10 He hath not dealt with us after our sins: nor rewarded us according to our wickedness.

11 For look how high the heaven is in comparison of the earth: so great is his mercy also toward them that fear him.

12 Look how wide also the east is from the west: so far hath he set our sins from us.

13 Yea, like as a father pitieth his own children: even so is the Lord merciful unto them that fear him.

14 For he knoweth whereof we are made: he remembereth that we are but dust.

15 The days of man are but as grass: for he flourisheth as a flower of the field.

16 For as soon as the wind goeth over it, it is gone: and the place thereof shall know it no more.

17 But the merciful goodness of the Lord endureth for ever and ever upon them that fear him: and his righteousness upon children's children;

18 Even upon such as keep his covenant: and think upon his commandments to do them.

19 The Lord hath prepared his seat in heaven: and his kingdom ruleth over all.

20 O praise the Lord, ye angels of his, ye that excel in strength: ye that fulfil his commandment, and hearken unto the voice of his words.

21 O praise the Lord, all ye his hosts: ye servants of his that do his pleasure.

22 O speak good of the Lord, all ye works of his, in all places of his dominion : praise thou the Lord, O my soul.

EVENING PRAYER.

PSALM CIV.

PRAISE the Lord, O my soul : O Lord my God, thou art become exceeding glorious, thou art clothed with majesty and honour.

2 Thou deckest thyself with light as it were with a garment : and spreadest out the heavens like a curtain.

3 Who layeth the beams of his chambers in the waters : and maketh the clouds his chariot, and walketh upon the wings of the wind.

4 He maketh his angels spirits : and his ministers a flaming fire.

5 He laid the foundations of the earth : that it never should move at any time.

6 Thou coveredst it with the deep like as with a garment : the waters stood above the mountains.

7 At thy rebuke they fled : at the voice of thy thunder they hasted away.

8 They go up as high as the hills, and down to the valleys beneath : even unto the place which thou hast appointed for them.

9 Thou hast set them their bounds which they shall not pass : neither turn again to cover the earth.

10 He sendeth the springs into the valleys which run among the hills.

11 All beasts of the field drink thereof: and the wild asses quench their thirst.

12 Beside them shall the fowls of the air have their habitation : and sing among the branches.

13 He watereth the hills from above : the earth is filled with the fruit of thy works.

14 He bringeth forth grass for the cattle : and green herb for the service of men.

15 That he may bring food out of the earth, and wine that maketh glad the heart of man : and oil to make him a cheerful countenance, and bread to strengthen man's heart.

16 The trees of the Lord also are full of sap : even the cedars of Libanus which he hath planted.

17 Wherein the birds make their nests : and the fir-trees are a dwelling for the stork.

18 The high hills are a refuge for the wild goats : and so are the stony rocks for the conies.

19 He appointed the moon for certain seasons : and the sun knoweth his going down.

20 Thou makest darkness, and it is night : wherein all the beasts ot tne forest do move.

21 The lions roaring after their prey : do seek their meat from God.

22 The sun ariseth, and they get them away together : and lay them down in their dens.

23 Man goeth forth to his work, and to his labour : until the evening.

24 O Lord, how manifold are thy works : in wisdom hast thou made them all ; the earth is full of thy riches.

25 So is the great and wide sea also : wherein are things creeping innumerable, both small and great beasts.

26 There go the ships, and there is that leviathan : whom thou hast made to take his pastime therein.

27 These wait all upon thee : that thou mayest give them meat in due season.

28 When thou givest it them, they gather it : and when thou openest thine hand, they are filled with good.

29 When thou hidest thy face, they are troubled : when thou takest away their breath, they die, and are turned again to their dust.

30 Thou sendest forth thy Spirit, they are created : and thou renewest the face of the earth.

31 The glorious Majesty of the Lord shall endure for ever : the Lord shall rejoice in his works.

32 The earth shall tremble at the look of him : if he do but touch the hills, they shall smoke.

33 I will sing unto the Lord as long as I live : I will praise my God while I have my being.

34 And so shall my words please him : my joy shall be in the Lord.

35 As for sinners, they shall be consumed out of the earth, and the ungodly shall come to an end : praise thou the Lord, O my soul, praise the Lord.

MORNING PRAYER.

PSALM CVII.—Part I.

O GIVE thanks unto the Lord, for he is gracious : and his mercy endureth for ever.

2 Let them give thanks whom the Lord hath redeemed : and delivered from the hand of the enemy ;

3 And gathered them out of the lands, from the east, and from the west : from the north, and from the south.

4 They went astray in the wilderness out of the way : and found no city to dwell in.

5 Hungry and thirsty : their soul fainted in them.

6 So they cried unto the Lord in their trouble : and he delivered them from their distress.

7 He led them forth by the right way : that they might go to a city of habitation.

8 O that men would therefore praise the Lord for his goodness : and declare the wonders that he doeth for the children of men !

9 For he satisfieth the longing soul : and filleth the hungry soul with goodness ;

10 Such as sit in darkness and in the shadow of death : being fast bound in misery and iron.

11 Because they rebelled against the words of the Lord : and lightly regarded the counsel of the Most Highest ;

12 He also brought down their heart through heaviness : they fell down, and there was none to help them.

13 Then they cried unto the Lord in their trouble : and he delivered them out of their distress.

14 For he brought them out of darkness, and out of the shadow of death : and brake their bonds in sunder.

15 O that men would therefore praise the Lord for his goodness : and declare the wonders that he doeth for the children of men !

16 For he hath broken the gates of brass : and smitten the bars of iron in sunder.

17 Foolish men are plagued for their offence : and because of their wickedness.

18 Their soul abhorreth all manner of meat : and they draw near unto the gates of death.

19 Then they cry unto the Lord in their trouble : and he delivereth them out of their distress.

20 He sent his word, and healed them : and they were saved from their destruction.

21 O that men would therefore praise the Lord for his goodness : and declare the wonders that he doeth for the children of men !

22 That they would offer unto him the sacrifice of thanksgiving : and tell out his works with gladness !

EVENING PRAYER.

PSALM CVII.—Part II.

THEY that go down to the sea in ships: and occupy their business in great waters ;

2 These men see the works of the Lord: and his wonders in the deep.

3 For at his word the stormy wind ariseth: which lifteth up the waves thereof.

4 They are carried up to the heaven, and down again to the deep: their soul melteth away because of the trouble.

5 They reel to and fro, and stagger like a drunken man: and are at their wit's end.

6 Then they cry unto the Lord in their trouble: and he delivereth them out of their distress.

7 For he maketh the storm a calm: so that the waves thereof are still.

8 Then they are glad, because they are at rest: so he bringeth them unto the haven where they would be.

9 O that men would therefore praise the Lord for his goodness: and declare the wonders that he doeth for the children of men !

10 That they would exalt him also in the congregation of the people: and praise him in the assembly of the elders.

11 Who turneth the floods into a wilderness: and the water-springs into dry ground.

12 A fruitful land maketh he barren: for the wickedness of them that dwell therein.

13 Again, he maketh the wilderness a standing water: and water-springs of a dry ground.

14 And there he setteth the hungry: that they may build them a city to dwell in ;

15 That they may sow their land, and plant vineyards: to yield them fruits of increase.

16 He blesseth them so that they multiply exceedingly : and suffereth not their cattle to decrease.

17 Again, when they are diminished, and brought low : through oppression, through any plague or trouble ;

18 Though he suffer them to be evil entreated through tyrants : and let them wander out of the way in the wilderness ;

19 Yet helpeth he the poor out of misery : and maketh him households like a flock of sheep.

20 The righteous will consider this, and rejoice : and the mouth of all wickedness shall be stopped.

21 Whoso is wise will ponder these things : and they shall understand the lovingkindness of the Lord.

MORNING PRAYER.

PSALM CXI.

I WILL give thanks unto the Lord with my whole heart : secretly among the faithful, and in the congregation.

2 The works of the Lord are great : sought out of all them that have pleasure therein.

3 His work is worthy to be praised, and had in honour : and his righteousness endureth for ever.

4 The merciful and gracious Lord hath so done his marvellous works : that they ought to be had in remembrance.

5 He hath given meat unto them that fear him : he will be ever mindful of his covenant.

6 The works of his hands are verity and judgment : and all his commandments are true.

7 They stand fast for ever and ever : and are done in truth and equity.

8 He sent redemption unto his people : he hath commanded his covenant for ever ; holy and reverend is his Name.

9 The fear of the Lord is the beginning of wisdom : a good understanding have all they that do thereafter : the praise of it endureth for ever.

PSALM CXII.

BLESSED is the man that feareth the Lord : he hath great delight in his commandments.

2 His seed shall be mighty upon earth : the generation of the faithful shall be blessed.

3 Riches and plenteousness shall be in his house : and his righteousness endureth for ever.

4 Unto the godly there ariseth up light in the darkness : he is merciful, loving, and righteous.

5 A good man is merciful, and lendeth : and will guide his words with discretion.

6 Surely he shall not be moved : and the righteous shall be had in everlasting remembrance.

7 He will not be afraid of any evil tidings : for his heart standeth fast, and believeth in the Lord.

8 He hath dispersed abroad, and given to the poor : and his righteousness remaineth for ever ; his horn shall be exalted with honour.

9 The ungodly shall see it, and it shall grieve him : he shall gnash with his teeth, and consume away ; the desire of the ungodly shall perish.

PSALM CXIII.

PRAISE the Lord, ye servants of his : O praise the Name of the Lord.

2 Blessèd be the Name of the Lord : from this time forth for evermore.

3 The Lord's Name is praised : from the rising up of the sun unto the going down of the same.

4 The Lord is high above all heathen: and his glory above the heavens.

5 Who is like unto the Lord our God, who hath his dwelling so high: and yet humbleth himself to behold the things that are in heaven and earth?

6 He taketh up the simple out of the dust: and lifteth the poor out of the mire;

7 That he may set him with the princes: even with the princes of his people.

8 He maketh the barren woman to keep house: and to be a joyful mother of children.

EVENING PRAYER.

PSALM CXIV.

WHEN Israel came out of Egypt, and the house of Jacob from among the strange people;

2 Judah was his sanctuary: and Israel his dominion.

3 The sea saw that, and fled: Jordan was driven back.

4 The mountains skipped like rams: and the little hills like young sheep.

5 What aileth thee, O thou sea, that thou fleddest: and thou Jordan, that thou wast driven back?

6 Ye mountains, that ye skipped like rams: and ye little hills, like young sheep?

7 Tremble, thou earth, at the presence of the Lord: at the presence of the God of Jacob;

8 Who turned the hard rock into a standing water and the flint-stone into a springing well.

PSALM CXV.

NOT unto us, O Lord, not unto us, but unto thy Name give the praise: for thy loving mercy, and for thy truth's sake

2 Wherefore shall the heathen say : Where is now their God?

3 As for our God, he is in heaven : he hath done whatsoever pleased him.

4 O Israel, trust thou in the Lord : he is their succour and defence.

5 Ye house of Aaron, put your trust in the Lord : he is their helper and defender.

6 Ye that fear the Lord, put your trust in the Lord : he is their helper and defender.

7 The Lord hath been mindful of us, and he shall bless us : even he shall bless the house of Israel ; he shall bless the house of Aaron.

8 He shall bless them that fear the Lord, both small and great.

9 The Lord shall increase you more and more : you and your children.

10 Ye are the blessed of the Lord : who made heaven and earth.

11 All the whole heavens are the Lord's : the earth hath he given to the children of men.

12 The dead praise not thee, O Lord : neither any that go down into silence.

13 But we will praise the Lord : from this time forth for evermore. Praise the Lord.

MORNING PRAYER.

PSALM CXVI.

I AM well pleased that the Lord hath heard the voice of my prayer ;

2 That he hath inclined his ear unto me : therefore will I call upon him as long as I live.

3 The snares of death compassed me round about: and the pains of hell gat hold upon me.

4 I found trouble and heaviness, and I called upon the name of the Lord : O Lord, I beseech thee, deliver my soul.

5 Gracious is the Lord, and righteous: yea, our God is merciful.

6 The Lord preserveth the simple : I was in misery, and he helped me.

7 Turn again then unto thy rest, O my soul: for the Lord hath rewarded thee.

8 And why? thou hast delivered my soul from death : mine eyes from tears, and my feet from falling.

9 I will walk before the Lord : in the land of the living.

10 I believed, and therefore have I spoken ; but I was sore troubled: I said in my haste, All men are liars.

11 What reward shall I give unto the Lord: for all the benefits which he hath done unto me ?

12 I will receive the cup of salvation : and call upon the Name of the Lord.

13 I will pay my vows now in the presence of all his people : right dear in the sight of the Lord is the death of his saints.

14 Behold, O Lord, how that I am thy servant : I am thy servant, and the son of thine handmaid ; thou hast broken my bonds in sunder.

15 I will offer to thee the sacrifice of thanksgiving : and will call upon the Name of the Lord.

16 I will pay my vows unto the Lord, in the sight of all his people : in the courts of the Lord's house, even in the midst of thee, O Jerusalem. Praise the Lord.

PSALM CXVII.

O PRAISE the Lord, all ye heathen : praise him, all ye nations.

2 For his merciful kindness is ever more and more towards us: and the truth of the Lord endureth for ever. Praise the Lord.

EVENING PRAYER.

PSALM CXVIII.

O GIVE thanks unto the Lord, for he is gracious: because his mercy endureth for ever.

2 Let Israel now confess, that he is gracious: and that his mercy endureth for ever.

3 Let the house of Aaron now confess: that his mercy endureth for ever.

4 Yea, let them now that fear the Lord confess: that his mercy endureth for ever.

5 I called upon the Lord in trouble: and the Lord heard me at large.

6 The Lord is on my side: I will not fear what man doeth unto me.

7 The Lord taketh my part with them that help me: therefore shall I see my desire upon mine enemies.

8 It is better to trust in the Lord: than to put any confidence in man.

9 It is better to trust in the Lord: than to put any confidence in princes.

10 All nations compassed me round about: but in the Name of the Lord will I destroy them.

11 They kept me in on every side, they kept me in, I say, on every side: but in the Name of the Lord will I destroy them.

12 They came about me like bees, and are extinct even as the fire among the thorns: for in the Name of the Lord I will destroy them.

13 Thou hast thrust sore at me, that I might fall: but the Lord was my help.

14 The Lord is my strength and my song: and is become my salvation.

15 The voice of joy and health is in the dwelling of the righteous: the right hand of the Lord bringeth mighty things to pass.

16 The right hand of the Lord hath the pre-eminence: the right hand of the Lord bringeth mighty things to pass.

17 I shall not die, but live: and declare the works of the Lord.

18 The Lord hath chastened and corrected me: but he hath not given me over unto death.

19 Open me the gates of righteousness: that I may go into them, and give thanks unto the Lord.

20 This is the gate of the Lord: the righteous shall enter into it.

21 I will thank thee: for thou hast heard me, and art become my salvation.

22 The same stone which the builders refused: is become the head-stone of the corner.

23 This is the Lord's doing: and it is marvellous in our eyes.

24 This is the day which the Lord hath made: we will rejoice and be glad in it.

25 Help me now, O Lord: O Lord, send us now prosperity.

26 Blessed be he that cometh in the Name of the Lord: we have wished you good luck, ye that are of the house of the Lord.

27 God is the Lord, who hath showed us light: bind the sacrifice with cords, yea, even unto the horns of the altar.

28 Thou art my God, and I will thank thee: thou art my God, and I will praise thee.

29 O give thanks unto the Lord, for he is gracious: and his mercy endureth for ever.

MORNING PRAYER.

PSALM CXIX.

BLESSED are those that are undefiled in the way:
and walk in the law of the Lord.

2 Blessed are they that keep his testimonies : and
seek him with their whole heart.

3 For they who do no wickedness : walk in his ways.

4 Thou hast charged : that we should diligently keep
thy commandments.

5 O that my ways were made so direct : that I might
keep thy statutes !

6 So shall I not be confounded : while I have respect
unto all thy commandments.

7 I will thank thee with an unfeigned heart : when I
shall have learned the judgments of thy righteousness.

8 I will keep thy statutes : O forsake me not utterly.

WHEREWITHAL shall a young man cleanse his
way ? Even by ruling himself after thy word.

2 With my whole heart have I sought thee : O let
me not go wrong out of thy commandments.

3 Thy words have I hid within my heart : that I
might not sin against thee.

4 Blessed art thou, O Lord : O teach me thy statutes.

5 With my lips have I been telling : of the judgments of thy mouth.

6 I have had as great delight in the way of thy
testimonies : as in all manner of riches.

7 I will talk of thy commandments : and have respect
unto thy ways.

8 My delight shall be in thy statutes : and I will not
forget thy word.

O DO well unto thy servant: that I may live, and keep thy word.

2 Open thou mine eyes: that I may see the wondrous things of thy law.

3 I am a stranger upon earth: O hide not thy commandments from me.

4 My soul breaketh out for the very fervent desire: that it hath alway unto thy judgments.

5 Thou hast rebuked the proud: and cursed are they that do err from thy commandments.

6 O turn from me shame and rebuke: for I have kept thy testimonies.

7 Princes also did sit and speak against me: but thy servant is occupied in thy statutes.

8 For thy testimonies are my delight: and my counsellors.

M Y soul cleaveth to the dust: O quicken thou me, according to thy word.

2 I have acknowledged my ways, and thou heardest me: O teach me thy statutes.

3 Make me to understand the way of thy commandments: and so shall I talk of thy wondrous works.

4 My soul melteth away for very heaviness: comfort thou me according to thy word.

5 Take from me the way of lying: and cause thou me to make much of thy laws.

6 I have chosen the way of truth: and thy judgments have I laid before me.

7 I have stuck unto thy testimonies: O Lord, confound me not.

8 I will run the way of thy commandments: when thou hast set my heart at liberty.

EVENING PRAYER.

TEACH me, O Lord, the way of thy statutes : and
I shall keep it unto the end.

2 Give me understanding, and I shall keep thy law :
yea, I shall keep it with my whole heart.

3 Make me to go in the path of thy commandments :
for therein is my desire.

4 Incline my heart unto thy testimonies : and not to
covetousness.

5 O turn away mine eyes, lest they behold vanity :
and quicken thou me in thy way.

6 O stablish thy word in thy servant : that I may
fear thee.

7 Take away the rebuke that I am afraid of : for thy
judgments are good.

8 Behold, my delight is in thy commandments : O
quicken me in thy righteousness.

LET thy loving mercy also come unto me, O Lord :
even thy salvation, according unto thy word.

2 So shall I make answer unto him that reproacheth
me : for my trust is in thy word.

3 O take not the word of thy truth utterly out of my
mouth : for my hope is in thy judgments.

4 So shall I alway keep thy law : yea, for ever and
ever.

5 And I will walk at liberty : for I seek thy commandments.

6 I will speak of thy testimonies also even before
kings : and will not be ashamed.

7 And my delight shall be in thy commandments :
which I have loved.

8 My hands also will I lift up unto thy commandments, which I have loved : and my study shall be in
thy statutes.

O THINK upon thy servant, as concerning thy word: wherein thou hast caused me to put my trust.

2 The same is my comfort in my trouble: for thy word hath quickened me.

3 The proud have had me exceedingly in derision: yet have I not shrunk from thy law.

4 For I remembered thine everlasting judgments, O Lord: and received comfort.

5 I am horribly afraid for the ungodly: that forsake thy law.

6 Thy statutes have been my songs: in the house of my pilgrimage.

7 I have thought upon thy Name, O Lord, in the night-season: and have kept thy law.

8 This I had: because I kept thy commandments.

THOU art my portion, O Lord: I have promised to keep thy law.

2 I made my humble petition in thy presence with my whole heart: O be merciful unto me, according to thy word.

3 I called mine own ways to remembrance: and turned my feet unto thy testimonies.

4 I made haste, and prolonged not the time: to keep thy commandments.

5 The congregations of the ungodly have robbed me: but I have not forgotten thy law.

6 At midnight I will rise to give thanks unto thee: because of thy righteous judgments.

7 I am a companion of all them that fear thee: and keep thy commandments.

8 The earth, O Lord, is full of thy mercy: O teach me thy statutes.

MORNING PRAYER.

O LORD, thou hast dealt graciously with thy servant: according unto thy word.

2 O teach me true understanding and knowledge:
for I have believed thy commandments.

3 Before I was troubled I went wrong: but now I
have kept thy word.

4 Thou art good and gracious: O teach me thy
statutes.

5 The proud have imagined a lie against me: but I
will keep thy commandments with my whole heart.

6 Their heart is fat as brawn: but my delight hath
been in thy law.

7 It is good for me that I have been in trouble: that
I may learn thy statutes.

8 The law of thy mouth is dearer unto me: than
thousands of gold and silver.

THY hands have made me and fashioned me: O
give me understanding, that I may learn thy commandments.

2 They that fear thee will be glad when they see
me: because I have put my trust in thy word.

3 I know, O Lord, that thy judgments are right:
and that thou, of very faithfulness, hast caused me to
be troubled.

4 O let thy merciful kindness be my comfort: according to thy word unto thy servant.

5 O let thy loving mercies come unto me, that I may
live: for thy law is my delight.

6 Let the proud be ashamed, for they go wickedly
about to destroy me: but I will be occupied in thy
commandments.

7 Let such as fear thee, and have known thy testimonies: be turned unto me.

8 O let my heart be sound in thy statutes : that I be not ashamed.

M Y soul hath longed for thy salvation : and I have a good hope because of thy word.

2 Mine eyes long for thy word: saying, O when wilt thou comfort me?

3 For I am become like a bottle in the smoke : yet do I not forget thy statutes.

4 How many are the days of thy servant : when wilt thou be avenged of them that persecute me?

5 The proud have digged pits for me : which are not after thy law.

6 All thy commandments are true : they persecute me falsely ; O be thou my help.

7 They had almost made an end of me upon earth : but I forsook not thy commandments.

8 O quicken me after thy lovingkindness : and so shall I keep the testimonies of thy mouth.

O LORD, thy word : endureth for ever in heaven.

2 Thy truth also remaineth from one generation to another : thou hast laid the foundation of the earth, and it abideth.

3 They continue this day according to thine ordinance : for all things serve thee.

4 If my delight had not been in thy law : I should have perished in my trouble.

5 I will never forget thy commandments : for with them thou hast quickened me.

6 I am thine, O save me : for I have sought thy commandments.

7 The ungodly laid wait for me, to destroy me : but I will consider thy testimonies.

8 I see that all things come to an end : but thy commandment is exceeding broad.

M

EVENING PRAYER.

LORD, what love have I unto thy law: all the day long is my study in it.

2 Thou through thy commandments hast made me wiser than mine enemies: for they are ever with me.

3 I have more understanding than my teachers: for thy testimonies are my study.

4 I am wiser than the aged: because I keep thy commandments.

5 I have refrained my feet from every evil way: that I may keep thy word.

6 I have not shrunk from thy judgments: for thou teachest me.

7 O how sweet are thy words unto my taste: yea, sweeter than honey unto my mouth.

8 Through thy commandments I get understanding: therefore I hate all evil ways.

THY word is a lantern unto my feet: and a light unto my path.

2 I have sworn, and am steadfastly purposed: to keep thy righteous judgments.

3 I am troubled above measure: quicken me, O Lord, according to thy word.

4 Let the free-will offerings of my mouth please thee, O Lord: and teach me thy judgments.

5 My soul is alway in my hand: yet do I not forget thy law.

6 The ungodly have laid a snare for me: but yet I swerved not from thy commandments.

7 Thy testimonies have I claimed as mine heritage for ever: and why? they are the very joy of my heart.

8 I have applied my heart to fulfil thy statutes alway: even unto the end.

I HATE them that imagine evil things : but thy law do I love.

2 Thou art my defence and shield : and my trust is in thy word.

3 Away from me, ye wicked : I will keep the commandments of my God.

4 O establish me according to thy word, that I may live : and let me not be disappointed of my hope.

5 Hold thou me up, and I shall be safe : yea, my delight shall be ever in thy statutes.

6 Thou hast trodden down all them that depart from thy statutes : for they imagine but deceit.

7 Thou puttest away all the ungodly of the earth like dross : therefore I love thy testimonies.

8 My flesh trembleth for fear of thee : and I am afraid of thy judgments.

I DEAL with the thing that is lawful and right : O give me not over unto mine oppressors.

2 Make thou thy servant to delight in that which is good : let not the proud oppress me.

3 Mine eyes are wasted away with looking for thy health : and for the word of thy righteousness.

4 O deal with thy servant according unto thy loving mercy : and teach me thy statutes.

5 I am thy servant: O grant me understanding, that I may know thy testimonies.

6 It is time for thee, Lord, to lay to thine hand : for they have destroyed thy law.

7 For I love thy commandments : above gold and precious stones.

8 Therefore I esteem all thy precepts concerning all things to be right : and all false ways I utterly abhor.

MORNING PRAYER.

THY testimonies are wonderful : therefore doth my soul keep them.

2 When thy word goeth forth : it giveth light and understanding unto the simple.

3 I opened my mouth, and drew in my breath : for my delight was in thy commandments.

4 O look thou upon me, and be merciful unto me : as thou usest to do unto those that love thy Name.

5 Order my steps in thy word : and so shall no wickedness have dominion over me.

6 O deliver me from the wrongful dealings of men : and so shall I keep thy commandments.

7 Show the light of thy countenance upon thy servant : and teach me thy statutes.

8 Mine eyes gush out with water : because men keep not thy law.

RIGHTEOUS art thou, O Lord : and true are thy judgments.

2 The testimonies that thou hast commanded : are exceeding righteous and true.

3 My zeal hath even consumed me : because mine enemies have forgotten thy words.

4 Thy word is tried to the uttermost : and thy servant loveth it.

5 I am small, and of no reputation : yet do I not forget thy commandments.

6 Thy righteousness is an everlasting righteousness : and thy law is the truth.

7 Trouble and heaviness have taken hold upon me : yet is my delight in thy commandments.

8 The righteousness of thy testimonies is everlasting : O grant me understanding, and I shall live.

I CALL with my whole heart: hear me, O Lord, I will keep thy statutes.

2 Yea, even unto thee do I call: help me, and I shall keep thy testimonies.

3 Early in the morning do I cry unto thee: for in thy word is my trust.

4 Mine eyes prevent the night-watches: that I may be occupied in thy words.

5 Hear my voice, O Lord, according unto thy loving-kindness: quicken me, according as thou art wont.

6 They draw nigh that of malice persecute me: and are afar from thy law.

7 Be thou nigh at hand. O Lord: for all thy commandments are true.

8 As concerning thy testimonies, I have known long since: that thou hast founded them for ever.

O CONSIDER mine adversity, and deliver me: for I do not forget thy law.

2 Avenge thou my cause, and deliver me: quicken me, according to thy word.

3 Health is far from the ungodly: for they regard not thy statutes.

4 Great is thy mercy, O Lord: quicken me, as thou art wont.

5 Many there are that trouble me, and persecute me: yet do I not swerve from thy testimonies.

6 It grieveth me when I see the transgressors: because they keep not thy law.

7 Consider, O Lord, how I love thy commandments: O quicken me, according to thy lovingkindness.

8 Thy word is true from everlasting: all the judgments of thy righteousness endure for evermore.

EVENING PRAYER.

PRINCES have persecuted me without a cause :
but my heart standeth in awe of thy word.

2 I am as glad of thy word : as one that findeth great
spoils.

3 As for lies, I hate and abhor them : but thy law do
I love.

4 Seven times a day do I praise thee : because of
thy righteous judgments.

5 Great is the peace that they have who love thy
law : and they are not offended at it.

6 Lord, I have looked for thy saving health : and
done after thy commandments.

7 My soul hath kept thy testimonies : and loved
them exceedingly.

8 I have kept thy commandments and testimonies :
for all my ways are before thee.

LET my complaint come before thee, O Lord : give
me understanding, according to thy word.

2 Let my supplication come before thee : deliver me,
according to thy word.

3 My lips shall speak of thy praise : when thou hast
taught me thy statutes.

4 Yea, my tongue shall sing of thy word : for all thy
commandments are righteous.

5 Let thine hand help me : for I have chosen thy
commandments.

6 I have longed for thy saving health, O Lord : and
in thy law is my delight.

7 O let my soul live, and it shall praise thee : and
thy judgments shall help me.

8 I have gone astray like a sheep that is lost : O
seek thy servant, for I do not forget thy commandments.

PSALM CXXI.

I WILL lift up mine eyes unto the hills : from whence cometh my help.

2 My help cometh even from the Lord : who hath made heaven and earth.

3 He will not suffer thy foot to be moved : and he that keepeth thee will not sleep.

4 Behold, he that keepeth Israel : shall neither slumber nor sleep.

5 The Lord himself is thy keeper : the Lord is thy defence upon thy right hand.

6 So that the sun shall not smite thee by day : neither the moon by night.

7 The Lord shall preserve thee from all evil : yea, it is even he that shall keep thy soul.

8 The Lord shall preserve thy going out and thy coming in : from this time forth for evermore.

MORNING PRAYER.

PSALM CXXIII.

UNTO thee I lift up mine eyes : O thou that dwellest in the heavens.

2 Behold, even as the eyes of servants look unto the hand of their masters, and as the eyes of a maiden unto the hand of her mistress : even so our eyes wait upon the Lord our God, until he have mercy upon us.

3 Have mercy upon us, O Lord, have mercy upon us : for we are utterly despised.

4 Our soul is filled with the scornful reproof of the wealthy : and with the despitefulness of the proud.

PSALM CXXIV.

IF the Lord himself had not been on our side, now may Israel say: if the Lord himself had not been on our side, when men rose up against us;

2 They had swallowed us up quick: when they were so wrathfully displeased at us.

3 Yea, the waters had drowned us: and the stream had gone over our soul.

4 The deep waters of the proud: had gone over our soul.

5 But praised be the Lord: who hath not given us over for a prey unto their teeth.

6 Our soul is escaped, even as a bird out of the snare of the fowler: the snare is broken, and we are delivered.

7 Our help standeth in the name of the Lord: who hath made heaven and earth.

PSALM CXXV.

THEY that put their trust in the Lord shall be even as the mount Sion: which cannot be removed, but standeth fast for ever.

2 The hills stand about Jerusalem: even so standeth the Lord round about his people, from this time forth for evermore.

3 For the rod of the ungodly shall not rest upon the lot of the righteous: lest the righteous put their hand unto wickedness.

4 Do well, O Lord: unto those that are good and true of heart.

5 As for such as turn back unto their own wickedness: the Lord shall lead them forth with the evil-doers; but peace shall be upon Israel.

PSALM CXXVI.

WHEN the Lord turned again the captivity of Sion: then were we like unto them that dream.

2 Then was our mouth filled with laughter: and our tongue with joy.

3 Then said they among the heathen: The Lord hath done great things for them.

4 Yea, the Lord hath done great things for us: whereof we rejoice.

5 Turn our captivity, O Lord: as the rivers in the south.

6 They that sow in tears: shall reap in joy.

7 He that now goeth on his way weeping, and beareth forth good seed: shall doubtless come again with joy, and bring his sheaves with him.

EVENING PRAYER.

PSALM CXXVII.

EXCEPT the Lord build the house: their labour is but lost that build it.

2 Except the Lord keep the city: the watchman waketh but in vain.

3 It is but lost labour that ye haste to rise up early, and so late take rest, and eat the bread of carefulness: for so he giveth his beloved sleep.

4 Lo, children and the fruit of the womb: are an heritage and gift that cometh of the Lord.

5 Like as the arrows in the hands of the giant: even so are the young children.

6 Happy is the man that hath his quiver full of them: they shall not be ashamed when they speak with their enemies in the gate.

PSALM CXXVIII.

BLESSED are all they that fear the Lord: and walk in his ways.

2 For thou shalt eat the labours of thine hands: O well shall it be with thee, and happy shalt thou be.

3 Thy wife shall be as the fruitful vine: upon the walls of thine house;

4 Thy children like olive-branches: round about thy table.

5 Lo, thus shall the man be blessed: that feareth the Lord.

6 The Lord from out of Sion shall so bless thee: that thou shalt see Jerusalem in prosperity all thy life long;

7 Yea, that thou shalt see thy children's children: and peace upon Israel.

PSALM CXXX.

OUT of the deep have I called unto thee, O Lord: Lord, hear my voice.

2 O let thine ears consider well: the voice of my complaint.

3 If thou, Lord, wilt be extreme to mark what is done amiss: O Lord, who may abide it?

4 But there is mercy with thee: therefore shalt thou be feared.

5 I look for the Lord; my soul doth wait for him: in his word is my trust.

6 My soul fleeth unto the Lord before the morning watch: I say, before the morning watch.

7 O Israel, trust in the Lord: for with the Lord there is mercy, and with him is plenteous redemption.

8 And he shall redeem Israel: from all his sins.

PSALM CXXXI.

LORD, I am not high-minded: I have no proud looks.

2 I do not exercise myself in great matters : which are too high for me.

3 But I refrain my soul, and keep it low, like as a child that is weaned from his mother : yea, my soul is even as a weaned child.

4 O Israel, trust in the Lord : from this time forth for evermore.

PSALM CXXXIII.

BEHOLD, how good and joyful a thing it is : brethren, to dwell together in unity.

2 It is like the precious ointment upon the head, that ran down unto the beard : even unto Aaron's beard, and went down to the skirts of his clothing.

3 Like as the dew of Hermon : which fell upon the hill of Sion.

4 For there the Lord promised his blessing : and life for evermore.

MORNING PRAYER.

PSALM CXXXV.

PRAISE the Lord, laud ye the Name of the Lord : O ye servants of the Lord ;

2 Ye that stand in the house of the Lord : in the courts of the house of our God.

3 O praise the Lord, for the Lord is gracious : O sing praises unto his Name, for it is lovely.

4 For why ? the Lord hath chosen Jacob unto himself : and Israel for his own possession.

5 For I know that the Lord is great : and that our Lord is above all gods.

6 Whatsoever the Lord pleased, that he did in heaven, and in earth : and in the sea, and in all deep places.

7 He bringeth forth the clouds from the ends of the world: and sendeth forth lightnings with the rain, bringing the winds out of his treasures.

8 Thy Name, O Lord, endureth for ever: so doth thy memorial, O Lord, from one generation to another.

9 For the Lord will avenge his people: and be gracious unto his servants.

10 Praise the Lord, ye house of Israel: praise the Lord, ye house of Aaron.

11 Praise the Lord, ye house of Levi: ye that fear the Lord, praise the Lord.

12 Praised be the Lord out of Sion: who dwelleth at Jerusalem.

PSALM CXXXVIII.

I WILL give thanks unto thee, O Lord, with my whole heart: even before the gods will I sing praises unto thee.

2 I will worship toward thy holy temple, and praise thy Name, because of thy lovingkindness and truth: for thou hast magnified thy Name, and thy word, above all things.

3 When I called upon thee, thou heardest me: and enduedst my soul with much strength.

4 All the kings of the earth shall praise thee, O Lord: when they hear the words of thy mouth.

5 Yea, they shall sing in the ways of the Lord: that great is the glory of the Lord.

6 For though the Lord be high, yet hath he respect unto the lowly: as for the proud, he beholdeth them afar off.

7 Though I walk in the midst of trouble, yet shalt thou refresh me: thou shalt stretch forth thy hand upon the furiousness of mine enemies, and thy right hand shall save me.

8 The Lord shall make good his lovingkindness

toward me: yea, thy mercy, O Lord, endureth for ever; forsake not then the works of thine own hands.

EVENING PRAYER.

PSALM CXXXIX.

O LORD, thou hast searched me out, and known me: thou knowest my down-sitting and mine uprising; thou understandest my thoughts long before.

2 Thou art about my path, and about my bed: and spiest out all my ways.

3 For lo, there is not a word in my tongue: but thou, O Lord, knowest it altogether.

4 Thou hast fashioned me behind and before: and laid thine hand upon me.

5 Such knowledge is too wonderful and excellent for me: I cannot attain unto it.

6 Whither shall I go then from thy Spirit: or whither shall I go then from thy presence?

7 If I climb up into heaven, thou art there: if I go down to hell, thou art there also.

8 If I take the wings of the morning: and remain in the uttermost parts of the sea;

9 Even there also shall thy hand lead me: and thy right hand shall hold me.

10 If I say, Peradventure the darkness shall cover me: then shall my night be turned into day.

11 Yea, the darkness is no darkness with thee, but the night is as clear as the day: the darkness and light to thee are both alike.

12 For my reins are thine: thou hast covered me in my mother's womb.

13 I will give thanks unto thee, for I am fearfully and wonderfully made: marvellous are thy works; and that my soul knoweth right well.

14 My substance was not hid from thee when I was made in secret: and curiously wrought in the lowest parts of the earth.

15 Thine eyes did see my substance yet being imperfect: and in thy book were all my members written;

16 Which day by day were fashioned: when as yet there was none of them.

17 How dear are thy counsels unto me, O God: O how great is the sum of them!

18 If I should count them, they are more in number than the sand: when I awake, I am present with thee.

19 Try me, O God, and seek the ground of my heart: prove me, and examine my thoughts.

20 Look well if there be any way of wickedness in me: and lead me in the way everlasting.

MORNING PRAYER.

PSALM CXLI.

LORD, I call upon thee, haste thee unto me: and consider my voice when I cry unto thee.

2 Let my prayer be set forth in thy sight as the incense: and the lifting up of my hands as the evening sacrifice.

3 Set a watch, O Lord, before my mouth: and keep the door of my lips.

4 O let not mine heart be inclined to any evil thing: let me not be occupied in ungodly works with the men that work wickedness; and let me not eat of their dainties.

5 Let the righteous rather smite me friendly: and reprove me.

6 Mine eyes look unto thee, O Lord God: in thee is my trust; O cast not out my soul.

7 Keep me from the snare that they have laid for me : and from the traps of the wicked doers.

PSALM CXLII.

I CRIED unto the Lord with my voice : yea, even unto the Lord did I make my supplication.

2 I poured out my complaints before him : and showed him of my trouble.

3 When my spirit was in heaviness, thou knewest my path : in the way wherein I walked have they secretly laid a snare for me.

4 I looked also upon my right hand : and saw there was no man that would know me.

5 I had no place to flee unto : and no man cared for my soul.

6 I cried unto thee, O Lord, and said : Thou art my hope and my portion in the land of the living.

7 Consider my complaint : for I am brought very low.

8 O deliver me from my persecutors : for they are too strong for me.

9 Bring my soul out of prison, that I may give thanks unto thy Name : which thing if thou wilt grant me, then shall the righteous resort unto my company.

EVENING PRAYER.

PSALM CXLIII.

HEAR my prayer, O Lord, and consider my desire : hearken unto me, for thy truth and righteousness' sake.

2 And enter not into judgment with thy servant : for in thy sight shall no man living be justified.

3 My spirit is vexed within me : and my heart within me is desolate.

4 Yet do I remember the time past ; I muse upon all thy works : yea, I exercise myself in the works of thy hands.

5 I stretch forth my hands unto thee: my soul gaspeth unto thee as a thirsty land.

6 Hear me, O Lord, and that soon, for my spirit waxeth faint : hide not thy face from me, lest I be like unto them that go down into the pit.

7 O let me hear thy lovingkindness betimes in the morning; for in thee is my trust : show thou me the way that I should walk in; for I lift up my soul unto thee.

8 Deliver me, O Lord, from mine enemies : for I flee unto thee to hide me.

9 Teach me to do the thing that pleaseth thee ; for thou art my God : let thy loving Spirit lead me forth into the land of righteousness.

10 Quicken me, O Lord, for thy Name's sake : and for thy righteousness' sake bring my soul out of trouble.

PSALM CXLIV.

BLESSED be the Lord my strength : who teacheth my hands to war, and my fingers to fight ;

2 My hope and my fortress, my castle and deliverer, my defender, in whom I trust : who subdueth my people that is under me.

3 Lord, what is man, that thou hast such respect unto him : or the son of man, that thou so regardest him ?

4 Man is like a thing of nought : his time passeth away like a shadow.

5 Bow thy heavens, O Lord, and come down: touch the mountains, and they shall smoke.

6 Cast forth thy lightning, and tear them : shoot out thine arrows, and consume them.

7 Send down thine hand from above : deliver me, and take me out of the great waters, from the hand of strange children ;

8 Whose mouth talketh of vanity : and their right hand is a right hand of wickedness.

9 I will sing a new song unto thee, O God : thou dost give victory unto kings, and hast delivered David thy servant from the peril of the sword.

10 Save me, and deliver me from the hand of strange children : whose mouth talketh of vanity, and their right hand is a right hand of iniquity ;

11 That our sons may grow up as the young plants : and our daughters may be as the polished corners of the temple ;

12 That our garners may be full and plenteous with all manner of store : that our sheep may bring forth thousands and ten thousands in our streets ;

13 That our oxen may be strong to labour, that there may be no decay : no leading into captivity, and no complaining in our streets.

14 Happy are the people that are in such a case : yea, blessed are the people who have the Lord for their God.

MORNING PRAYER.

PSALM CXLV.

I WILL magnify thee, O God, my King : and I will praise thy Name for ever and ever.

2 Every day will I give thanks unto thee : and praise thy Name for ever and ever.

3 Great is the Lord and marvellous, worthy to be praised : there is no end of his greatness.

4 One generation shall praise thy works unto another : and declare thy power.

5 As for me, I will be talking of thy worship : thy glory, thy praise, and thy wondrous works.

6 So that men shall speak of the might of thy marvellous acts : and I will also tell of thy greatness.

7 The memorial of thine abundant kindness shall be showed : and men shall sing of thy righteousness.

8 The Lord is gracious and merciful : long-suffering, and of great goodness.

9 The Lord is loving unto every man : and his mercy is over all his works.

10 All thy works praise thee, O Lord : and thy saints give thanks unto thee.

11 They show the glory of thy kingdom : and talk of thy power.

12 That thy power, thy glory, and the mightiness of thy kingdom : might be known unto men.

13 Thy kingdom is an everlasting kingdom : and thy dominion endureth throughout all ages.

14 The Lord upholdeth all such as fall : and lifteth up all those that are bowed down.

15 The eyes of all wait upon thee, O Lord : and thou givest them their meat in due season.

16 Thou openest thine hand : and fillest all things living with plenteousness.

17 The Lord is righteous in all his ways : and holy in all his works.

18 The Lord is nigh unto all them that call upon him : yea, all such as call upon him faithfully.

19 He will fulfil the desire of them that fear him : he also will hear their cry, and will help them.

20 The Lord preserveth all them that love him : but all the ungodly will he destroy.

21 My mouth shall speak the praise of the Lord : and let all flesh give thanks unto his holy Name for ever and ever.

PSALM CXLVI.

PRAISE the Lord, O my soul; while I live will I praise the Lord: yea, as long as I have any being, I will sing praises unto my God.

2 O put not your trust in princes, nor in any child of man: for there is no help in them.

3 For when the breath of man goeth forth, he returneth to his earth: and then all his thoughts perish.

4 Blessed is he that hath the God of Jacob for his help: and whose hope is in the Lord his God;

5 Who made heaven and earth, the sea, and all that therein is: who keepeth his promise for ever;

6 Who helpeth them to right that suffer wrong: who feedeth the hungry.

7 The Lord looseth men out of prison: the Lord giveth sight to the blind.

8 The Lord helpeth them that are fallen: the Lord careth for the righteous.

9 The Lord careth for the strangers; he defendeth the fatherless and widow: as for the way of the ungodly, he turneth it upside down.

10 The Lord thy God, O Sion, shall be King for evermore: and throughout all generations.

EVENING PRAYER.

PSALM CXLVII.

O PRAISE the Lord, for it is a good thing to sing praises unto our God: yea, a joyful and a pleasant thing it is to be thankful.

2 The Lord doth build up Jerusalem: and gather together the outcasts of Israel.

3 He healeth those that are broken in heart : and giveth medicine to heal their sickness.

4 He telleth the number of the stars; and calleth them all by their names.

5 Great is our Lord, and great is his power : yea, and his wisdom is infinite.

6 The Lord setteth up the meek : and bringeth the ungodly down to the ground.

7 O sing unto the Lord with thanksgiving : sing praises unto our God;

8 Who covereth the heaven with clouds, and prepareth rain for the earth : and maketh the grass to grow upon the mountains, and herb for the use of men.

9 Who giveth fodder unto the cattle : and feedeth the young ravens that call upon him.

10 He hath no pleasure in the strength of an horse : neither delighteth he in any man's legs.

11 But the Lord's delight is in them that fear him : and put their trust in his mercy.

12 Praise the Lord, O Jerusalem : praise thy God, O Sion.

13 For he hath made fast the bars of thy gates : and hath blessed thy children within thee.

14 He maketh peace in thy borders : and filleth thee with the flour of wheat.

15 He sendeth forth his commandment upon the earth : and his word runneth very swiftly.

16 He giveth snow like wool : and scattereth the hoar-frost like ashes.

17 He casteth forth his ice like morsels : who is able to abide his frost ?

18 He sendeth out his word, and melteth them : he bloweth with his wind, and the waters flow.

19 He showeth his word unto Jacob : his statutes and ordinances unto Israel.

20 He hath not dealt so with any nation : neither have the heathen knowledge of his laws.

PSALM CXLVIII.

O PRAISE the Lord of heaven: praise him in the height.

2 Praise him, all ye angels of his : praise him, all his host.

3 Praise him, sun and moon : praise him, all ye stars and light.

4 Praise him, all ye heavens : and ye waters that are above the heavens.

5 Let them praise the Name of the Lord: for he spake the word, and they were made ; he commanded, and they were created.

6 He hath established them for ever and ever : he hath given them a law which shall not be broken.

7 Praise the Lord upon earth: ye dragons, and all deeps ;

8 Fire and hail, snow and vapours : wind and storm, fulfilling his word ;

9 Mountains and hills: fruitful trees and all cedars ;

10 Beasts and all cattle : creeping things and feathered fowls ;

11 Kings of the earth and all people: princes and all judges of the world ;

12 Young men and maidens, old men and children, praise the Name of the Lord: for his Name only is excellent, and his praise above heaven and earth.

13 He shall exalt the horn of his people, all his saints shall praise him: even the children of Israel, even the people that serveth him.

PSALM CL.

O PRAISE God in his holiness : praise him in the firmament of his power.

2 Praise him in his noble acts : praise him according to his excellent greatness.

3 Let every thing that hath breath : praise the Lord.

FORM AND MANNER

OF

ORDAINING CANDIDATES

FOR THE

WESLEYAN-METHODIST MINISTRY.

After the singing of an appropriate Hymn, and the offering up to God of extemporary prayer for his blessing upon the entire service, the names of the Candidates for ordination shall be read aloud. The following Scriptures, or a part of them, shall then be read by the President of the Conference.

Matthew xxviii. 18.

JESUS came and spake unto them, saying, All power is given unto me in heaven and in earth. Go ye therefore, and teach all nations, baptizing them in the name of the Father, and of the Son, and of the Holy Ghost; teaching them to observe all things whatsoever I have commanded you: and, lo, I am with you alway, even unto the end of the world.

Luke xii. 35.

LET your loins be girded about, and your lights burning; and ye yourselves like unto men that wait for their Lord, when he will return from the wedding; that when he cometh and knocketh, they may open unto him immediately. Blessed are those servants, whom the Lord when he cometh shall find watching: verily I say unto you, that he shall gird himself, and make them to sit down to meat, and will come forth and serve them. And if he shall come in the second watch, or come in the third watch, and find them so, blessed are those servants.

John x. 1.

VERILY, verily, I say unto you, He that entereth not by the door into the sheepfold, but climbeth up some other way, the same is a thief and a robber. But he that entereth in by the door is the shepherd of the sheep. To him the porter openeth ; and the sheep hear his voice : and he calleth his own sheep by name, and leadeth them out. And when he putteth forth his own sheep, he goeth before them, and the sheep follow him : for they know his voice. And a stranger will they not follow, but will flee from him : for they know not the voice of strangers. This parable spake Jesus unto them : but they understood not what things they were which he spake unto them. Then said Jesus unto them again, Verily, verily, I say unto you, I am the door of the sheep. All that ever came before me are thieves and robbers : but the sheep did not hear them. I am the door : by me if any man enter in, he shall be saved, and shall go in and out, and find pasture. The thief cometh not but for to steal, and to kill, and to destroy : I am come that they might have life, and that they might have it more abundantly. I am the good shepherd : the good shepherd giveth his life for the sheep. But he that is an hireling, and not the shepherd, whose own the sheep are not, seeth the wolf coming, and leaveth the sheep, and fleeth : and the wolf catcheth them, and scattereth the sheep. The hireling fleeth because he is an hireling, and careth not for the sheep. I am the good shepherd, and know my sheep, and am known of mine. As the Father knoweth me, even so know I the Father : and I lay down my life for the sheep. And other sheep I have, which are not of this fold : them also I must bring, and they shall hear my voice ; and there shall be one fold, and one shepherd.

John xxi. 15.

JESUS saith to Simon Peter, Simon, son of Jonas, lovest thou me more than these ? He saith unto him, Yea, Lord ; thou knowest that I love thee. He said unto him, Feed my lambs. He saith to him again the second time, Simon, son of Jonas, lovest thou me ? He saith unto him, Yea, Lord ; thou knowest that I love thee. He saith unto him, Feed my sheep. He said unto him the third time, Simon, son of Jonas, lovest thou me ? Peter was grieved because he said unto him the third time, Lovest thou me ? and he said unto him, Lord, thou knowest all things : thou knowest that I love thee. Jesus saith unto him, Feed my sheep.

Acts xx. 17.

FROM Miletus Paul sent to Ephesus, and called the Elders of the church. And when they were come to him, he said unto them, Ye know from the first day that I came into Asia, after what manner I have been with you at all seasons, serving the Lord with all humility of mind, and with many tears and temptations which befell me by the lying in wait of the Jews : and how I kept back nothing that was profitable unto you, but have showed you, and have taught you publicly, and from house to house, testifying both to the Jews, and also to the Greeks, repentance toward God, and faith toward our Lord Jesus Christ. And now, behold, I go bound in the spirit unto Jerusalem, not knowing the things that shall befall me there : save that the Holy Ghost witnesseth in every city, saying, that bonds and afflictions abide me. But none of these things move me, neither count I my life dear unto myself, so that I might finish my course with joy, and the ministry which I have received of the Lord Jesus, to testify the Gospel of the grace of God. And now, behold, I know that ye all, among whom I have gone preaching the kingdom of God, shall see my face no more. Wherefore I take you to record this day, that I am pure from the blood of all men. For I have not shunned to declare unto you all the counsel of God. Take heed therefore unto yourselves, and to all the flock, over which the Holy Ghost hath made you Overseers, to feed the church of God, which he hath purchased with his own blood. For I know this, that after my departure shall grievous wolves enter in among you, not sparing the flock. Also of your own selves shall men arise, speaking perverse things, to draw away disciples after them. Therefore watch, and remember, that for the space of three years I ceased not to warn every one night and day with tears. And now, brethren, I commend you to God, and to the word of his grace, which is able to build you up, and to give you an inheritance among all them who are sanctified. I have coveted no man's silver, or gold, or apparel : yea, ye yourselves know, that these hands have ministered unto my necessities, and to them that were with me.

Ephes. iv. 7.

UNTO every one of us is given grace according to the measure of the gift of Christ. Wherefore he saith, When he ascended up on high, he led captivity captive, and gave gifts unto men. (Now that he ascended, what is it but that he also descended first into the lower parts of the earth? He that descended is the same also that ascended far above all things.)

N

And he gave some, Apostles; and some, Prophets; and some, Evangelists; and some, Pastors and Teachers; for the perfecting of the saints, for the work of the ministry, for the edifying of the body of Christ: till we all come in the unity of the faith, and of the knowledge of the Son of God, unto a perfect man, unto the measure of the stature of the fulness of Christ.

And that done, the President shall say unto the Candidates as hereafter followeth:

YOU have heard, Brethren, as well in your private examination, as in the exhortation which was now made to you, and in the holy lessons taken out of the Gospel, and the writings of the Apostles, of what dignity, and of how great importance, this office is, whereunto ye are called. And now again we exhort you, in the Name of our Lord Jesus Christ, that you have in remembrance, into how high a dignity, and to how weighty an office and charge, ye are called; that is to say, to be Messengers, Watchmen, and Stewards of the Lord; to teach and to premonish, to feed and to provide for, the Lord's family; to seek for Christ's sheep that are dispersed abroad, and for his children who are in the midst of this naughty world, that they may be saved through Christ for ever.

Have always, therefore, printed in your remembrance how great a treasure is committed to your charge. For they are the sheep of Christ, which he bought with his death, and for whom he shed his blood. The church and congregation whom you must serve is his Spouse and his Body. And if it shall happen, the same church, or any member thereof, do take any hurt or hinderance by reason of your negligence, ye know the greatness of the fault, and also the horrible punishment that will ensue. Wherefore consider with yourselves the end of your ministry towards the children of God, towards the

Spouse and Body of Christ; and see that you never cease your labour, your care, and diligence, until you have done all that lieth in you, according to your bounden duty, to bring all such as are or shall be committed to your charge, unto that agreement in the faith and knowledge of God, and to that ripeness and perfectness of age in Christ, that there be no place left among you, either for error in religion, or for viciousness in life.

Forasmuch then as your office is both of so great excellency, and of so great difficulty, ye see with how great care and study ye ought to apply yourselves, as well that ye may show yourselves dutiful and thankful unto that Lord who hath placed you in so high a dignity; as also to beware that neither you yourselves offend, nor be occasion that others offend. Howbeit ye cannot have a mind and will thereto of yourselves; for that will and ability is given of God alone : therefore ye ought, and have need, to pray earnestly for his Holy Spirit. And seeing that you cannot by any other means compass the doing of so weighty a work, pertaining to the salvation of man, but with doctrine and exhortation taken out of the holy Scriptures, and with a life agreeable to the same ; consider how studious ye ought to be in reading and learning the Scriptures, and in framing the manners both of yourselves, and of them that specially pertain unto you, according to the rule of the same Scriptures : and for this self-same cause, how ye ought to forsake and set aside (as much as you may) all worldly cares and studies.

We have good hope that you have all weighed and pondered these things with yourselves long before this time ; and that you have clearly determined, by God's grace, to give yourselves wholly to this office, whereunto it hath pleased God to call you : so that, as much as lieth in you, you will apply yourselves wholly to this one thing, and draw all your cares and studies this way; and that you will continually pray to God the Father, through the mediation of our only Saviour Jesus Christ, for the heavenly assistance of the Holy Ghost; that, by daily reading and weighing of the Scriptures, ye may wax riper and stronger in your ministry; and that ye may so endeavour, from time to time, to sanctify the lives of you and yours, and to fashion them after the rule and doctrine of Christ, that ye may be wholesome and godly examples and patterns for the people to follow.

And now, that this present congregation of Christ here assembled may also understand your minds and wills in these things, and that this your promise may the more move you to do your duties; ye shall answer plainly to these things, which we, in the name of God, and his church, shall demand of you touching the same.

DO you trust that you are inwardly moved by the Holy Ghost to take upon you this office and ministration, to serve God for the promoting of his glory, and the edifying of his people?

Answer. I trust so.

The President.

ARE you persuaded that the holy Scriptures contain sufficiently all doctrine required of necessity for eternal salvation through faith of Jesus Christ? And are you determined, out of the said Scriptures, to instruct the people committed to your charge; and to teach nothing, as required of necessity to eternal salvation, but that which you shall be persuaded may be concluded and proved by the Scripture?

Answer. I am so persuaded, and have so determined, by God's grace.

The President.

A S you are to exercise your ministry under the direction of the Wesleyan-Methodist Conference, I have further to inquire, whether you have read the first four volumes of Mr. Wesley's Sermons, and his Notes on the New Testament; and whether you believe that the system of doctrine therein contained is in accordance with the holy Scriptures?

Answer. I have read them, and do so believe.

The President.

I HAVE also to ask you, whether you have read the Large Minutes of the Conference; and believe that the general system of discipline contained therein is agreeable to the holy Scriptures; and whether you will maintain and enforce it in the societies which shall be committed to your charge?

Answer. I have read them, and do so believe and resolve.

The President.

W ILL you then give your faithful diligence, always so to minister the Doctrine and Sacraments, and the Discipline of Christ, as the Lord hath commanded?

Answer. I will do so, by the help of the Lord.

The President.

W ILL you be ready, with all faithful diligence, to banish and drive away all erroneous and strange doctrines contrary to God's word; and to use both public and private admonitions and exhortations, as well to the sick as to the whole, within your district, as need shall require, and occasion shall be given?

Answer. I will, the Lord being my helper.

The President.

WILL you be diligent in prayers, and in reading of the holy Scriptures, and in such studies as help to the knowledge of the same, laying aside the study of the world and the flesh ?

Answer. I will endeavour so to do, the Lord being my helper.

The President.

WILL you be diligent to frame and fashion your own selves, and your families, (if you have, or shall have any,) according to the doctrine of Christ ; and to make both yourselves and them, as much as in you lieth, wholesome examples and patterns to the flock of Christ ?

Answer. I shall apply myself thereto, the Lord being my helper.

The President.

WILL you maintain and set forwards, as much as lieth in you, quietness, peace, and love among all Christian people, and especially among them that are or shall be committed to your charge ?

Answer. I will do so, the Lord being my helper.

The President.

WILL you reverently obey your chief Ministers, unto whom is committed the charge and government over you ; following with a glad mind and will their godly admonitions, and submitting yourselves to their godly judgments ?

Answer. I will do so, the Lord being my helper.

Then shall the President say,

ALMIGHTY God, who hath given you this will to do all these things ; Grant also unto you strength and power to perform the same ; that he may accomplish his work which he hath begun in you; through Jesus Christ our Lord. *Amen.*

Then the President shall move the Congregation present to pray, saying thus to them :

BRETHREN, it is written in the Gospel of Saint Luke, that our Saviour Christ continued the whole night in prayer, before he did choose and send forth his twelve Apostles. It is written also in the Acts of the Apostles, that the Disciples who were at Antioch did fast and pray before they laid hands on Paul and Barnabas, and sent them forth. Let us therefore, following the example of our Saviour Christ, and his Apostles, first fall to prayer, before we admit and send forth these persons presented unto us to the work whereunto we trust the Holy Ghost hath called them.

After this the Congregation shall be desired, secretly in their Prayers, to make their humble supplications to God for all these things ; for which Prayers there shall be silence kept for a space.

The following Prayers shall then be read by the President.

ALMIGHTY God, giver of all good things, Mercifully behold these thy servants now called to the office and work of Ministers and Pastors in thy church; and replenish them so with the truth of thy doctrine, and adorn them with innocency of life, that both by word and good example they may faithfully serve thee in this office, to the glory of thy Name, and the edification of thy church ; through the merits of our Saviour Jesus Christ, who liveth and reigneth with thee and the Holy Ghost, world without end. *Amen.*

ALMIGHTY God, and heavenly Father, who of thine infinite love and goodness towards us hast given to us thy only and most dearly beloved Son Jesus Christ, to be our Redeemer, and the Author of everlasting life; who, after he had made perfect our redemption by his death, and was ascended into heaven, sent abroad into the world his Apostles, Prophets, Evangelists, Teachers, and Pastors; by whose labour and ministry he gathered together a great flock in all parts of the world, to set forth the eternal praise of thy holy Name: For these so great benefits of thy eternal goodness, and for that thou hast vouchsafed to call these thy servants here present to the same office and ministry appointed for the salvation of mankind, we render unto thee most hearty thanks, we praise and worship thee; and we humbly beseech thee, by the same thy blessed Son, to grant unto all who either here or elsewhere call upon thy holy Name, that we may continue to show ourselves thankful unto thee for these and all other thy benefits; and that we may daily increase and go forwards in the knowledge and faith of thee and thy Son by the Holy Spirit. So that as well by these thy Ministers, as by them over whom they shall be appointed thy Ministers, thy holy Name may be for ever glorified, and thy blessed kingdom enlarged; through the same thy Son Jesus Christ our Lord, who liveth and reigneth with thee in the unity of the same Holy Spirit, world without end. *Amen.*

ALMIGHTY God, and most merciful Father, Grant, we beseech thee, to these thy servants such grace, that they may evermore be ready to spread abroad thy Gospel, the glad tidings of reconciliation with thee; and use the authority given them, not to destruction, but to salvation; not to hurt, but to help: so that, as wise and faithful servants, giving to thy family their portion in due season, they may at last be received into everlasting joy; through Jesus Christ our Lord, who, with thee and the Holy Ghost, liveth and reigneth, one God, world without end. *Amen.*

When these Prayers are done, the President, and other Ministers present, shall lay their Hands severally upon the Head of every one of the Candidates, who shall humbly kneel upon their knees, the President saying,

MAYEST thou receive the Holy Ghost for the office and work of a Christian Minister and Pastor, now committed unto thee by the imposition of our hands. And be thou a faithful Dispenser of the Word of God, and of his holy Sacraments; In the Name of the Father, and of the Son, and of the Holy Ghost. *Amen.*

Then the President shall deliver to every one of them kneeling, the Bible into his hand, saying,

TAKE thou authority to preach the Word of God, and to administer the holy Sacraments in the Congregation.

Then shall the President address the following admonition to the Candidates who have been ordained :

BRETHREN, give heed unto reading, exhortation, and doctrine. Think upon the things contained in the Holy Bible, which we have now delivered unto you. Be diligent in them, that the increase coming thereby may be manifest unto all men. Take heed unto yourselves and to the doctrine ; for by so doing you shall both save yourselves and them that hear you. Let each of you be to the flock of Christ a Shepherd, not a wolf: feed them, devour them not. Hold up the weak, heal the sick, bind up the broken, bring again the outcasts, seek the lost. Be so merciful,.

that you be not too remiss ; so minister discipline, that you forget not mercy ; that when the Chief Shepherd shall appear, you may receive the never-failing crown of glory ; through Jesus Christ our Lord. *Amen.*

Then shall be offered by the President the following Prayer :

MOST merciful Father, we beseech thee to send down upon these thy servants thy heavenly blessing ; and so endue them with thy Holy Spirit, that they preaching thy word, may not only be earnest to reprove, beseech, and rebuke, with all patience and doctrine ; but also may be, to such as believe, wholesome examples in word, in conversation, in love, in faith, in chastity, and in purity ; that faithfully fulfilling their course, at the latter day they may receive the crown of righteousness laid up by the Lord, the righteous Judge, who liveth and reigneth one God with the Father and the Holy Ghost, world without end. *Amen.*

Next shall follow the administration of the Lord's Supper, the persons newly ordained first receiving that holy sacrament, and then such other Ministers and private Christians as may conveniently join in the service.

ARTICLES OF RELIGION.

I. OF FAITH IN THE HOLY TRINITY.

THERE is but one living and true God, everlasting, without body or parts; of infinite power, wisdom, and goodness; the Maker and Preserver of all things both visible and invisible. And in unity of this Godhead there are three Persons, of one substance, power, and eternity; the Father, the Son, and the Holy Ghost.

II. OF THE WORD OR SON OF GOD, WHO WAS MADE VERY MAN.

THE Son, who is the Word of the Father, the very and eternal God, of one substance with the Father, took man's nature in the womb of the blessed Virgin; so that two whole and perfect natures, that is to say, the Godhead and Manhood, were joined together in one person, never to be divided; whereof is one Christ, very God, and very man, who truly suffered, was crucified, dead, and buried, to reconcile his Father to us, and to be a sacrifice, not only for original guilt, but also for the actual sins of men.

III. OF THE RESURRECTION OF CHRIST.

CHRIST did truly rise again from the dead, and took again his body, with all things appertaining to the perfection of man's nature; wherewith he ascended into heaven, and there sitteth, until he return to judge all men at the last day.

IV. OF THE HOLY GHOST.

THE Holy Ghost, proceeding from the Father and the Son, is of one substance, majesty, and glory, with the Father and the Son, very and eternal God.

V. OF THE SUFFICIENCY OF THE HOLY SCRIPTURES FOR SALVATION.

HOLY Scripture containeth all things necessary to salvation: so that whatsoever is not read therein, nor may be proved thereby, is not to be required of any man that it should be believed as an article of the faith, or be thought requisite or necessary to salvation. In the name of the holy Scripture we do understand those canonical Books of the Old and New Testament, of whose authority was never any doubt in the church.

Of the Names of the Canonical Books.

Genesis,
Exodus,
Leviticus,
Numbers,
Deuteronomy,
Joshua,

Judges,

Ruth,

The First Book of Samuel,

The Second Book of Samuel,

The First Book of Kings,

The Second Book of Kings,

The First Book of Chronicles,

The Second Book of Chronicles,

The Book of Ezra,

The Book of Nehemiah,

The Book of Esther,

The Book of Job,

The Psalms,

The Proverbs,

Ecclesiastes, or the Preacher,

Cantica, or Songs of Solomon,

Four Prophets the greater,

Twelve Prophets the less.

All the Books of the New Testament as they are commonly received, we do receive, and account canonical.

VI. OF THE OLD TESTAMENT.

THE Old Testament is not contrary to the New: for both in the Old and New Testament everlasting life is offered to mankind by Christ, who is the only Mediator between God and man, being both God and man. Wherefore they are not to be heard, who feign that the old Fathers did look only for transitory promises. Although the law given from God by Moses, as touching ceremonies and rites, doth not bind Christians, nor ought the civil precepts thereof of necessity to be received in any commonwealth ; yet, notwithstanding, no Christian whatsoever is free from the obedience of the commandments which are called Moral.

VII. OF ORIGINAL OR BIRTH SIN.

ORIGINAL sin standeth not in the following of Adam, (as the Pelagians do vainly talk,) but it is the corruption of the nature of every man, that naturally is engendered of the offspring of Adam; whereby man is very far gone from original righteousness, and of his own nature inclined to evil, and that continually.

VIII. OF FREE WILL.

THE condition of man after the fall of Adam is such, that he cannot turn and prepare himself by his own natural strength and works to faith, and calling upon God: wherefore we have no power to do good works pleasant and acceptable to God, without the grace of God by Christ preventing us, that we may have a good will, and working with us when we have that good will.

IX. OF THE JUSTIFICATION OF MAN.

WE are accounted righteous before God only for the merit of our Lord and Saviour Jesus Christ, by faith, and not by our own works or deservings: wherefore, that we are justified by faith only, is a most wholesome doctrine, and very full of comfort.

X. OF GOOD WORKS.

ALTHOUGH good works, which are the fruits of faith, and follow after justification, cannot put away our sins, and endure the severity of God's judgment; yet they are pleasing and acceptable to God in

Christ, and spring out of a true and lively faith, inso-much that by them a lively faith may be as evidently known, as a tree is discerned by its fruit.

XI. WORKS OF SUPEREROGATION.

VOLUNTARY works besides, over and above, God's commandments, which they call works of supererogation, cannot be taught without arrogancy and impiety. For by them men do declare, that they do not only render unto God as much as they are bound to do, but that they do more for his sake than of bounden duty is required; whereas Christ saith plainly, " When ye have done all that is commanded you, say, We are unprofitable servants."

XII. OF SIN AFTER JUSTIFICATION.

NOT every sin willingly committed after justifi-cation is the sin against the Holy Ghost, and unpardonable. Wherefore the grant of repentance is not to be denied to such as fall into sin after justifica-tion : after we have received the Holy Ghost, we may depart from grace given, and fall into sin, and by the grace of God rise again, and amend our lives. And therefore they are to be condemned who say, they can no more sin as long as they live here, or deny the place of forgiveness to such as truly repent.

XIII. OF THE CHURCH.

THE visible church of Christ is a congregation of faithful men, in which the pure word of God is preached, and the sacraments duly administered according to Christ's ordinance, in all those things that of necessity are requisite to the same.

XIV. OF PURGATORY.

THE Romish doctrine concerning purgatory, pardons, worshipping and adoration, as well of images as of reliques, and also invocation of saints, is a fond thing vainly invented, and grounded upon no warrant of Scripture, but repugnant to the word of God.

XV. OF SPEAKING IN THE CONGREGATION IN SUCH A TONGUE AS THE PEOPLE UNDERSTAND.

IT is a thing plainly repugnant to the word of God, and the custom of the primitive church, to have public prayer in the church, or to minister the sacraments, in a tongue not understood by the people.

XVI. OF THE SACRAMENTS.

SACRAMENTS ordained of Christ are not only badges or tokens of Christian men's profession; but rather they are certain signs of grace and God's good will toward us, by the which he doth work invisibly in us, and doth not only quicken, but also strengthen and confirm our faith in him.

There are two sacraments ordained of Christ our Lord in the Gospel; that is to say, baptism, and the supper of the Lord.

Those five commonly called sacraments, that is to say, confirmation, penance, orders, matrimony, and extreme unction, are not to be counted for sacraments of the Gospel, being such as have partly grown out of the *corrupt* following of the Apostles; and partly are states of life allowed in the Scriptures, but yet have not the like nature of baptism and the Lord's supper, because they have not any visible sign or ceremony ordained of God.

The sacraments were not ordained of Christ to be gazed upon, or to be carried about; but that we should duly use them. And in such only as worthily receive the same, they have a wholesome effect or operation: but they that receive them unworthily purchase to themselves condemnation, as St. Paul saith.

XVII. OF BAPTISM.

BAPTISM is not only a sign of profession, and mark of difference, whereby Christians are distinguished from others that are not baptized; but it is also a sign of regeneration, or the new birth. The baptism of young children is to be retained in the church.

XVIII. OF THE LORD'S SUPPER.

THE supper of the Lord is not only a sign of the love that Christians ought to have among themselves one to another, but rather is a sacrament of our redemption by Christ's death: insomuch that to such as rightly, worthily, and with faith receive the same, the bread which we break is a partaking of the body of Christ, and likewise the cup of blessing is a partaking of the blood of Christ.

Transubstantiation, or the change of the substance of bread and wine in the supper of the Lord, cannot be proved by holy writ; but is repugnant to the plain words of Scripture, overthroweth the nature of a

sacrament, and hath given occasion to many super-
stitions.

The body of Christ is given, taken, and eaten in the
supper only after an heavenly and spiritual manner:
and the mean whereby the body of Christ is received
and eaten in the supper is faith.

The sacrament of the Lord's supper was not by
Christ's ordinance reserved, carried about, lifted up, or
worshipped.

XIX. OF BOTH KINDS.

THE cup of the Lord is not to be denied to the lay-
people; for both the parts of the Lord's supper,
by Christ's ordinance and commandment, ought to be
ministered to all Christians alike.

XX. OF THE ONE OBLATION OF CHRIST FINISHED UPON THE CROSS.

THE offering of Christ, once made, is that perfect
redemption, propitiation, and satisfaction for all
the sins of the whole world, both original and actual;
and there is none other satisfaction for sin but that
alone. Wherefore the sacrifice of masses, in the which
it is commonly said that the Priest doth offer Christ
for the quick and the dead, to have remission of pain or
guilt, is a blasphemous fable, and dangerous deceit.

XXI. OF THE MARRIAGE OF MINISTERS.

THE Ministers of Christ are not commanded by
God's law either to vow the estate of single life,
or to abstain from marriage: therefore it is lawful for
them, as for all other Christians, to marry at their own
discretion, as they shall judge the same to serve best to
godliness.

XXII. OF THE RITES AND CEREMONIES OF CHURCHES.

IT is not necessary that rites and ceremonies should in all places be the same, or exactly alike; for they have been always different, and may be changed according to the diversity of countries, times, and men's manners, so that nothing be ordained against God's word. Whosoever, through his private judgment, willingly and purposely doth openly break the rites and ceremonies of the church to which he belongs, which are not repugnant to the word of God, and are ordained and approved by common authority, ought to be rebuked openly, that others may fear to do the like; as one that offendeth against the common order of the church, and woundeth the consciences of weak brethren.

Every particular church may ordain, change, or abolish rites and ceremonies, so that all things be done to edification.

XXIII. OF THE RULERS OF THE BRITISH DOMINIONS.

THE King's Majesty, with his Parliament, hath the chief power in all the British dominions; unto whom the chief government of all estates in all causes doth appertain; and is not, nor ought to be, subject to any foreign jurisdiction.

XXIV. OF CHRISTIAN MEN'S GOODS.

THE riches and goods of Christians are not common, as touching the right, title, and possession of the same, as some do falsely boast. Notwithstanding, every man ought, of such things as he possesseth, liberally to give alms to the poor, according to his ability.

XXV. OF A CHRISTIAN MAN'S OATH.

AS we confess that vain and rash swearing is forbidden Christian men, by our Lord Jesus Christ, and James his Apostle; so we judge that the Christian religion doth not prohibit that a man may swear when the Magistrate requireth, in a cause of faith and charity, so it be done, according to the Prophet's teaching, in justice, judgment, and truth.

THE END.

ROCHE. PRINTER, 25, HOXTON-SQUARE, LONDON.

Trieste

Trieste Publishing has a massive catalogue of classic book titles. Our aim is to provide readers with the highest quality reproductions of fiction and non-fiction literature that has stood the test of time. The many thousands of books in our collection have been sourced from libraries and private collections around the world.

The titles that Trieste Publishing has chosen to be part of the collection have been scanned to simulate the original. Our readers see the books the same way that their first readers did decades or a hundred or more years ago. Books from that period are often spoiled by imperfections that did not exist in the original. Imperfections could be in the form of blurred text, photographs, or missing pages. It is highly unlikely that this would occur with one of our books. Our extensive quality control ensures that the readers of Trieste Publishing's books will be delighted with their purchase. Our staff has thoroughly reviewed every page of all the books in the collection, repairing, or if necessary, rejecting titles that are not of the highest quality. This process ensures that the reader of one of Trieste Publishing's titles receives a volume that faithfully reproduces the original, and to the maximum degree possible, gives them the experience of owning the original work.

We pride ourselves on not only creating a pathway to an extensive reservoir of books of the finest quality, but also providing value to every one of our readers. Generally, Trieste books are purchased singly - on demand, however they may also be purchased in bulk. Readers interested in bulk purchases are invited to contact us directly to enquire about our tailored bulk rates. Email: customerservice@triestepublishing.com

You May Also Like

ISBN: 9780649066155
Paperback: 144 pages
Dimensions: 6.14 x 0.31 x 9.21 inches
Language: eng

Heath's Modern Language Series. Atala

François-René de Chateaubriand & Oscar Kuhns

ISBN: 9780649639663
Paperback: 188 pages
Dimensions: 6.14 x 0.40 x 9.21 inches
Language: eng

The Lost Found, and the Wanderer Welcomed

W. M. Taylor

You May Also Like

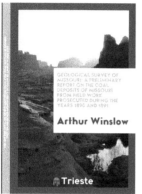

Geological Survey of Missouri: A Preliminary Report on the Coal Deposits of Missouri from Field Work Prosecuted During the Years 1890 and 1891

Arthur Winslow

ISBN: 9780649691807
Paperback: 244 pages
Dimensions: 6.14 x 0.51 x 9.21 inches
Language: eng

Longmans' English Classics; Dryden's Palamon and Arcite

William Tenney Brewster

ISBN: 9780649565733
Paperback: 170 pages
Dimensions: 6.14 x 0.36 x 9.21 inches
Language: eng

www.triestepublishing.com

You May Also Like

ISBN: 9780649333158
Paperback: 84 pages
Dimensions: 6.14 x 0.17 x 9.21 inches
Language: eng

Report of the Department of Farms and Markets, pp. 5-71

Various

Catalogue of the Episcopal Theological School in Cambridge Massachusetts, 1891-1892

Various

ISBN: 9780649324132
Paperback: 78 pages
Dimensions: 6.14 x 0.16 x 9.21 inches
Language: eng

You May Also Like

Three Hundred Tested Recipes

Various

ISBN: 9780649352142
Paperback: 88 pages
Dimensions: 6.14 x 0.18 x 9.21 inches
Language: eng

A Basket of Fragments

Anonymous

ISBN: 9780649419418
Paperback: 108 pages
Dimensions: 6.14 x 0.22 x 9.21 inches
Language: eng

Find more of our titles on our website. We have a selection of thousands of titles that will interest you. Please visit

www.triestepublishing.com

Lightning Source UK Ltd.
Milton Keynes UK
UKHW01f0835050618
323752UK00005B/318/P